TO SCALE
THE SKIES

TO SCALE THE SKIES

The Story of Group Captain
J.C. 'Johnny' Wells DFC & BAR

PETER CORNWELL

First published 2011 by Spellmount,
an imprint of The History Press
The Mill, Brimscombe Port
Stroud, Gloucestershire, GL5 2QG
www.thehistorypress.co.uk

British Library Cataloguing in Publication Data.
A catalogue record for this book is available from the British Library.

ISBN 978 0 7524 6353 7
Typesetting and origination by The History Press
Printed in the EU for The History Press.

CONTENTS

ABBREVIATIONS

AA	Anti-Aircraft	DFC	Distinguished Flying Cross
A&AEE	Aeroplane & Armament Experimental Establishment	DFM	Distinguished Flying Medal
ACı	Aircraftman First Class	DSC	Distinguished Service Cross
ADGB	Air Defence Great Britain	DSO	Distinguished Service Order
AFC	Air Force Cross	ELS	Emergency Landing Strip
ALG	Advance Landing Ground	FAA	Fleet Air Arm
AOC	Air Officer Commanding	F/L	Flight Lieutenant
ATC	Air Training Corps	F/Sgt	Flight Sergeant
ATS	Armament Training Station	F/O	Flying Officer
		FTS	Flying Training School
BAFO	British Air Forces of Occupation	G/C	Group Captain
		GCC	Group Control Centre
BLPI	British Liaison Party Iraq	GM	George Medal
BOAC	British Overseas Airways Corporation	GOC	General Officer Commanding
CBE	Commander of the British Empire	HMS	His Majesty's Ship
		HQ	Headquarters
C-in-C	Commander-in-Chief	IO	Intelligence Officer
CO	Commanding Officer	KCB	Knight Commander of the Bath
DCM	Distinguished Conduct Medal	KD	Khaki Drill

LAC	Leading Aircraftman	RNVR	Royal Naval Volunteer Reserve
MC	Military Cross		
MEAF	Middle East Air Force	R/P	Rocket Projectile
MM	Military Medal	R/T	Radio Telegraphy
MO	Medical Officer	SAO	Senior Administration Officer
MRCP	Mobile Radar Control Post		
		SASO	Senior Air Staff Officer
NATO	North Atlantic Treaty Organisation	SFTS	Service Flying Training School
NCO	Non-commissioned Officer	SITREP	Situation Report
		S/L	Squadron Leader
OBE	Order of the British Empire	2TAF	2nd Tactical Air Force
		TUC	Trades Union Congress
OC	Officer Commanding	UN	United Nations
OHMS	On His Majesty's Service	USAAF	United States Army Air Force
ORB	Operations Record Book		
OTU	Operational Training Unit	USAF	United States Air Force
		VE	Victory in Europe
P/O	Pilot Officer	VHF	Very High Frequency
QBI	Signal code for bad weather	WAAF	Women's Auxiliary Air Force
RFC	Royal Flying Corps	W/C	Wing Commander
RLG	Relief Landing Ground	W/O	Warrant Officer
RM	Royal Marines	WRAF	Women's Royal Air Force
RN	Royal Navy		
RNAS	Royal Naval Air Service	WSM	Wing Sergeant Major
RNR	Royal Naval Reserve	W/T	Wireless Telegraphy

INTRODUCTION

This book owes its existence to a chance conversation between two school-boys and the fact that the father of one subsequently recognised a photograph of a celebrated goat among the souvenirs of an RAF pilot. First thanks are therefore due to my good friend John Vasco and his son Jamie for bringing the collection of the late Johnny Wells to my attention and for introducing me to his niece, Mrs Margaret Goff.

With her permission, I was allowed to inspect a wealth of documents, photographs and material relevant to Johnny's RAF career that remained in the keeping of the family. While his meticulously compiled logbooks revealed a rich source of information on his varied flying experiences, his surviving letters gave an equally fascinating insight into the character of the man himself – a rich vein of material further enhanced by his wide selection of photographs. For allowing me full access to all of this, copying me dozens of documents and answering my many questions, I am most grateful. Margaret Goff has been most generous with her time and enthusiastic in her support of the project from my first hesitant suggestion that she might consider entrusting me with the biography of her late uncle. I can only hope that she feels that I have done his story full justice.

Given this prime source material, any gaps in the family records were more than adequately filled by documents held in the National Archives at Kew and by selected published works as acknowledged in the bibliography. But for personal memories and anecdotes to flesh out the often sterile official accounts and add considerable colour to Johnny Wells' story, I am indebted to some of those who knew him and flew alongside him. For their time and most generous hospitality whilst sharing memories of the man and their shared experiences, and for answering my questions, I am therefore grateful to: the late Wing Commander Roland 'Bee' Beamont, CBE DSO★ DFC★

DFC (USA) DL FRAeS; the late Squadron Leader Lawrence 'Pinky' Stark, DFC★ AFC; Flight Lieutenant Sir Alec 'Joe' Atkinson, KCB DFC; and Flight Lieutenant Sydney 'Darkie' Hanson, MBE. Others who also provided valuable assistance were Peter Brookes of the Sheringham Museum; Jim Earnshaw of the No 609 (West Riding) Squadron Association; and fellow aviation historian Chris Goss, whose extensive photo collection once again proved invaluable. I thank them all.

My old friend and mentor, the late Bruce Robertson, generously cast an editorial eye over the completed text and offered several helpful suggestions. He also offered many photographs from his extensive private collection depicting aircraft flown by Johnny Wells during his early career. I was pleased to have had this final opportunity to once more share time with one of the founding fathers of the British aviation historian movement and regret that he did not see it reach fruition.

Peter Cornwell
Girton, Cambridge
May 2011

1

SHERINGHAM SHANNOCKS

Yellaway, yellaway, hear me great loud rattle,
Fly away, fly away, never more you'll settle

Norfolk children's rhyme

John Christopher Wells was born on 28 May 1912, in Sheringham on the north Norfolk coast; sea air in his lungs and salt water in his veins. The latest addition to an unbroken line spanning more than four generations of Norfolk fishermen, he was the youngest of three children, his sister Margaret being six years older and his brother Robert three.

Under normal circumstances, Johnny would have followed in his father's footsteps, and those of his grandfather and great-grandfather before him, by becoming an inshore fisherman. But he was a 'Mad Shannocks', as tradition along this wild stretch of coast labels those who are Sheringham born – for their 'shannying' or wild and reckless risk-taking, and born into a period of great social and economic upheaval. And with such change comes fresh opportunities and challenges. Dragging a mean and perilous living from the cruel North Sea was not for him. He would break with family tradition and choose a different element to shape his life. He would take to the air.

He grew up in Lower Sheringham, a popular seaside resort a few miles west of Cromer, set ''twixt sea and pine' as described in the publicity posters of the day. The neighbouring parish, Upper Sheringham, sheltered from the on-shore breezes a mile further inland, had a neat cluster of grey stone cottages set around All Saints church and the adjacent tavern. Surrounded by gently rolling hills and thick woodland, Sheringham sprawled between grassy, gorse-covered cliffs rising a hundred feet or so above its wide, sandy beaches. Eastward, the coast curved away towards Cromer, while from Sheringham

Leas, high above the western promenade, the horizon was dominated by the sweep of Blakeney Point 10 miles to the west along the coast.

Sheringham, a quiet, relaxed place, shunned the blatantly vulgar displays and fairground attractions of other resorts. Yet despite more than a whiff of gentile pretension on the sea air, it had a particular charm which held its visitors in thrall and was in essence a modest little town offering an honest and hearty welcome.

Little has changed there over the years. The High Street slopes gently down towards the seafront from the Victorian railway station alongside the main road to Cromer. And at a fork in the road, just down from St Peter's church, a squat clock tower sits in the shadow of buildings whose upper storeys are decorated in the mock-Tudor style so favoured by Victorian builders. Further down the street, at the lower end of town, a quaint jumble of grey pebble-built cottages crowd the seafront, all connected by a maze of alleys, cuts and closes, interspersed with shops, inns and boarding houses. A coastguard station and two lifeboat houses completed the picture-postcard scenery.

Heavy wooden window shutters are still fitted to most seafront properties, for winters here can be bleak. Biting North Sea winds and fierce storms, which in Johnny's youth were constantly undermining the cliffs, force those foolish souls who do venture outside in such weather to stay well wrapped up, with teeth clenched tight against the wind. But during the long, hot summer months, the local population of around 2,000 or so was swelled by swarms of visitors descending on the village by road and rail. The Midland and Great Northern Railway, King's Lynn to Norwich line, provided a good connection, via nearby Holt, to the quaint Hornby Dublo-like platform of Sheringham Halt.

Apart from this seasonal influx of visitors and the lucrative holiday trade, most of the local community gained a living from farming the acres of wheat and barley fields surrounding the village. Many harvested the sea. Like most towns and villages along this stretch of the Norfolk coast, Sheringham boasted its own fishing fleet with close to 300 boats and fishing smacks in its heyday. When Johnny was born, fishing was already in decline and the local fleet had reduced to about 75 boats and some 120 fishermen.

But, depending on weather and season, the fishing here could still be good with large catches of codling, skate, plaice, mackerel and herring being landed. The noise and bustle of boats competing to land their catches on to beaches festooned with wet sails, ropes and nets would have been familiar to young Johnny. Growing up in a family which owed its livelihood to the sea, he was often found playing amongst the wicker baskets and wooden boxes which littered the high water mark, crammed with crabs, lobsters and whelks en route to markets in Norwich and London.

Only a handful of the Sheringham fleet were luggers fitted for deep-sea fishing, most being in-shore boats like that operated by Johnny's father, John Cox Wells, a third generation fisherman. Most of his catch went straight to the family fish shop in town, Grice's, owned and run by his wife Mabel's family.

The Grices were another old Sheringham fishing family, Johnny's maternal grandfather, Robert Henry Grice, being greatly respected in the town. He owned the fish shop and was an elected member of the Urban District Council as well as being town crier, and served on the Sheringham lifeboat, the *Henry Ramey Upcher*. He also represented the town on the Eastern District Sea Fisheries Committee.

Another of Mabel's relations was a prominent member of the Fishery Board, serving aboard the vessel *Protector*. So Johnny's home life was dominated by talk of the weather and of the sea, and the house cluttered with bulky clothing, oilskins, sea boots and all the other paraphernalia associated with boats and fishing. His mother, a resolute and determined woman, did insist on keeping things neat and tidy and would spend hours trying to get the smell of fish off her hands before attending church every Sunday.

The Wells family had been fishermen and landowners on this coast for as far back as anyone cared to remember. Family folklore had it that years before, Johnny's great-great-grandfather had made a tidy sum selling land to the famous landscape artist Repton when Sheringham Park was being created for the Upcher family. Exactly what had happened to this fabled fortune was unclear, but through a series of inter-connected wills over the years a distant relative, a solicitor in Norwich, inherited most of it.

The sea had taken Johnny's great-grandfather in 1863, lost overboard and drowned at the age of 27, leaving a young widow with children to raise – a common enough occurrence in any fishing community in those days. Families who depended on the sea for a living were used to enduring such tragedies and many a child in Sheringham was raised without ever knowing a father.

Grandfather, John Philip Wells, another well-known local character and fisherman, had survived years at sea to settle into fairly comfortable retirement on an income largely derived from letting holiday apartments in the village. With the Grand Hotel and every other accommodation in the neighbourhood often full to overflowing during the summer months, this was a useful sideline for many local families and Johnny's grandfather advertised holiday apartments during the season. For years, Elim House, his property in Mill Lane, was a favourite holiday haunt for many families of 'regulars'.

With father often away at sea and mother busy in the fish shop, Margaret, Robert and young Johnny, were looked after by Dora Farrow, a distant cousin on their mother's side of the family. Throughout their early childhood Dora cared for the children as if they were her own and they all loved her dearly. But when Johnny was about 7 or 8 years of age, the family moved to Grimsby leaving Dora behind. It was an awful wrench for all of them.

Grimsby offered their father the chance of working the big deep-sea boats, which may have lacked the independence of running his own boat but carried none of the associated costs. It was a move borne of necessity. Times were very hard and there was little money to spare, particularly during the hard winter months when fishing often proved impossible due to the weather. The lure of a better, more reliable income proved irresistible. But before long it became clear that things weren't working out as planned and by 1922 the fiercely independent Mabel had had quite enough of Grimsby and her increasingly unreliable husband and she returned to her family in Sheringham with the three children.

They quickly settled back into the familiar routine of Sheringham life with its close-knit community. Most families here were interrelated over generations so they were surrounded by family and friends. To make ends meet, Mabel went back to what she knew best and opened another fish shop in West Runton, on the Cromer Road.

The children all attended the local council school where Johnny, always a bright and inquisitive child, emerged as a star pupil, regularly topping his class year after year. But once school was over he was as adventurous and playful as any boy his age, a popular playmate with a wide circle of friends, and a frequent patron of the cinema down the Cromer Road where he regularly surrendered his hard-earned coppers. With a shock of fine brown hair and bright hazel eyes, he grew up an active and athletic boy who never walked anywhere if he could get there by running, and would happily spend hours exploring the local countryside or playing on the beach with friends. He blossomed mentally and physically and shot up in height, soon outstripping his elder brother Robert.

On warm summer evenings, he was probably one of the dusty young urchins who would squat on the kerb outside the open-air theatre at Arcade Lawn to ogle the 'toffs' from the hotels along West Promenade who arrived in all their finery for the concert parties, attracted by popular entertainers of the day such as Leslie Henson, Jack and Claude Hulbert, or Cicely Courtnedge.

He grew up in a loving and affectionate family, mother and children remaining very close throughout their lives. Mabel raised them to cherish virtues she had been brought up to value herself: honesty, integrity and probity. The Grice family was full of people to look up to and take pride in: relations, however distant, who inspired great respect and deep admiration in young Johnny.

Meantime, Johnny's father stayed behind in Grimsby trying to make a living. He was away, often for days on end, far out in the North Sea, and contact with the family back in Sheringham was at best sporadic. Inevitably they became increasingly estranged and he soon became a background figure, rarely mentioned or discussed, particularly within earshot of the children.

On the face of it, there was little or nothing in Sheringham that would fuel a young boy's imagination or spark any interest in flying. For sure, Johnny would have known all about 'the first German bomb to fall in England in World War I' which had dropped in Whitehall Close, off Wyndham Street, early in the Great War. But this stray missile from Zeppelin L4 in January 1915 was surely scant reason for him to decide on a career in the Royal Air Force.

Did he, perhaps, on a hot summer's day lie up on the cliffs watching the occasional aircraft drift high overhead, the murmur of its engine merging with the hum of insects and the dull roar of the surf? Did he ever ride his treasured bicycle the 6 miles or so along dusty lanes to the nearest airfield at Holt? Here a landing ground had been established during the Great War as a satellite to the RNAS air station at Great Yarmouth and Zeppelin chasers had been based. But Johnny would have found no trace of them remaining and the grass knee-high.

The reality is probably far less romantic. In May 1926 Johnny would have been 14 years old, which was school-leaving age. That same month the TUC called a general strike in support of the coal miners and 4 million workers downed tools. The tottering British economy was in serious trouble. Employers and successive governments alike had failed to tackle rising taxation and the crippling costs of the First World War, and workers were ill-prepared to sacrifice hard-won improvements in their working conditions and living standards. A period of economic doldrums threatened which would last a decade and continue well into the 1930s. Prospects for a young lad about to leave school were bleak indeed.

Many head teachers, aware of the opportunities presented by the RAF Apprenticeship Scheme, actively encouraged lads with good educational standards and the necessary aptitude to consider the RAF for a future career. So it is highly likely that an approach from his headmaster, Mr S.E. Day, was how Johnny and the family first came to learn of the exciting possibility of an RAF apprenticeship.

Estcourt Day, headmaster of Sheringham Council School, was the source of great encouragement and support to his young student, offering sound advice and good counsel to the family which undoubtedly helped them reach certain decisions concerning Johnny's future. He also provided this glowing reference:

It gives me great pleasure to testify to the splendid character of John Wells late pupil of my school. During the last twelve months of his school career

Wells was senior boy and as such held positions of responsibility and trust. Throughout I have always found him honest, straightforward and trustworthy. He has always been most punctual, keen on his work and most willing to oblige. In 1925 he was awarded the Character Prize for the school, this being the result of voting from his own school fellows. I have no hesitation in recommending him as a youth of high moral character and feel sure he will do his duty thoroughly and willingly wherever he is.

S. Estcourt Day, Head Master.

It must have seemed like a godsend, as there was a growing awareness within the family that Johnny should avoid going to sea like so many of his forebears. He was gifted and bright, and, whilst it was probably never discussed openly, everyone accepted that young Johnny could have a bright future ahead of him. Besides, it was a very flattering thing for Johnny to be recommended so highly by his headmaster, a fact that an immensely proud mother would have undoubtedly shared with those who enquired after him in casual conversation over the shop counter.

Luckily, Johnny's elder sister and brother were both bringing money into the household, making it a lot easier to entertain any future for young Johnny beyond that of simply earning a living. Equally bright, his sister Margaret had quit school at 14 years of age to start work to help make ends meet and bring some extra money into the household purse. His brother Robert had a post round and worked alongside their mother in the fish shop, as well as a weekend job lighting the fires in Beeston church before services.

With the economy in the doldrums, the armed services were one of the few avenues which still offered a young man a decent chance of a career. They would even teach you a useful trade. Hadn't one of Johnny's uncles on his mother's side, John Edmund Grice, done well for himself in the Royal Navy? Joining as a boy cadet, he had served aboard HMS *Princess Royal* during the Great War, rising to become the youngest warrant officer in the service. Rumour had it that he would soon be commissioned as an officer which was some achievement for a Sheringham lad, educated at the local school, but it just went to show what was possible.

So, with Mr Day's help, the necessary application forms were completed and sent off. A prompt acknowledgement duly arrived. There was a stiff entrance examination to be taken, consisting of two three-hour papers. According to his mentor, Mr Day, of the 500 or so boys who would sit the examination across the whole country that June, only the top 200 would be selected. So extra coaching was the order of the next few weeks. Finally, the great day came, and although Johnny felt that he had done his best and was quietly confident, it was a tense time awaiting the results.

In due course a buff OHMS envelope fluttered through the letter box and with fingers trembling with excitement and anticipation, Johnny tore it open. Anxiously he scanned the contents trying to make sense of it all. He had to read it twice before the truth dawned: A list of successful entrants to the 'Limited Competitive Examination for the Entry of Aircraft Apprentices' included his name. He was placed 103rd out of 467 and had 'gained entrance to the RAF Apprentice School at Halton'. Delighted at his success, Johnny was nevertheless a little surprised at his somewhat humble rating after enjoying top place at Sheringham Council School for so long. Clearly he was moving up a grade and would need to buckle down to some serious study to stay in the race. But as his mother was quick to point out, many of the other successful applicants came from prestigious sounding schools or even technical colleges. He was to report within the week and a travel warrant and joining instructions were enclosed. He was to be an airman.

2

TRENCHARD BRAT

On 31 August 1927, 561960 Boy Aircraft Apprentice John Christopher Wells, along with 300 or so other would-be erks, arrived at a small railway station in rural Buckinghamshire en route to RAF No 1 School of Technical Training at Halton.

Alighting from the train, they were greeted by a loud-voiced flight sergeant who checked their names against his list and shepherded them all into waiting trucks for the journey to Halton, about 4 miles from Aylesbury amongst the rolling Chiltern hills. Bouncing around in the back of the lorry, Johnny viewed the passing scenery with interest. It was decidedly different to the wide horizons and levels of his native East Anglia.

On arrival at Halton, Johnny found himself allotted a member of 'C' Squadron, in No 4 Apprentices Wing. They were harried into groups and formed up on the grey tarmac parade ground facing a flagpole flanked by an anti-aircraft gun, a relic from the Great War. The RAF standard fluttered weakly in the breeze. Blank windows of the tall, red-brick barrack blocks surrounding the square gazed down on them. Suddenly, they were all feeling strangely subdued, out of place and very, very civilian.

After a few words of welcome from an astonishingly immaculate officer who turned out to be the CO, Wing Commander W.C. Hicks no less, they stomped off to be medically examined and were then sworn in as aircraft apprentices – no turning back now.

Next they were issued with mattresses, blankets and pillows, directed to their dormitories, and shown how to make up their beds. Then, a brief tour of the ablutions: heavily disinfected toilets and a long washroom with rows of taps and bowls down one side and open shower cubicles opposite, before adjourning to the mess hall for tea. Here they queued at the serving hatches for bread and margarine with a dollop of jam, a slab of fruit cake and a steaming cup of dark brown tea drawn from enormous urns and served in thick china mugs emblazoned with the RAF crest. Perched on a bench and jostling for elbow room at one of the long mess tables, Johnny munched his way through it amidst the excited chatter around him and reflected on his introduction to service life. So this would be home for the next three years – not bad at all!

The following morning, after reveille at an obscenely early hour, they stumbled through ablutions and off to breakfast. Two lads from each mess table collected what was on offer from the kitchen hatch, carried it back and dished it out to the others with much hurried passing of plates and ribald comments on the size of some portions which came under close scrutiny. Suitably fortified, everyone was then ushered to the barber's shop from where they emerged a little later like shorn lambs.

Next the clothing store, where they shuffled along in front of a counter to be issued with uniforms: breeches, puttees, boots, high-necked 'choker' tunic, peaked cap, stiff overalls, socks and underwear – the lot. Most things were issued in threes: one to wear, one to wash and one spare for kit inspection, which added considerably to the overall bulk. On top of which came a bewildering assortment of boot brushes, cleaning kit, plates, mug, knife, fork and spoon, webbing, towels, their very own bath plug, and a huge kit bag to carry it all.

Staggering under the load, they returned to their billets and changed into uniform, swapping items of clothing with one another in an effort to find something that approximated a decent fit. Struggling into coarse, unfamiliar uniforms was an uncomfortable yet exciting experience for the young apprentices. Civilian clothes were parcelled up and addressed home before they expectantly viewed results. They were starting to look something like proper airmen, 'with most artificial waist and more artificial chest and rump' as Johnny described himself, though most still felt and certainly looked distinctly less than military.

An inveterate correspondent, Johnny wrote regular letters to his sister Margaret back home in Sheringham throughout his time at Halton. Every week or so he would describe his latest adventures and, fortunately, many of these letters have survived. They provide fascinating insights into his character and his impressions, with often graphic descriptions of the typical experiences of a Halton apprentice in the late 1920s. Written in his characteristic neat, confident hand, they display obvious affection, a keen sense of observation, and a wicked sense of humour.

Obviously one early mystery, that of winding unfamiliar puttees around calves, took hours of practice to master amidst much hilarity. But like everything else at Halton he soon got used to them:

Some poor laddie got into a terrible mess with his putees. Somehow he wound them round both knees and after tugging first one end and then the other for half an hour he finally finished with half of them round his neck and was in danger of slow asphyxiation. Beastly things puttees. They are put on so tightly that when at last I staggered back to the barracks and removed them from the shanks, the pins and needles arrived by the truck.

The RAF, or more accurately its predecessor the RFC, had been at Halton since 1917 when it took over a military site there as a training centre. But not until plans were being finalised for the future of the post-war RAF did the concept of Halton fully emerge. It was the brainchild of Hugh Trenchard, the 'father of the RAF', who in 1920 announced plans for an Aircraft Apprenticeship Scheme for boys of good education and physical fitness. Under this scheme, boys 15 to 17 years of age would sign on for twelve years' regular RAF service, the first three of which would be spent at Halton being trained as ground technicians and tradesmen. No 1 Apprentice Wing, with 1,000 entrants, first formed there on 22 October 1925 and regular intakes had followed ever since, Johnny joining the sixteenth entry.

Halton was a huge complex of buildings and it was not long before Johnny and his new chums were off exploring their surroundings and looking around:

I had a squint inside the school on Saturday. Through one doorway labelled 'Lab' I espied a queer chunk of engineering which seemed to suggest weird and wonderful evolutions, however we could not investigate on the spot ... We next trailed into the lecture hall, an imposing room with tiers and tiers of seats towering skywards, all nicely carpeted and distempered in bale buff and dark brown, and with a white dome. We gaped into the maths rooms which looked so dry that we retreated to the hockey pitch where we maimed each others' legs with painful hard hockey clubs and a much harder ball.

Their first few weeks were spent in learning basic drill and settling into the disciplines of service life: reveille at 0630 hours, ablutions and a quick cup of cocoa, before falling in outside the barrack blocks in shorts and singlets for thirty minutes' exercise. Come rain or snow, the physical training instructor kept them on their toes until they glowed – then a most welcome breakfast, often the best meal of the day. After that, following daily routine orders, there was inspection by the duty officer before a period of hearty drill under the steadfast gaze of Wing Sergeant Major Lea – irreverently known to all and sundry as 'Annabelle'.

Most of the senior NCOs were ex-Brigade of Guards, recruited to lick the infant RAF into shape, so discipline at the wing was harsh. Every Friday a dormitory inspection took place and woe betide any group who failed to reach the required standard; fatigues or loss of privileges were regular features of life at Halton. One of Johnny's early letters home describes a fairly typical daily round:

> We have had a strenuous day today and when we came off the square limp and fatigued everybody was blessing vaccination and unsympathetic Sergeant Majors. We have early meals here, brekker being at 7.00, dinner at 12.30 and tea at 4.30, so that by the middle of the evening we are famished and have to retire to the NAAFI where one Eccles cake cost 1 1/2d and an extra halfpenny is clapped on everything for luck. They are so mean that they take the wrappers off the Sharps Creamy Toffees because free gifts can be obtained from them. Some of the chaps are waxing eloquent over it because they are within fifty or so of the required 500 wrappers!

The workshop complex was vast, covering a few acres, with workshops adjacent to each other and set out in long rows. Here budding apprentices learned their trade, under Squadron Leader MacLean, and the work was painstaking, often literally so, but the atmosphere more relaxed than the discipline of the wing.

They were to spend the whole of their first year working on a solid block of cast iron learning several basic skills. One side of the iron block had to be filed flat, and two even parallel grooves cut down the centre. Then you had to chip away the ridges which stood proud as a result of all this effort and file the surface perfectly flat again. Working at crowded benches in a huge noisy workshop, young inexperienced hands wielded heavy hammers, files and surgically sharp chisels. The din was incredible and the resultant damage to fingers and knuckles had to be seen to be believed. Gradually the skills of measuring, marking off and working to fine limits of a thousandth of an inch were mastered.

During this period, preliminary tests were conducted to start assessing the suitability of each apprentice for selection to specific trades: airframes, engines, armament or transport. Johnny found himself earmarked as a potential engine fitter which suited him just fine. It seemed to have a lot more about it than simply patching and repairing airframes, although he had to admit that the armourer's job had a certain appeal – handling bombs, machine guns, ammunition and the like. All very exciting and war-like.

Every afternoon, apart from Wednesday, was spent in the workshops learning technical skills whilst periods in the machine shop, welding shop, foundry, metal shop and blacksmiths further extended their technical knowledge. After a year mastering basic theory and practice, they were ready to transfer to the hangars to start work on the real thing.

Workshop schoolrooms conducted by experienced NCO fitters, many of them ex-naval engine room artificers and sporting dustcoats complete with stripes denoting their rank, were set up in each corner of the hangars. Here Johnny and his fellow engine apprentices were introduced to the baffling complexities of the modern aero engine, starting with the fundamental principles of internal combustion before moving on to the differences between in-line, radial and rotary engines.

The tutors knew their trade inside out and would pass on their knowledge to small groups of a dozen or so rapt apprentices, dressed in the obligatory overalls, who clustered around perched upon benches in front of the blackboard. Instruction was clear and questions encouraged at every stage and sessions were often enlivened with humour or some colourful anecdote culled from the instructors' lurid past.

Sessions were interspersed with practical tuition, again done in small groups so that everyone got hands-on experience. Using motor engines at first, they progressed on to low-powered aero engines. They bench-stripped and re-assembled engine components and entire motors until they could practically do it blindfolded. Within a few months they were tackling major overhauls and refits. Gradually, they laid bare the mysteries of engines, carburettors and magnetos; superchargers and pumps; filters, fuel and hydraulic systems; and a myriad of other topics, until they were deemed proficient enough to graduate on to more modern high-powered radial and in-line aero engines.

Much of the training was done with engine in situ on the aircraft, which meant working in the open in all weathers. It was here that they turned theory into practice and started to gain the skills that would be required of them. Everything was done under the expert tuition and constant supervision of the instructors, some of whom, Johnny and his cronies soon learned, had barks worse than their bites:

Things are at the usual mid-term state. One ghastly engine (complete with final exam) just over. Tomorrow we start on our last – the famous Napier Lion. Naturally we change our instructors & we get a bull-necked Lancashireman – Wilkins by name instead of the long suffering Ware. I believe he is a happy soul & if he did not expect you to file to .0005" of arc dimension he would be alright. Anyway I have seen him laugh – so must be alright. Anybody who can face us & laugh has some innards!

We were put on washing down some machines & the day & water being very hot, interest in washing flagged somewhat, so a little liveliness was clearly indicated. The soft soap which we had been using … made lovely snowballs only slightly more odiferous & messy than self respecting snow. Still it stuck where it hit & that is the main thing. There were twelve of us altogether & three machines. The ensuing battle was exactly what you might expect & believe me was highly satisfactory from every point of view, which is more than can be said for the machines. After that … bootless & sockless we skidded nicely over the main planes in real Swiss style & rubbed in the superfluous soap. The next operation was washing it off so we tied huge dusters on our wamps & paddled to & fro from numerous water tubs all over the planes. Rinsing being the next process more water was brought, the dusters changed & more paddling ensued; the result being highly satisfactory to everyone & the planes a model of industry & energy. Altogether the 'drome course was a good time & we are very sorry to return to the old routine.

Many early graduates of the Halton Apprenticeship Scheme, on joining regular RAF units, were met with a degree of jealousy, suspicion or downright contempt by the more seasoned veterans serving in the squadrons. These 'old sweats', many of whom were approaching expiry of their service contracts, felt threatened by the apprentices' higher educational standards and feared for their jobs. They dubbed the Halton boys 'Trenchard's Brats', a disparaging put-down which the apprentices learned to accept willingly and later adopted with a perverse but fierce pride. After all, they were as steeped in the heritage of the RAF and as jealous of its traditions as those who had learned them the 'hard way'. But attitudes began to change when the Halton apprentices' knowledge and skills became self-evident to the most hardened sceptic. Yet even when they became widely acknowledged as the finest tradesmen in RAF service, 'brats' they remained and do so to this day.

As well as their technical training, general schooling and physical well-being, the day-to-day routine of squadron life made additional demands on an apprentices' time with a variety of tasks and extra responsibilities.

I was on the fire picket last week. Exciting times! At 6.00 pm precisely last Friday when we had just put our weary rumps upon the forms in the dining hall, the fire buzzer buzzed. Instant commotion! Uproar! Then a ruddy blush for the door! In record time we hied across the square to the drill shed and grabbed the fire cart right heartily. Bill Hicks, the Wing Commander, rolled up ten minutes later and trailed up and down the bored ranks. It was only an alarm! Groans. The whistle went and we dashed back to the jolly old rations. As in duty bound, the fateful eight had to wait until the square was empty. Dolefully we rushed back to the feast. Alas snaffled – gone to the unknown! Starving we retired to the Naafi. Such is life!

An ambitious project undertaken by apprentices during Johnny's first year was the construction from scratch of a full-size biplane. Once completed and test flown, it was handed over to the Halton Station Flight who maintained it in first-class trim and flying condition – as was to be expected. It became a familiar sight in the sky around Halton and a constant reminder to every apprentice of what could be achieved.

The following July, someone on the staff decided that it would be 'an absolutely beezer idea' to convert the biplane into a monoplane. This was another major undertaking but, as the instructors recognised, an excellent learning vehicle for those involved in the design, planning, drawing, construction, rigging and bench testing. It was a project that had the potential to cover practically the entire syllabus. Gallons of midnight oil later, with the conversion done, all the necessary flight tests completed and the Certificate of Airworthiness duly granted, there was much celebration. Only then was it announced to the astonished assembly of proud young apprentices that their new 'Halton Mono' was to be entered in the next King's Cup Air Race!

In the weeks leading up to the big event, growing excitement and anticipation on the station approached fever pitch. The forthcoming race became the sole topic of conversation with endless discussions on the relative merits of each new entrant and their previous form. Newspapers were eagerly scanned and aviation journals scoured for any scrap of information. Meantime, the aircraft itself was lavished with attention, fine-tuned and streamlined to a standard hitherto only dreamt of. Confidence grew.

On the day of the race only a small select group from Halton were allowed to attend but news of the result preceded their return. Leading the race and only 2 miles from the finish, the Halton entry had run out of petrol and had been forced to land – literally something of a come-down, but a magnificent performance of which they could all feel justifiably proud. Or so it was said at the time.

On top of classroom theory and practical work, every apprentice had to attend a full round of instructional films, demonstrations and technical lectures, some of them delivered by leading experts in the field:

I had a perfectly ripping evening last week at a lecture on 'Slotted Wings' by Handley Page. The gathering was of course select & the front benches were eminent technical officers & others of like ilk. We were the back benchers. Brother Page ambled happily through his notes & slides (90% shown upside down) & then came the discussion – and the fun.

His first victim was a Squadron Leader of great renown who 'midst respectful silence asked a question about the air eddies over the upper surface of the planes wings & said they were most noticeable at a certain part. Brother Page armed with lengthy pointer & smirking broadly indicated a spot on the diagram & said, 'You mean there?' His Highness replied in the affirmative &

then – 'Well they don't, it's here!' from H.P. pointing to another spot a yard away & grinning expansively. His Highness just sank down weakly upon his unsympathetic chair whilst we rocked & choked at his foaming dial.

Another ass from the centre of the assembly then got up sprightly & expounded at painful length speaking with his usual plummy voice. He wound up with great stress, lifting his eyebrows to soaring heights by way of effect. Dead silence followed this learned tirade & then H.P. said, "Fraid I don' quite git yer!' The learned friend fairly gobbled, then grew gloriously red whilst guffaws that were nearly muffled arose from the back benches. Deflation finally set in & he sat down perspiring.

We began to take a lively interest at this point & by the time the lecture closed down we were shrieking at the answers thrown around to the learned by H.P.

Clearly an accomplished speaker, Handley Page obviously knew a thing or two about putting a message across and had gauged his audience to a tee.

Two days a week were also spent on school studies in order to raise apprentices' standard of general education to at least matriculation level. Mathematics, science, technical drawing and English were drummed into them under the supervision of the headmaster, Mr H.A. Cox, and Sunday morning church parade punctuated each week, helping to keep track of the days, with religious services conducted in a converted hangar.

There was also a fairly regular stream of visiting dignitaries and foreign delegations, all keen to learn what they could of the RAF Apprentice Scheme in general and Halton in particular. Without doubt, it was an impressive facility and a much-admired jewel in the RAF crown. Over a single four-month period between March and July 1928, Halton hosted visits by the King of Afghanistan, the Czechoslovakian Air Attaché, a delegation of French officers and three officers from the Imperial Japanese Army. One of Johnny's letters captures something of such occasions from an apprentice's viewpoint:

We had our annual inspection by the AOC on Monday. We played at soldiers until 11am whilst the Wing band played a mournful dirge on bagpipes or bellowed brazenly from trumpets. They turned on some flutes by way of a treat (?) & that just about settled it. Had it not been for the OC persisting in saying 'Flights florm flours' it would have been a disaster.

But it was not all work and 'bull', for sports and physical education also featured on the syllabus. Of average height and build, Johnny stood 5ft 8in and enjoyed such activities, particularly cross-country running. Every Wednesday afternoon was set aside for sports, weather permitting, or even it seems when not:

Yesterday it rained Halton rain. It just fell. Consequently all games were off and some bright spark had an inspiration – X country. We set off and trailed down the Wendover Road for about a mile and two hills. Then we broke off and squelched happily up a morass labelled 'Farm Road' and waded muddily another ½ mile till we came to the worst hill in Bucks. It was chalk, it was wet, and it was raining Halton rain on the worst hill in Bucks up which we were supposed to run. Terrific groans.

We treadmilled up the skyline. It took ages. At last we reached the top and plunged into the wood, and incidentally more water. We wallowed through twigs and beautiful foliage. Knee-deep we emerged to the tipmost top (or topmost tip?). Then we had to descend. We did. A winding path led temptingly downwards covered by a carpet of brown autumnal leaves. Tempted, we rushed and we fell. The leaves were two feet deep and wet. The jolly old wamps kicked up the Persian carpet in a sloppy exhaust. I caught somebody's wake and thirsted for revenge. I forged ahead and gave him my wake. Not 'arf. He was smothered. Happy, I continued. The gradient took its effect. My feet seemed to revolve. I tore my way through leaf and twig and arrived in record time at the bottom. A clear way lay ahead and I let it rip. I mowed 'em down like hay. I was done in when the Naafi gates heaved in sight and I staggered wetly upstairs leaving my trail as I proceeded.

Apprentices at Halton were members of a Flight within a Squadron, like the house system in public schools, and teams representing each Flight competed for the many sports cups and prizes to be won throughout the year. The better sportsmen amongst them could graduate to the squadron team, but only the very best of them stood any chance of qualifying to represent the wing. Johnny, a good runner, was less keen on other sports and this obviously included boxing:

We had a shriek last Wednesday. In the afternoon we all had to go and watch the boxing. After a time we felt bored … thus when we were told we had to watch it again the next night we groaned. At 9.00 pm feeling utterly fed up with boxing and boxers who were afraid to tap each other, we (my chum and I) trailed off and then turned in. At 11.00 pm the others turned up … we grinned happily from the jolly old blankets. The others raged. Tired as they were, the temptation to a pillow fight was not to be resisted. Therefore at 11.00 pm Room 6 was an uproar and after a strenuous twenty minutes we crawled back to bed and encored the efforts of some unhappy lads who were trying to make their beds, the lights having gone out at just after 11.15.

On 28 May 1930, Johnny, reaching the exalted age of 18, achieved 'man status' in the eyes of His Majesty's Royal Air Force. His salary was doubled to a full guinea a week which undoubtedly helped with the cost of the cigarettes he was now officially permitted to smoke, although he had already been doing so for some time, risking a day's detention had he been caught. After nearly three years in the service, to the vocal distress of his mother but barely concealed mirth of his sister, Johnny was also developing a very colourful vocabulary.

By now, Johnny and his cronies were old hands and fast becoming well versed in the ways of the service; younger, less experienced apprentices being considered fair game:

> Here all the lamp-posts bearing fire alarms are painted with horizontal red & white stripes for half their height. Some wag told some poor innocent 'rooks' to line up at one for their first haircut indicating lamp-post to assure them that the adjoining building was the barbers. A doleful line accumulated its members patiently waiting for the doors to open. At last they did & the Wing Sergeant Major came in sight tapping belt in a satisfied manner. His brilliant optics then lighted on the line in front of him & popped out of his head in the approved manner. A minute of vain gurgling & this dignitary then quietly enquired what they wanted outside the Sergeants Mess!
>
> The timid line having restored themselves to their feet after the polite enquiry replied 'Haircuts' in various keys & tones. The WSM then developed a mild fit for he landed the first one a beauty & then carried on moving down the steadfast though wavering line in record time. The line needless to say soon dispersed & melted gradually & painfully away whilst the WSM hitching pantaloons & belt made his way to his car.

Now WSM 'Annabelle' Lea was inordinately proud of his motorcar, which Johnny describes as a 'super extra-special two-seater coupe sports model', a source of considerable interest and amusement:

> It was bought expressly to do one of the officers in the eye as (he) has just got a rare saloon car which quite outdid the WSM's Fiat. Now the WSM's car is glorious to look at but makes a terrible row when the engine is going. When Symington (Flt Lt Archibald Symington MC) first got his the WSM drew up in his Fiat pretty silently & viewed the other car with the eye of the owner-driver, noting polished black leather covering etc etc. His engine purred happily away & he asked the other respectfully when he was going to start his engine at which Brother Symington grinned & glided happily away. The engine had been going all the while! Curses from the WSM.

The WSM however gets this latest creation, a Hillman, in reply & we are waiting to see what his rival will do. I think the WSM has bitten off a big bit this time because the rival happens to be Symington of the soup family & has thousands of quids laying around as a matter of course. Yesterday he had his Hillman engine running & Symington told him to 'shut off that damned row'. More curses from WSM which of course are just what we like. I don't know what he will do if Symington rolls up in a Rolls on Monday.

Meantime, his studies were progressing well:

I staggered up for a 'Board' on the Jupiter engine yesterday morning. The examiner (an expert) has unfortunately a mouth like the cross-section of a bad pear … & I was almost moved to mild hilarity. However I was only there for fifteen minutes (others had fifty) & so soon staggered back to the fold. I was nearly last to go from our crowd so had all the answers off pat. He seemed quite peeved – my Colgate treated molars seemed to transfix him & negate all his efforts to make me contradict my theoretical expoundings. Tomorrow I go forth again like a lamb to the slaughter – this will occur thrice more in all.

Quick and keen to learn, Johnny was a good scholar and figured well in examinations which didn't escape the notice of his wing commander, who wrote, 'You have done very well in this paper and I am pleased with it. Your work shows that you can be relied upon to give a good account of yourself in any emergency.' Exactly what sort of emergency prompted this comment or what the wing commander had in mind is unfortunately not recorded, but another of Johnny's letters possibly contains a clue:

We were practising starting up the engine in a Flycatcher & an instructor (Hopper by name) was perched on a step ladder just by the cockpit dealing out the information to the gallant A/A (Aircraft Apprentice) in the cockpit. This brilliant lad had forgotten to adjust the throttle lever & it was in the full open position. Well she started & so did Hopper! The engine was doing twice the revolutions she should have been & as the bus was chocked down the airscrew created such a slipstream that it blew (Hopper) off the top of the step ladder … the whole affair swept away in the direction of the tail! They finished in a nice heap by the rudder having flown the intervening space.

Meanwhile the old engine was roaring away & the A/A in the cockpit was happily waiting for the instructor to operate said throttle. As you will gather Hopper had somewhat shifted his position & after a nerve-racking time the A/A in the cockpit looked around. Hopper not being on the horizon the A/A's eyes went up about 7 inches & the bus went up the chocks. Hopper still being deprived of wind another he-man arrived & shut off the engine. Naturally we were howling away with mirth but our 'old man' had the wind-up properly.

Time was also found for social activities, apprentices being allowed to 'walk out' occasionally, complete with obligatory cane carried in the right hand. But for Johnny, the most abiding memories of his days at Halton involved the rituals of service life and its traditions. Lowering the colours every evening at sunset as the trumpeter sounded 'Flag Down' was a particular memory which stayed with him.

On 22 August 1930, after a welcome spell of leave spent at home in Sheringham, Johnny completed his three-year course. Back at Halton the long-awaited results of final examinations and trade tests were announced and Johnny learned that he had graduated as a Fitter (Aero Engines) with top grading as Leading Aircraftman. To achieve this he must have scored an 80 per cent pass mark at least, undoubtedly a fine result for a young man from the council school in Sheringham. He could feel justifiably proud of himself, for only around one in eight apprentices passed muster as LACs and 'put up their props'. As he confided to his sister Margaret with due modesty, 'I haven't done so dusty – compared with some of my contemporaries'.

Then, and all too soon it seemed, it was farewell to Halton with a passing-out ceremony, march past and salute taken by the new CO, W/C H.J.F. Hunter MC. It was a stirring and memorable occasion for all. Within a few days, swearing undying allegiance and everlasting comradeship, they dispersed with their first notices of posting. To Johnny's delight his stated preference being taken into account, he was to report to No 35 (Bomber) Squadron at Bircham Newton, in Norfolk, within easy reach of home; he was also given a forty-eight-hour pass.

3

BIRCHAM NEWTON

Bircham Newton, a large permanent RAF station, had sprung up due to rapid expansion during the First World War. It sported the most impressive guardhouse Johnny had ever seen, where he reported on arrival. With its neat, whitewashed, portico columns, it resembled a Greek temple and would not have been out of place on top of Mount Olympus. Ruining the illusion, military buildings and low hutments clustered around it, all over-shadowed by an immense water tower which dominated the area around the main entrance. Through its massive iron legs Johnny could see the tops of some huge sheds beyond, hangars that once housed giant Handley Page V/1500 four-engined bombers. Everything here seemed to be on a grand scale.

From the guardhouse, Johnny was directed to the barrack blocks opposite the parade ground further down the road. Hoisting his kitbag over his shoulder he made off through what resembled a building site. There seemed to be a lot of work going on, with gangs of civilian contractors everywhere. Picking his way through the mess, he reached 'Mons', an imposing two-storey barrack block that would be home for the foreseeable future. Being fairly new, the barracks had decent amenities and could accommodate sixty to seventy airmen in spartan comfort under the watchful eye of three resident NCOs. Johnny was shown around, allocated a bed and locker in one of the upstairs dormitories, and started settling in.

Apart from all the building work, things were strangely quiet. The entire station had a haunted air about it and Johnny soon learned that he had arrived in the middle of a month-long period of leave. Bircham Newton's two squadrons, Nos 35 and 207, had only just returned from Upper Heyford after a major exercise. Such activities, he was reliably informed, were a significant part of station life for both squadrons were organised and trained as special service units which could pack up and move quickly, even abroad if necessary in the event of an emergency.

Johnny's unit, No 35 Squadron, a day bomber squadron, had disbanded after the First World War to reform in March 1929 as part of the Air Defence of Great Britain (ADGB), the forerunner of what later became RAF Fighter Command. The squadron had recently exchanged its vintage DH9A bombers for Fairey IIIFs, a general-purpose aircraft used extensively by the RAF and the Fleet Air Arm in a variety of roles. The squadron, organised into three flights, each of six aircraft, with a Headquarters Flight of four, was commanded by S/L B.E. Harrison AFC. Johnny found himself allocated to 'A' Flight under Flight Lieutenant A. Jones.

As LAC Fitter (Aero Engine), Johnny's main concern was keeping the water-cooled Napier Lion XI engines up to scratch. But he was confident that, given his Halton training, he would soon find his way around the bowels of the 570hp power plant and the intricacies of its lubrication and cooling systems.

Normally, on posting to squadrons, Halton apprentices, or 'ex-boys' to use the service parlance of the day, were required to work for a full year under supervision of an experienced fitter. But many of these older men with years of service under their belts, finding themselves threatened by the educational standards introduced by the Trenchard scheme, resented the intrusion of these Trenchard Brats who were not only well educated but also technically proficient. Many old stalwarts in the technical trades, who had learned their craft the hard way through years of service in the RFC or RNAS, had to meet the new standards or quit the service on completion of their contracts. As a result, Halton apprentices sometimes met with mixed receptions or experienced a rough passage on joining their first squadrons.

Johnny, who had already 'made the grade' as LAC and sported the propeller badges on his sleeve to prove it, had no such trouble and settled in quickly. On more than one occasion his natural good humour and infectious grin saw him through any potential difficulty, and well before the end of the usual year of working under instruction and assisting other fitters, he was entered for trade tests to confirm his proficiency to work unsupervised. The tests, which were conducted at the RAF depot at West Drayton, turned out to be much the same as Johnny's final examination at Halton: a basic filing test in the morning followed by a verbal examination on engines in the afternoon. He sailed through.

Completing your first Aircraft Serviceability Form after the daily inspection of an engine was another milestone in a young fitter's career. So, after a suitable period of instruction, and assisting in this routine but vital task, Johnny was finally deemed ready to do one on his own. Sleep the night before was difficult.

The great day eventually dawned, but his flight sergeant was almost matter-of-fact as he thrust the necessary docket towards him, his fingers stained a curious shade of sallow brown from years of exposure to nicotine, oil and 'Grease – Yellow – General Purpose'. But 'Flight' became more solicitous as they picked their way across the hangar towards the waiting aircraft. 'Don't cut corners lad,' he muttered through his moustache. 'Do things just the way you've been shown and you'll do fine. And if you're not sure about something, don't take chances – just ask.' They stopped in front of a IIIF and, checking the serial number against the docket clutched firmly in Johnny's hand, he gave him a friendly pat on the shoulder, 'Here you are – she's all yours'.

'She's all yours.' The words seemed to echo in Johnny's head as Flight's footsteps receded back across the hangar towards his shanty wooden cubicle lodged in the corner. Johnny experienced something of that indefinable emotion that can link man and machine. Reaching out he touched the engine cowling, patting the polished metal as he would a favourite dog. Then, stuffing the all-important docket deep into an overall pocket, he reached for his tools.

Following the familiar routine until he was satisfied that everything was in order, Johnny signed off the aircraft with something of a flourish and with a considered degree of nonchalance. But shortly afterwards, feeling more than a little apprehensive after signing himself responsible for several thousands of pounds worth of His Majesty's aircraft, he watched it start up, take off and climb steadily away into the wide blue yonder. To his immense relief, nothing fell off.

Some time later, when it returned and landed, he made sure that he just happened to be around to casually enquire of the pilot how it had gone. 'It ran sweet as a nut, dear boy, sweet as a nut. Absolutely top notch,' was the pilot's casual response as he clambered down from the cockpit wrestling with his scarf. Johnny's face creased into an enormous grin and inwardly he glowed with pride. Out of sight behind him, even his flight sergeant allowed himself a quiet smile.

In most squadrons, ground crew had the chance to occupy a rear seat and take to the air, many of them getting the bug and subsequently applying for a transfer to aircrew. It was a practice the service was happy to encourage, for airmen flying in the aircraft they were responsible for servicing was sound policy, and pilots putting in flying time for their logbooks were always pleased to take up a willing passenger.

Johnny's first chance came on 30 April 1931, seven months after joining the squadron, when he joined Sergeant Fox for a fifteen-minute local flight in Fairey IIIF J9822. His Form 414 Flying Logbook, impeccably completed in his neat, firm hand, unfortunately gives no clue as to his impressions of his first flight. But it was another two weeks before he again took to the air, also with Sergeant Fox, after which flights together became more frequent.

Johnny found the IIIF a very steady machine in the air, a 'gentleman's aircraft' the pilots called it, and apparently it was relatively easy to fly though not to everyone's liking. During a recent visit to England by the famous American aviator Charles Lindbergh, he had flown one and commented:

> A cavernous cockpit filled with nothing but smell and noise and me, supported by great shuddering wings strung together by random struts and wire and string. The engine sounded somehow as if it had been running since the beginning of time but that it would go on till the end.

Johnny was a regular back-seat passenger in J9822 over the following months, with a succession of pilots including, on one occasion, the new CO, S/L Brown. Swathed in bulky flying clothing, with Sidcot suit, sheepskin-lined flying boots, leather flying helmet, goggles and gloves, he felt very much at home in the air.

A fresh spate of exercises started in July 1931 when, on successive days, No 35 Squadron flew sorties over West India Docks, which they 'bombed' from 13,000ft and were 'intercepted' by opposing fighters. Silver-doped Bulldogs and Furies sporting vivid squadron colours on their fuselages and upper wings snarled and darted about their formation. The squadron also flew photo reconnaissance missions over Aldershot and Salisbury Plain where the army exercised their tanks. Unfortunately, Johnny, not included, remained back at Bircham Newton but still taking every opportunity for an occasional local flight.

The following month, the entire squadron flew off to Andover, but the exercises planned there were cut short by bad weather. No sooner back at Bircham Newton, they flew a series of long-distance formation flights at high altitude for the benefit of the medical officer, who examined every pilot and gunner after each flight. Then, in October, there was a full-blown mobilisation exercise which involved them having to pack up, de-camp, travel across country and set up at Sealand. There they were duly inspected, after which they re-packed, de-camped and returned to Bircham Newton – a round trip of over 300 miles. Still under training, Johnny languished back at Bircham Newton but enjoyed more frequent flights.

During the following week, the squadron was engaged in 'bombing' sorties to Birmingham, Bristol and Lincoln. Some were abandoned due to low cloud, but this made no difference to the workload of the squadron fitters and riggers. However, with the rapid approach of winter and deteriorating weather conditions, flying activity reduced, coming as something of a welcome relief. The squadron had completed a hectic period of training and had done well – it was now time to reflect on what had been learned and prepare for the future.

Johnny had his own period of reflection. He had now been with the squadron for over a year and recognised the advantages he enjoyed over those in the other services. He knew that the RAF was no place for senseless, unheeding discipline. Every airman had a responsible task to perform and was expected to do it well, with care, and to the very best of his ability. This brought its own self-discipline and real sense of responsibility. The reliability of 'your' aircraft and the safety of its crew were literally in your hands. It was a duty that Johnny accepted willingly and cherished.

By the end of the year he had accumulated over thirty hours flying, mainly local flights, with the occasional cross-country trip to North Weald or Cranwell, and some map-reading instruction thrown in for good measure. Not surprisingly, he found the tantalising prospect of flying as a career increasingly occupying his thoughts. Finally reaching a decision, he requested a formal interview with his flight commander and applied to re-muster as an air gunner.

From January 1932 he was in the air as often as the weather allowed, on a variety of tasks: cross-country flights, formation practice, navigation and map-reading, manning the rear camera gun and pinpoint photography of specified 'bombing' targets. With an improvement in the weather the squadron returned to the familiar round of exercises while Johnny continued to grab every opportunity he could to fly, adding twelve hours a month to his logbook.

On 9 March, he experienced a few exciting moments and his first flying accident. Piloted by Sergeant Fox, their Fairey IIIF (J9785) suffered sudden and total engine failure on take-off. There was no warning, the engine just died on them. This was a potentially dangerous situation, but Fox, an experienced and competent pilot, kept his head and didn't attempt to turn back to the airfield. He kept the aircraft heading straight ahead in a level glide while he selected a safe place to put down.

They force-landed near South Creake, and all was going well until they ran into a deep furrow which tipped the aircraft up on its nose. Fortunately it didn't go over the vertical so they were both able to pull the quick-release pins on their Sutton harness and scramble down to the ground. The poor old IIIF suffered nothing worse than a bent prop and some dents in the engine cowling, which hardly warranted the attention of the large group of mechanics who turned up to gloat. Someone even produced a camera to record the incident for posterity, a smiling Johnny Wells leaning nonchalantly against the wing and clearly highly amused by the whole affair. Such accidents were gratifyingly rare on the squadron but they certainly enlivened the daily routine.

In April, in another busy week of exercises, the squadron mounted twenty photo-bombing raids on Scunthorpe, Thrapston, Andover and Highbridge. To his delight, Johnny was included on two sorties accompanying Pilot Officers Bax and Jenkins on successive days returning with excellent photographs of their target at Thrapston taken from 3,000ft. Four more days of intensive bombing practice back at Bircham Newton followed.

All this frantic activity preceded a squadron move to Duxford for a week of affiliation exercises. Here, Johnny and the other air gunners defended themselves with camera guns against attacks by the Bristol Bulldogs of No 19 (Fighter) Squadron – all most thrilling and very 'Hell's Angels'. Then, within days of their return to Bircham Newton on 15 May 1932, the entire squadron moved to No 1 Armament Training Camp at North Coates Fitties on the bleak mudflats south of Grimsby.

They spent the next five weeks over the mouth of the Humber Estuary on bombing and air-firing practice. Flying with Sergeant Fox or with Flying Officer Webb, Johnny completed more than thirty flights over the ranges at North Coates, dropping a total of seventy-six bombs, some of them live. He also fired almost 2,000 rounds with his Lewis gun at ground targets and towed drogues to complete the necessary tests for his official classification as an air gunner.

With the whiff of cordite still in their nostrils and all feeling decidedly war-like, the squadron returned to Bircham Newton barely two weeks before another move, this time to Hawkinge on the south coast. Johnny flew with F/O Webb in J9822 for the duration of this week-long air exercise, ADGB clearly being dead set on maintaining a high state of preparedness in its squadrons.

On their return, they immediately set in hand preparations to re-equip with new aircraft, the first Fairey Gordon Is arriving at Bircham Newton on 26 July 1932 to replace their Fairey IIIFs. This involved everyone familiarising themselves with the new machines, for while the Gordon airframe was basically the same old Fairey IIIF, it was powered by an Armstrong Siddeley Panther radial rather than the familiar Napier Lion engine. In fact, some of the aircraft received were simply old IIIFs re-engined, though most of the new equipment was manufactured as Gordons.

Johnny missed out on all this excitement because towards the end of August he was packed off to the Air Armament School at Eastchurch on the Isle of Sheppey to join No 72 Air Gunners Course. A hectic six weeks followed, with Johnny making two flights on most days over the Leysdown ranges dropping practice bombs and air-to-ground firing from Westland Wapitis. He returned to the squadron in early October, a fully fledged air gunner, having obtained very respectable results in his handling of the Vickers and Lewis guns, and individual air-firing and bombing tests. He could now clear Nos 1, 2, 3 and 4 stoppages and, at the drop of a hat, would expound at length of the respective merits of bombs and ammunition, be they armour-piercing, incendiary, high-explosive, tracer, TNT or Amatol. He was starting to feel much more a part of things.

During his absence a new station commander had taken over, Wing Commander Raymond Collishaw DSO DSC DFC: a dynamic Canadian whose exploits as a naval fighter pilot during the war, and later fighting the Communists in southern Russia, were the talk of the mess. The squadron had also completed re-equipping and, as part of the reorganisation, Johnny found himself transferred to F/L Greenlaw's 'C' Flight, which was short of a qualified air gunner. He managed to get in three long flights in one of their new Gordons (K2685) before a visit from the AOC who arrived to inspect the squadron on 31 October.

Within days of this, Johnny received news that his father had died. Granted immediate compassionate leave, he returned home to Sheringham before travelling north to Cleethorpes to attend the funeral, accompanied by his brother Robert. Apparently, some months earlier, their father had been seriously injured when caught between a boat and the dock. He had been badly crushed and hadn't fully recovered from his injuries when he suffered another collapse and died in the ambulance on the way to hospital. The funeral was a brief and sombre occasion, during which small knots of mourners eyed each other curiously across the aisle, and after the service nodded or exchanged a few words before departing their various ways. Duty done, Johnny was glad to get back to his unit although it had been nice to see the family again.

In February 1933, S/L Brown left the squadron prior to taking command of the Air Armament School at Eastchurch; his successor, S/L J.F. Gordon DFC, only stayed with the squadron for two months before S/L V. Buxton took over on 5 May. There was a fairly regular turnover of officers and pilots during Johnny's time with the squadron and he got to fly with most of them, although his regular pilot in 'C' Flight was F/O Foster-Packer.

Johnny soon recognised what a difference the individual style or flair of a pilot made to the aircraft's performance and handling. Some seemed to have to wrestle with the controls forcing the machine to do what they wanted, while others worked with the machine guiding it gently but firmly without fuss. It was, he supposed, all a question of feel – a bit like riding a horse.

With his growing love of flying he soon began to realise that re-mustering as an air gunner was not going to be enough for him. He wanted to be a pilot and was firm in his conviction, knowing full well how difficult a step it would be for a ranker like himself. He mulled the idea around for a while and talked it through with one or two of the older members of the squadron. One of them, a feisty little corporal, had served as an air gunner and flown several hundred hours over the North West Frontier, as he was very fond of reminding anybody prepared to listen. If only they had posted him to the Western Front in 1916, it seemed, the Fokker scourge would have been over at a stroke. But his well-worn tunic was adorned with several campaign ribbons and his knowledge and flying experience proved useful to Johnny who pumped him for information.

Air Ministry Pamphlet No 15 explained the seemingly long and arduous path from ex-apprentice to pilot, and in optimistic terms. Johnny read it from cover to cover several times. According to this, there were a series of preliminary interviews before a final interview, as well as the stringent physical and medical examinations to pass. So, armed with as much information as he could muster, Johnny eventually took the plunge by formally applying for pilot training 'through the proper channels'. Much to his surprise, and despite much banter from all his mates who were at pains to remind him that the extra flying pay he could look forward to would barely cover the cost of his funeral, no one scoffed at the idea or tried to talk him out of it. Most of them wished him well.

In May 1933, the squadron moved to North Coates Fitties for its annual camp and another month of practice bombing and air firing, during which the Secretary of State for Air, the Marquis of Londonderry and the Under Secretary, Sir Phillip Sassoon, paid them a visit. It was obviously open season for visitors, for S/L Buxton had to dash back to Bircham Newton on the 25th when the AOC visited the station during their absence.

Throughout late June and early July, the squadron was occupied in affiliation exercises with the Bristol Bulldog fighters of Nos 111 and 54 Squadrons before flying off to Tangmere, on the Sussex coast, for a week of exercises. These involved two opposing forces attacking or defending each others territory which provided an invaluable experience for all those taking part and also helped to develop the RAF's ground control and communication systems. Johnny was scheduled to crew one of the eleven Gordons taking part.

Within a couple of days of arriving at Tangmere, they flew their first sortie when, shortly after 6 p.m. on 18 July, S/L Buxton took off at the head of ten Gordons to make a dummy attack on the airfield at RAF Bicester. Johnny was aboard K2690 flown by F/O Earle as the formation climbed slowly to 7,000ft and followed the coast down to the Isle of Wight before crossing into 'enemy' territory at Southampton.

Shortly after 7 p.m., somewhere over Compton, they were attacked by a gaggle of Bulldogs whose black zigzag markings identified them as No 17 Squadron machines. The fighters broke off their attacks after about four minutes cavorting around the Gordons, who maintained tight formation and dived down through the cloud layer to 5,000ft setting course direct for Bicester. There they made two dummy runs over the target and flew back via Swindon and Hurst Castle, beating off more attacks from some Hawker Furies near Quarley Hill, before landing back at Tangmere after more than three hours in the air.

When the target photographs were analysed later, it was decided that they had not done too badly. On their first bombing run they recorded an error of only 115yd, which was adjudged 'a palpable hit', but their second run over the target missed the mark by about a quarter of a mile. Everyone satisfied themselves that this lapse was due to a sudden change in wind direction over the target area, but it had all seemed so much easier when they had been practising at North Coates.

The following evening, shortly before 7 p.m., they were off again. This time the target was Wantage railway station, 60 miles away to the north-west, and Johnny had a change of aircraft, flying with Sergeant Jackson in K1762. It was a beautiful evening and pleasantly warm, as the squadron climbed west along the coast in close formation. Laid out below him, Johnny could see the whole of the Isle of Wight and the great sweep of coast all the way from Poole Harbour to Beachy Head which lay behind them.

To confuse the opposing defences they formed up with some Gordons from No 40 Squadron. Together both squadrons crossed the 'enemy' lines near Gosport, heading north at just under 7,000ft until, east of Winchester, No 40 broke away to seek their own target. Johnny exchanged a cheery wave with his opposite number in one of their Gordons as it veered away.

Reaching Wantage, two runs over the target went unopposed, despite the sudden appearance of the Hawker Furies of No 25 Squadron. These dainty but menacing fighters seemed to have trouble getting themselves into anything remotely like proper attack formation as the Gordons, their business done, headed away south to land back at Tangmere in the gathering dusk shortly before 9 p.m.

Dawn the next morning saw more feverish activity at the No 35 Squadron dispersal as aircraft were prepared for an early morning 'show' again to RAF Bicester. F/L Jones, the 'A' Flight commander, was leading the formation and they were off the ground by 5 a.m., with Johnny back in K2690, this time piloted by his usual pilot F/O Foster-Packer. These early junkets were a distinct change from the balmy conditions they had enjoyed on the previous two evenings and Johnny was glad of an extra scarf or two to keep out the draughts at 6,000ft.

They flew over Angmering en route to their target, the ground completely shrouded in a solid layer of cloud at 3,000ft, so no flying by Visual Flight Rules on this trip. One of the Gordons dropped out of formation, the 'B' Flight Commander, F/L Thackray, signalling a 'wash-out' as his aircraft, with propeller idling, slowly disappeared from sight. It managed to put down in a field east of Clandon Wood, and neither Thackray nor his passenger, LAC Fishlock, was injured.

Somewhere just north of Oxford the rest of the squadron started letting down through the cloud layer and popped out below it to find the target dead ahead of them. Top marks to whoever was navigating even it was by dead-reckoning! Two brisk attacks in less than six minutes and the squadron was on its way to Martlesham Heath, where they landed at 7.30 a.m., in time for breakfast. There was no sign of any fighters this trip – obviously far too early in the day for them.

Exercises over, the squadron returned to Bircham Newton and started preparations for the annual leave period over the entire month of August. But all too soon, summer leave was over and they returned to Bircham Newton and the familiar squadron routine. This was interrupted on 12 October 1933 when, after weeks of formation practice, the squadron drew admiring gasps from the crowds attending Hull Civic Week with a dazzling display of immaculate set-piece formations as they wheeled and turned most prettily, high above East Park. Spectators may have been a little less impressed had they but known that the entire drill was being controlled and orchestrated by W/T from an aircraft circling 5 miles away.

New Year 1934 arrived, celebrations enlivened by the news that the squadron had won the Armament Officers' Trophy Competition, so another feather in somebody's cap no doubt. This prompted an inspection by the AOC on 30 January amidst much swank and bullshine. But even this paled into insignificance when an inspection by King George V and Queen Mary took place on 24 May. Johnny was mildly surprised to see His Majesty wearing civilian dress during their tour of the station, with W/C Collishaw and Air Marshal Brooke-Popham, who commanded ADGB, in close attendance.

This great day in the squadron's calendar culminated in a formation fly-past by nine Gordons led by S/L Buxton. Taking off in close formation, they wheeled into V-formation on the turn prior to a fly-past, reforming into squadron formation before landing together in flights line astern. Had their Majesties been able to spot him, a very proud and upright LAC Wells occupied the rear cockpit of F/O Hargreaves' aircraft (K2690) on the extreme left of the formation. Did he risk a cheeky wave or was that simply a sloppy salute?

The following month was spent, as usual, over the ranges at North Coates Fitties as a prelude to annual leave. But just prior to this, Johnny was summoned by his flight commander, F/L Bates, who notified him of the date on which he should attend, 'at 09.00 hours or as soon thereafter as travelling facilities permit', the Central Medical & Air Crew Selection Board. His application for pilot training was proceeding.

Presenting himself as instructed, he felt much the same as he had on first arriving at Halton. There were about a dozen other young hopefuls in his group and he was pleased to note that most were LACs like himself with only a sprinkling of corporals. As they congregated in readiness for what was to come there was a lot of noisy shop talk and nervous banter at first, but the prevailing mood was one of cautious self-control apart from a few exagger-ated displays of seeming total indifference.

One by one they were called out for first interviews and in due course Johnny was summoned. He was glad to get started at last; the tension in the waiting room was becoming unbearable and any small talk had dried up long ago. He was led off into an adjoining room where his name and rank were announced as he threw up a furniture-rattling salute to the two officers who sat facing him across a table. One a group captain and the other a squadron leader – that much he would remember later. But as for their questions, which had all seemed fairly straightforward at the time, let alone his answers, he would have little recall. There had been some basic mathematics, he remem-bered, but nothing to worry someone who had passed the final exams at Halton. They had seemed most concerned with his reasoning skills and talked quite a lot about his ambition to become a pilot. What mattered most was that Johnny got through and progressed to the next interview which was the same sort of thing, only much tougher.

Later he emerged, not a little ruffled by the experience, but glowing with triumph with the magic words 'Accepted for Pilot' stamped across his docu-ments. He still had the Central Medical Board to get through, but with the main hurdle now behind him, he was confident that he would sail through that – which of course he did. He was on his way to becoming a pilot at last, and although he got the last of the oil from under his fingernails eventually, it would be some years before he lost the habit of carrying an adjustable span-ner, a screwdriver and a pair of pliers in his pocket.

4

TYRO PILOT

Terra firma – the more firma, the less terra.

Punch magazine

Johnny joined No 27 Course at No 5 FTS, on 2 October 1934, one of only ten "umble erks' like himself plus thirty-two officer candidates, but all aspiring pilots. This was a fairly typical cross-section which reflected the rampant class system prevalent at the time. Sealand was clearly a very busy station. Johnny noticed an encouraging assortment of aircraft taking off, landing and buzzing around the circuit.

On arrival they checked in and were escorted to their rooms where they dumped their kit and were issued with a neat wad of typed instructions. These notes guided them to their respective flights to meet their flight commanders. There Johnny, and the rest of his small group, was greeted by F/L Carter and the other instructors who would be in charge of their training for the entire course.

Their flying training would take about a year to complete, he told them, learning basic flying skills on Avro Tutors before graduating on to Bristol Bulldogs after about six months. Then, after a few encouraging words along the lines of 'There's a lot to be learned in a very short time so don't waste your time in the air', they all filed through to stores to draw flying kit.

Next, their printed programmes sent them scurrying off to the parachute shed where they were fitted with parachutes which prompted a few morbid comments. Back at their flights they were allocated a locker to stow their surplus flying kit. There was obviously no time to lose and, within hours of arriving, a somewhat startled Johnny found himself 2,000ft over Sealand in Avro Tutor (K3263) flown by F/O Spendlove, enjoying ten minutes of local flying 'to get the lie of the land'.

Not a moment was wasted: the crammed timetable was a triumph of organisation. Weather permitting, most mornings were spent in the air exploring the complexities of 'the effect of controls with engine, straight and level flight, stalling, spinning, climbing, gliding', and all manner and variety of turns. Afternoons were usually set aside for classwork on navigation, calculating course and speed, and meteorology. Johnny soon found that his background as an ex-Halton apprentice, plus over 400 hours' flying experience, gave him a distinct edge over some of the other pupils.

Every daylight hour possible was spent in the Avro 621 Tutor two-seat biplane. Fitted with dual controls, the Tutor was the standard RAF *ab initio* trainer of the period and a perfect machine for the job for it was robust but fairly docile. It had rather ugly square-tipped wings and was fitted with, rather than powered by, a seven-cylinder 240hp Armstrong-Siddeley Lynx IVC engine. Given its performance, flaps were obviously considered an unnecessary luxury and it also lacked any cockpit heating. So, despite a windscreen and an exhaust pipe which ran the length of the fuselage, Johnny's flights during that winter were thoroughly uncomfortable affairs. Swaddled in full winter flying kit of padded Sidcot suit with fur collar, thick socks, multitudinous scarves and gloves, and heavy fleece-lined flying boots, it was still freezing wedged in the open rear cockpit. But he was flying.

The long-suffering instructor sat in the forward cockpit and spoke to the pupil, who sat directly behind him, through a mouthpiece connected by flexible tubes to earpieces in the pupil's flying helmet. As they completed different manoeuvres, the instructor kept up a steady commentary explaining what was happening exactly as it happened. The words seldom varied and very soon this 'patter', as it was known, became ingrained into the pupil's memory. Johnny's instructor, Sergeant Tribe, would also resort to hand signals which were often more graphic but far less colourful than some of the language he used. Johnny claimed that the instructors could also communicate through the back of their heads and he became quite adept at interpreting every nuance or slight movement of the leather helmet in front of him.

The Tutor's take-off run was quite long, but when good and ready it would lift off without much interference from the pilot. It climbed sedately and was rumoured to have a top speed in excess of 140mph but Johnny never managed to coax it up to anything like that during all his time at FTS. The controls were nicely balanced, light and smooth, and everything was easily accessible. In short, and as far as Johnny was concerned, the Tutor was 'a real peach' of an aircraft.

Lesson 7 'Landing and Judging Distances' was very much an acquired skill. This was largely due to the fact that the dear old Tutor tended to 'hold off' the ground and float along quite happily a couple of feet above the ground until you eventually managed to coax it down or ran out of petrol. But when the Tutor did decide to return to earth, it was usually with a bone-shaking thump that rattled the teeth. Fortunately, it was a very forgiving aircraft and its stout undercarriage usually stood up to this sort of punishment, which was a lot more than Sergeant Tribe was prepared to do, judging from the language that emanated from the front cockpit when things went badly wrong. Along with much else, distance from the ground was eventually mastered and Johnny was soon waffling into neat three-point landings along with the best of them.

As was to be expected, there were occasional accidents, mostly minor, but there were also serious crashes. On 27 October 1934, within only three weeks of commencing their course, Acting P/O Eric Hall was killed. Such losses were part and parcel of service flying and something airmen got used to – even in peacetime – along with service funerals and they became quite experienced at slow marching with arms reversed.

Early one afternoon, about three days later, Johnny landed after an uneventful fifteen-minute flight around the airfield in Tutor K3252. Indicating for him to stay put, Sergeant Tribe clambered out of the front cockpit while Johnny sat enjoying the unfamiliar sight of an idling propeller flicking over ahead of him. 'That was fine,' Tribe shouted over the noise of the engine. 'Just watch your speed on the final approach. Look, you've done about 10 hours dual now and I reckon you're ready to go solo. What do you think?' Rendered temporarily speechless, Johnny managed what he hoped was an enthusiastic smile and a vigorous nod of the head.

'Fine,' said Tribe, 'we'll get you tested right away and then you can go off on your own.' Within two hours, Johnny had completed his test for solo with F/L Britton, a straightforward repeat of his earlier flight with Tribe, and was sent off on his own. Staring forward over the empty cockpit ahead of him, Johnny completed a simple ten-minute circuit of the airfield at 1,000ft and came in for an uneventful landing. His first solo flight was over before he had time to realise it. It had all happened so fast it was almost something of an anti-climax.

After that he spent as much time in the air as possible, clocking up flying hours and preparing for his fifteen-hour test with the flight commander, F/L Carter, which took place on 19 November. In the meantime, as he grew in confidence and experience, Sergeant Tribe introduced him to climbing turns, sideslipping and flying on instruments.

Flying on instruments, as the name implies, involved flying blind by locking a green canvas hood in place entirely covering the pupil's cockpit when required. Enveloped in deep gloom under this flapping contrivance, the hapless pupil would stare at his instruments and attempt to control the aircraft. Using a stopwatch in conjunction with the compass, he would attempt to steer a prescribed course without sight of the ground and with no knowledge of what was going on outside. It was unnerving and disorienting and, like most other student pilots, Johnny was not all that keen on it. But apart from this, he was often flying seven or eight times a day and enjoying every second of it.

Lesson 3, 'Taxying and Ground Handling', also formed an important element of the course and was a lesson that gave him some trouble at first. With no wheel brakes and an unsteerable tailskid, taxiing a Tutor could prove an exciting business, particularly if there was any sort of wind blowing. Turning on the ground was done using full rudder, a good burst of engine, opposite aileron into and across wind, and around you twirled: effortless and impressive when done properly – very much the dashing young airman.

Turning down wind, however, was an entirely different matter and gave Johnny a few problems until he had it mastered. You needed the merest touch of throttle, with aileron in the direction you wanted to turn, and had to remember to keep the stick well forward to stop the wind getting under your tail which could have potentially disastrous results. But in anything even approaching a fresh breeze the Tutor had a tendency to weathervane into wind and once or twice, on some early solo flights, an exasperated Johnny found himself waltzing around and around in very tight circles, still firmly earthbound and gagging on his own exhaust fumes. Eventually a couple of compassionate mechanics ran out and, taking firm hold of each wingtip, gleefully shepherded him back to safety.

Occasionally Sergeant Tribe managed to winkle him out of the Tutor to spend some time in a little wooden hut housing the Link Trainer, an ingenious contraption resembling a motorcycle sidecar with stubby wings. The Link, equipped with a basic cockpit layout complete with flying controls and instruments, was perched high off the ground attached by cables to an ingenious device tracing the course 'flown' by the pilot on to paper, thus plotting every false move.

Training on the Link was as disciplined and systematic as any training in the air. First a couple of familiarisation 'flights' to get a feel for the thing, then straight and level flying, followed by climbing and gliding, before progressing on to medium turns, gliding and climbing turns, fast turns and other manoeuvres. A lot of time on the Link was also spent 'under the hood', practising blind flying, essential before attempting any bad weather or night flying for real. Then the acid test: flying a neat triangular course. This sounded simple enough but was a severe test of any budding pilot's navigational skills and handling control, and many a pupil traced a spidery course before landing miles from their destination or 'crashed in flames' to howls of derision from those who sat outside awaiting their turn.

By early December, having successfully completed his thirty-hour test, Johnny started aerobatics with the imperturbable Sergeant Tribe taking him through loops, stall turns, slow rolls and the whole gamut of manoeuvres required of a qualified pilot. Then mid-April 1935, with over forty-five hours solo under his belt, Johnny was assessed by the chief flying instructor, S/L Beardsworth, who deemed him an 'average' pilot but ready to progress on to the Bristol Bulldog.

The Bulldog was a fighter and looked every inch of it: stumpy silver-doped fuselage, highly cambered wings and a potent nine-cylinder Jupiter engine which gave off a wonderful smell of hot castor oil. Apparently it would cruise quite comfortably at 130mph and was highly responsive, handling well. It had a cockpit simply awash with instruments, levers and instruction plates, and even the gun channels in the engine cowling remained in situ, although, of course, no guns were fitted. This was more like it! All this could easily turn a young aviator's head, and Johnny could almost feel the mantle of Mannock, Ball and McCudden hovering above his shoulders.

Sergeant Buchanan was responsible for training on Bulldogs, which followed roughly the same pattern as that on the Tutor. Dual instruction in a two-seat Bulldog Trainer covered basic handling and was followed, within two weeks in Johnny's case, by solo flights with ballast or, joy of joys, in a single-seat Bulldog IIA – a pukka fighter aircraft. His first flight in one of these beauties came on 13 June 1935.

He sat semi-prone, legs straddling the rudder bar, grasping the spade grip in his right fist, left hand closed around the ample throttle lever. The Bulldog rocked and bumped as he taxied down to the leeward side of the airfield for take-off, the aircraft constantly seeking to turn into wind as if impatient to take to the air. After the Tutor it felt decidedly skittish. He turned into the wind, took a quick look round to check the circuit and gently opened the throttle.

Bumping across the grass, the tail lifted almost immediately and the Bulldog simply soared off the ground. He levelled off for a few seconds to gather speed then, with stick held well back, he climbed away like a rocket to 5,000ft. With his heart in his mouth and his stomach somewhere back on the ground, Johnny was exultant. This was really flying! After a delirious forty-five minutes of loops and slow rolls he touched down at a high rate of knots, seeming to run on for ever. After which he flew the Bulldog IIA as often as possible, practising aerobatics, but interspersed with regular flights in the Bulldog Trainer or cross-country flights in a Tutor, with Sergeant Buchanan up front, to get in more navigation practice and lots more of the dreaded instrument flying.

On 30 April, the Under Secretary of State for Air, Sir Philip Sassoon, visited Sealand. But nothing was allowed to interfere with the training programme, Johnny making two flights that afternoon in Bulldog K3929. On 25 May 1935

Empire Air Day was celebrated when the station threw open its gates to the public, attracting over 6,500 people who thronged the hangars, swarmed all over the static displays of aircraft and enjoyed the flying displays which continued throughout the day and well into the early evening.

By the following August, No 27 Course was nearing completion with only final examinations and flying tests remaining before those qualifying became RAF pilots and receive the coveted wings to adorn the left breast of their tunics. Having already passed his Central Flying School, cross-country and air navigation tests the previous month, Johnny's final test with the chief flying instructor was scheduled for 22 August 1935.

The day dawned fine and bright with perfect flying conditions. S/L Beardsworth joined Johnny at the flight line and after a few words of instruction they clambered aboard Bulldog K3186 for his final test. Naturally somewhat nervous, for a great deal depended on it, Johnny found his thoughts and actions coming almost naturally. His training had taken over and any lingering anxiety seeming to vanish as he went through the familiar procedures and routines. He taxied out and took off with Sergeant Tribe's constant patter sounding in his head. After twenty-five minutes aloft on that sublime summer morning, S/L Beardsworth was satisfied and ordered him to land. It turned out to be Johnny's last flight at No 5 FTS. His ability as a pilot was assessed 'above the average', which was duly stamped and recorded in his flying logbook, a small volume with his neat entries recording more than fifty-eight hours dual and eighty-six hours solo to add to his previous flying experience – Johnny had accumulated over 563 flying hours.

Of the forty-two young pupil pilots who had come together the previous October all but six had completed the course and three had been awarded Special Distinctions. Six others were awarded Distinguished Passes, one of these being 561960 LAC J.C. Wells – an RAF pilot at last!

On 31 August, after a passing out parade and the award of wings by the AOC of No 23 (Training) Group, Air Commodore Breese, No 27 Course dispersed almost as quickly as it had come together barely eleven months before, the young pilots posted to squadrons at home and abroad. Clustering around the notice board an excited scrum eagerly scanned the posting list. Johnny had been selected as a bomber pilot and was posted to No 45 (B) Squadron at a place called Helwan. This sounded like somewhere in Cornwall or deepest Wales, but surprise turned to mounting excitement when he learned that it was in Egypt – he was going overseas.

5

MIDDLE EAST AIR FORCE

Three weeks later, on 20 September 1935, after an all too brief embarkation leave spent saying goodbye to family and friends, and a fairly rough crossing of the Bay of Biscay to Gibraltar and into the Mediterranean, his ship arrived at Port Said in Egypt. Threading a path through the busy harbour, home to the destroyers of the Mediterranean Fleet, the ship finally docked.

The jostling armies of dockside touts and babbling street vendors were a bit daunting at first, but Johnny and some other airmen were taken firmly in tow by a flight lieutenant who had been sent to meet them and they all managed to board the waiting transport safely enough. The airfield at Helwan lay a few miles south of the famous pyramids at Giza just outside Cairo: a vast, colourful, bustling, ramshackle city which Johnny would come to know well – full of fabulous sights, incredible sounds and smells, and teeming with life and the ever-present beggars.

His new unit, No 45 Squadron, was originally formed in 1916 as a fighter squadron. Disbanded after the First World War, it reformed in Egypt in 1921 only to be absorbed into another unit six years later. Resurrected again in April 1927 at Heliopolis, the squadron was deployed across Egypt and Palestine engaged in routine patrol duties, operating from its home base in Helwan. They flew the old familiar Fairey IIIFs but were about to re-equip as part of the on-going development and expansion of the RAF then taking place at home and overseas.

There was a definite air of expectancy about Helwan with everything very orderly and business-like. On arriving, Johnny had reported to the adjutant who promptly wheeled him in to meet S/L A.R. Churchman DFC. The CO, who had himself arrived only the previous month, welcomed him to the squadron and started putting him in the picture. It was a busy time for them for, only two days earlier, 'B' Flight under F/L Barlow had re-deployed five

Fairey IIIFs to Nairobi, over 2,000 miles south, to fly protection patrols along the Kenyan, Abyssinian and Italian borders in support of the King's African Rifles. Johnny quickly formed the impression that he could be in for some exciting times.

Policing these far-flung outposts of the British Empire was difficult and costly, and our limited military resources were often spread exceedingly thin. Even under Lord Trenchard's system of 'air control', advocating replacing costly fixed army garrisons with mobile squadrons of RAF aircraft operating in conjunction with armoured cars, to adequately cover the vast areas involved, was a problem. A constant balance had to be struck between being able to mount a prompt and effective response to any threat to British interests, and maintaining a presence or simply 'flying the flag'.

The runway at Helwan was hard-packed sand set immediately adjacent to the hangars. It became progressively softer the further you ventured from the landing strip. Then the desert stretched away to the far horizons; the terrain bare, bleak and barren, apart from the occasional clump of camel thorn. At least it was all fairly flat which made forced landings a lot easier to survive.

Johnny was assigned to a new 'D' Flight being formed as an addition to the squadron under F/L A.N. Luxmoore, also newly arrived. Johnny found that he was one of a number of pilots recently posted to the squadron to make up the strength; P/Os Hunter and Rampling arriving around the same time. The new flight was currently awaiting delivery of its aircraft which, Johnny was delighted to learn, would be Hawker Harts.

The Hawker Hart, with Rolls-Royce Kestrel engine, was the fastest single-engined bomber of the day and something akin to a racing aeroplane or a two-seat fighter. With a top speed of 184mph, even the best RAF fighter in service, the Bristol Bulldog, couldn't touch it. It could climb reasonably well, 10,000ft in about eight minutes, cruise along comfortably at 130mph and, in terms of overall performance and handling, was far superior to any other two-seat aircraft of the period. Why, it could even do aerobatics! Along with the other pilots forming 'D' Flight, Johnny couldn't wait to get his hands on one. Having drawn flying kit from stores and a short spell of dual on a Fairey IIIF with F/L Luxmoore, Johnny flew his first solo on type on 27 September. It was quite an experience for him after spending all those hours as a passenger in the rear cockpit five years before.

Their first Hart arrived that same week, others being delivered soon afterwards, and before too long they had received their full complement. Fast and powerful with their staggered, slightly swept-back wings, the rakish Harts of 'D' Flight lined up at dispersal, their highly polished aluminium engine cowlings reflecting the sun. Set slightly apart from the rest of the squadron, they made the old Fairey IIIFs look pretty tired and jaded by comparison.

After twenty minutes' dual with Luxmoore, and a thorough briefing on the petrol system, cockpit layout and controls, Johnny flew his first Hart solo on 30 September: a fifteen-minute circuit of the airfield at 1,000ft. It was a lot heavier on the controls than other aircraft he had flown, but the more experienced pilots seemed to throw the Hart around quite comfortably, and even the tightest of turns was just as smooth as you like. It had a roomy cockpit, warm and comfortable even at altitude, and the rear 'office' was equipped with a menacing Scarff-ring mounting for a Lewis gun. Due to engine torque, the Hart had a tendency to swing left on take-off which had to be countered quite firmly with bags of right rudder, and the take-off run was a lot longer than Johnny expected, the Hart seeming a mite reluctant to unstick from the ground. But, as he later learned, this was quite normal in warm climates and was something to do with the effect of the heat on air density.

Another characteristic of the Hart was that, due to the sharply tapered nose, you could see an awful lot ahead of you, and until you got used to it this gave the impression that you were in a constant dive. So landings could be tricky, particularly if there was any wind, because unless you brought the stick back smartly at exactly the right moment, the Hart would simply drop on to its well-sprung undercarriage and bounce straight back 6ft into the air like a startled gazelle. This could be most unsettling when you were hovering almost at a standstill, but Johnny soon learned to keep the stick well back and give it a good burst of throttle as she sank the last couple of feet. This usually did the trick and kept the Hart anchored firmly to the ground.

Weather conditions at Helwan were generally good for flying except in the short rainy season and during the Spring, when the oppressively hot Khamsin winds blew in off the Sahara, bringing impenetrable sandstorms which made all flying impossible. But clear skies and shimmering heat were the norm which meant very early starts each day before it got too hot to work.

Johnny rose at 5 a.m. daily to marvel at the spectacular sunrises, unlike anything he had ever seen: tier after tier of blue-grey stratus cloud striping the pale sky flushed vivid cream or pink as each layer in turn met the advancing rays of the sun which shimmered on the eastern horizon. Flying started at dawn and generally ceased in the early afternoon or as soon as the midday meal was over. In the heat of the day engines were often close to boiling, making engine cowlings too hot to handle, even with hands swathed in rags. Working under canvas awnings to screen them from the worse of the heat, mechanics also kept their tools covered for many a forgetful fitter had blistered fingers to remind him of the power of the sun.

Most of the pilots generally turned in as soon after dinner as was decently possible, usually about 9 p.m. The desert was incredibly still and quiet at night but could turn bitterly cold; however, during the summer months, even sleeping naked under a loose sheet and mosquito net, you generally tossed fitfully all night and woke soaked in perspiration. Apparently, one got used to it after a few years.

Dress was KD (khaki-drill) open-necked, short-sleeve shirt and shorts worn with knee-length socks and shoes, though many of the older hands simply threw khaki coveralls over their pyjamas in the morning, a slovenly practice officially frowned upon. Like many new arrivals, Johnny put his kit through the wash far more often than it warranted, which incurred a hefty laundry bill but soon achieved the faded look of a long-service flying type. This ensemble was usually topped off with an incongruous, yet extremely comfortable, solar topee as headgear which offered good protection from the sun. This was taken everywhere, although standard issue leather helmet and goggles were normally worn when flying.

Johnny rapidly gained in confidence on the Hart and was enjoying the flying. Floating high above the wide open wastes of desert, spreading away to the horizon far beyond the narrow fringe of vegetation bordering the Nile, was a heady experience. One warm early morning, when flying alone with only ballast in the rear cockpit for company and with the engine purring away steadily ahead of him, Johnny realised with some regret that he would soon have to land. Flying like this was a pure joy. He stuck the nose down to gain more speed and pulled the nose up in a spirited loop. It was a bad mistake.

At the top of the loop, Johnny fell on his shoulder straps and was hanging upside down with eyes bulging, staring at the ground a few thousand feet above his head, when there was an almighty bang shaking the aircraft from nose to tail. Frightened, he quickly half-rolled the aircraft level and checked that the wings were still attached, his mind racing. Something must have broken or had he collided with something – possibly a large bird? As he straightened out an equally loud clunk emanating from somewhere beneath his seat sent another tremor through the machine. In a flood of relief, it dawned on him what had happened. The Hart had an under-slung retractable radiator which it was deemed advisable to crank up and secure before going inverted. If you didn't, it had the disconcerting habit of abruptly dropping inboard under gravity, to the consternation of those aboard, as Johnny had just discovered to his cost. A mistake that he would never make again.

On several occasions during October 1935, squadron aircraft carried or escorted a number of high-ranking officers, including the GOC, AOC-in-C and AOC, on a round of official visits to far-flung units based across the Sudan and Iraq. And though it was preceded by weeks of tedious formation practice, the annual air pageant in Cairo provided some relief from the norm and, for the lucky ones, a spot of welcome leave.

Leave! In this part of the world it generally meant only few things, one being visiting the fleshpots of Cairo or Alexandria, where every desire known to man, woman or beast, if the stories were to be believed, could all be satisfied – at a price. No problem. Pay tended to accumulate when you were stationed in the desert for any length of time – there was bugger all to spend it on. Consequently, even a humble NCO could live in comparative luxury for a good few days on his back pay, staying at one of the many clubs or pensions in Cairo or Alexandria which exclusively catered for servicemen. In a frenzy of anticipation, best tunics were cleaned and pressed, buttons and boots polished to astonishing brilliance, and the squadron barber did excellent business.

Being based so close to Cairo, only forty minutes from Helwan by train, Johnny was able to spend most Saturday evenings there. One of his earliest letters home, written within a month of his arrival in Egypt, describes his impressions:

Nearly all Cairo is out of bounds. We are allowed in the centre of the city which has quite a healthy percentage of Europeans. Everywhere else is a turgid offence to the nostrils & I don't go much on the atmosphere at all, as viewed from the edge. We have to take taxis to pass through some parts … as they are apparently not quite conducive to the health of Europeans. All the police are armed with rifles & they look very queer. If any of our chaps go out in uniform they have to carry a nice shiny entrenching tool which is said to help a lot …

The cinemas are not too bad but the big snag is the seating accommodation. In order to combat the ravages of the bugs & ants, all the seats have to be made of wood or cane which seems to get awfully hard after a while. I haven't had any meals out yet, partly because those which we have in the Mess are so good & partly because I haven't found a decent looking place in Cairo yet. I suppose there are one or two good places, but up to now they all exude a pungent aroma which might arise from anything but food.

I haven't paid the customary visit to the Giza Pyramids yet, although I have flown over & round them dozens of times. They are only about six minutes away by air. I couldn't find the blessed Sphinx at first, but was eventually able to make it out. I suppose that one day I shall have to make the duty trip by land & have the usual snap taken whilst mounted on ass, horse or camel. It seems to be the usual & expected thing.

Within the next month he had done both. Another letter records a trip to Giza to visit the great pyramid of Cheops and the Sphinx.

We had to crawl along the horizontal tunnels & stagger up thousands (?) of steps to reach the upper chamber. It was awfully hot despite ventilation ducts provided by my old pal Pharoah way back. We saw the famous Sphinx but I thought that art & photography has been unduly kind to it. Probably Napoleon thought the same & that's why he knocked the nose off it.

These little expeditions are frightfully expensive so I rather think that I have seen quite enough from close range. They look much better from the air & at the same time are not spoilt by protracted arguments with drago-men & a thousand or two of wheedling, swindling & smelly natives. The glamour of the East is much better when viewed from a distance.

We had a wonderful lunch in Cairo. The first meal out since I arrived. It was an Italian establishment so of course we had it a la carte when we found out that the big cheese understood English! Cairo was put out of bounds again last night. One gathers that the wilful children have been naughty again. It is most inconvenient from our point of view & political suicide from theirs – though they can't see that yet.

Such diversions aside, established squadron routine remained largely undis-turbed despite rumours which were circulating that they were scheduled to return to England the following May, political situation permitting. Johnny's views were somewhat mixed: 'As I was entertaining grave doubts of returning within five long years, the news is definitely heartening although I have a slight "crush" on this place. To be in a spot with perpetual summer is a great thing.'

So it seems that, in spite of all the petty and irritating inconveniences, Egypt and Cairo were already wreathing some of their magic on him and Johnny was slowly succumbing to their charms, entranced by the sights and sounds which surrounded him: water sellers humping bloated goat-skins with their dangling brass cups, almond-eyed street urchins begging for baksheesh fol-lowing you down streets and alleys, tugging at your sleeve. Dusty horse-drawn gharries rattled by, their intricate brass-work decorations flashing in the sun. And, on street corners, outside ramshackle ahwas or coffee shops, men dressed in flowing galabiahs huddled together, tossing dice into well-worn backgam-mon boards and sharing the cool, aromatic smoke from bubbling shisha pipes. Shade could be sought in a cafe or dingy bar where drinks were twice the price if any 'entertainment' was provided, and which usually comprised a floor show involving an overweight belly dancer gyrating to the hideous wailing of pipes and throbbing drums. And throughout the day, rising high above all the noise like some descant, the shrill calls to prayer by the muezzin echoed from the towering minarets of mosques which covered the city.

Always most particular about his appearance, even at dawn up on the flight line, Johnny sported a rather handsome leather flying jacket which he had asked his sister to acquire for him. Privately purchased, she had sensibly selected a natty lightweight affair compared to the more bulky service issue, and it was obviously drawing admiring glances from other pilots in 'D' Flight:

> I expected a stout effort, but that is just the goods. Since I first appeared in it the other pilots have abandoned theirs finding the struggle far too unequal. As a consequence they groan every morning & 'dudder' continuously with cold. I am not sufficiently concerned to leave mine off in sympathy.

In the meantime, the squadron progressed with plans to re-equip. They were due to rearm, exchanging their Fairey IIIFs for Vickers Vincents, the first new aircraft arriving late in November. Re-equipment was completed by the end of the year, the squadron bidding farewell to its last two Fairey IIIFs on 9 December, when F/O Byram, who had joined the squadron the same time as Johnny, led them off to join the Kenyan contingent still at Nairobi.

It was there in Nairobi, where 'B' Flight formed RAF Kenya, that the squadron suffered its only casualties during Johnny's entire time with them. On 29 December 1935, F/O C.C. Francis was killed when his Fairey IIIF crashed just outside Nairobi; his passenger, Corporal H.J. Bryant, later died in hospital. These were the last squadron casualties involving the faithful old Fairey IIIF, for the following month the Kenya detachment also started re-equipping, but with Fairey Gordons.

Christmas far from home and family was a new experience for Johnny, but British military establishments the world over always rose to the occasion as only they could and he seems to have been looking forward to the festivities with some enthusiasm:

> It seems rather queer to have a Xmas under a cloudless sky. It is quite hot here today although dawn was decidedly nippy. Xmas arrangements are going forward well. There is a concert on the 19th. Fancy dress dance on the 21st. Flight dinner in Helwan on the 23rd & of course great spasms of excitement on 25th winding up with a posh dance at Heliopolis on the 28th. Quite a social week ahead!!

The fancy dress dance was themed on the adventures of Robin Hood and his Merry Men, one brave soul even electing to turn out as Maid Marion, and Christmas Day saw the arrival of Father Christmas himself in the rear cockpit of a Vickers Vildebeest. However, it was not a week of entirely hedonistic pleasure for the spiritual well-being of the squadron was clearly not overlooked:

I don't know what the atmosphere is going to be like in church on Xmas
morning, but expect it will be a bit th(hic!) I shall never forget the ...
Warrant Officer ... on the Sunday morning after a dance night when dis-
cussing simple hymn books. In trying to avoid a complete frontal attack on
the chaplain, he produced quite an aura around the revered head which
bade fair to upset the Episcopal equilibrium. Fortunately the organ started
up at full bore & the poor old padre beat a hasty retreat under cover of a
thundering chord. He tottered a bit, which I could quite understand, as
though I was at four yards range I hadn't the faintest doubt as to the cause of
the heady atmosphere.

With Christmas and the New Year over, and in a series of moves aimed at
reorganising deployment of RAF aircraft throughout the Middle East, the
Vincents of 'D' Flight No 14 Squadron flew in to Helwan to join No 45
Squadron, making it purely Vincent equipped. As a consequence, the Harts of
No 45 Squadron were designated to form 'D' Flight of No 6 (B) Squadron
which, as a result of the recent reorganisation, was to be entirely Hart equipped
– their Hawker Demons having already gone to No 29 Squadron at Amirya.

So with F/L Luxmoore leading, P/Os Blomfield, Hunter, Rampling and
Sergeant Wells, carrying Aircraftman Lincoln in the rear cockpit of K4473, left
Helwan on 6 January 1936 bound for No 6 Squadron at Ismailia.

6

ON ACTIVE SERVICE

Now, by my life, this day grows wondrous hot;
Some airy devil hovers in the sky,
And pours down mischief.

King John, Shakespeare

The flight of five No 45 Squadron Harts landed at Ismailia without incident, a sixth joining them two days later on 8 January 1936. Their new CO, S/L H.M. Massey MC, welcomed them and had them shown around and introduced to some of the other officers on the staff. All told, there were thirty pilots, organised in four flights. Johnny was pleased to note that while half of them were officers, the rest were NCO pilots like himself. He had been in a distinct minority at Helwan, not to say a bit of a curiosity, and had occasionally felt a bit like a fish out of water. Here, he would be among more of his own kind and able to relax and enjoy the company more easily.

Originally an Army Co-operation squadron, No 6 had proud traditions being one of the first RFC squadrons formed in January 1914. Unlike many other units which disbanded after the war, it enjoyed unbroken service, arriving in the Middle East soon after the armistice to help police northern Iraq against Turkish-backed rebels and marauding bands of tribesmen. Since October 1929, the squadron had been based at Ismailia in Egypt, with its 'C' Flight detached to Ramleh in Palestine, a particularly troubled region.

Most of their time was spent training in air-to-ground firing and bombing practice, Johnny and the rest of 'D' Flight engaging in some high-altitude bombing within days of arrival. There were also frequent calls for the squadron to fly search or supply missions for vehicles and aircraft lost or stranded in the desert. In the hot and dusty conditions, engine failures were not altogether uncommon during routine patrols, and invariably chose to occur at the farthest point from base.

At Ismailia news was received of the accession of King Edward VIII following the death of King George V and the flag was flown half-mast, but the following week, on 31 January, the squadron celebrated its twenty-second anniversary which was a much livelier affair. Work ceased at 1130hrs that morning for the festivities to begin. A fine time was had by all, despite the fact that the squadron football team managed to lose to the Station HQ side by one goal to nil.

The following week, most of the squadron were involved in a practice move to the landing ground at Qasaba, three transport aircraft taking the advance party, which was followed by fourteen Harts. Mobility was essential if the squadron was to cover the vast tracts required of them so the ability to operate from rudimentary desert airstrips, often at very short notice, was part of their stock in trade. Johnny was one of those who remained behind at Ismailia for bombing practice.

From the dusty strip at Qasaba, squadron aircraft spent the next two days reconnoitring a number of advance landing grounds across the Western Desert before returning to Ismailia on 8 February. Here they resumed air-to-ground firing and bombing practice with a full squadron attack on Brown's Bottom, a designated bombing range in Sinai, taking place on the 11th.

Later that week, 'D' Flight sent four aircraft off to Ramleh, where the detached 'C' Flight, under F/L J.H. Reynolds, had its base. Johnny flew one of the four aircraft and from Ramleh reconnoitred the advanced landing grounds east of the Wadi Araba. This could be tricky work as the landing grounds were not always manned. Smoke canisters had to be let out to get an idea of wind speed and direction before attempting a landing on these barren desert strips assumed to be clear of major obstacles even though a few low passes were made for a visual check.

The scenery was dramatic, the aircraft often flying through rugged canyons between towering cliffs of rock dwarfing them on either side. Flying like this could be a tricky business and a pilot needed good reflexes to counter the unpredictable air currents and eddies often met in such conditions. He also needed keen navigation skills to find his way across mile after mile of fairly featureless terrain. And this with your engine constantly at boiling point. It was real fun.

Johnny returned the following day having landed at Ma'an, south-east of the ancient cave-city of Petra; Wadi Rum, with its massive outcrops of red rock towering 500ft off the desert floor; and Aqaba, at the mouth of the Gulf – a round trip of some 350 miles. Other squadron aircraft repeated this exercise the following month with a grand tour of ALGs across the Nile Delta and Gulf of Suez, but Johnny missed out on this particular excursion.

The political situation in Palestine was deteriorating, the increasing scale of Jewish immigration and settlement in the region being the key dividing issue. Three years before, Hitler had come to power in Germany where increasingly anti-Semitic laws prompted a huge exodus of Jewish refugees and a resultant influx into Palestine. If the current immigration levels continued, close to 62,000 during 1935 alone, the Palestinian Arab would soon be in a minority and any hope of national independence gone forever. The stage was set for another outbreak of violence.

In the meantime, No 6 (B) Squadron maintained readiness with air-to-ground firing and bombing practice, reconnaissance flights to advanced landing grounds across the region, and refuelling and rearming practice all continuing throughout March 1936 alongside joint exercises with local police and ground troops.

By mid-April, growing tension between Arab and Jew finally boiled over into serious rioting, resulting in sixteen deaths in Jaffa alone. A general strike was called by the Arab Higher Committee, led by the Mufti of Jerusalem, and there were reports of murders, sabotage, arson attacks and widespread destruction of crops. Civil disobedience was rife and there was open hostility towards anyone in authority or those attempting to restore order. The Palestine garrison was being reinforced and the role of No 6 Squadron was to co-operate with local police and army units in suppressing any trouble. Suddenly, after years of nervous and troubled co-existence between Arab and Jew, Palestine was about to ignite.

On the 19th, the three flights based at Ismailia received instructions to prepare for a move to Palestine in accordance with the Armed Forces Internal Security Scheme. This caused much excitement at first, many in the squadron thinking that the balloon had gone up at last, but it turned out to be merely another practice – albeit on a much grander scale.

Trueforce Exercise No 3 was a full-scale rehearsal for what might yet surely come. It involved every flying unit in the entire command flying practice missions and operating in conjunction with ground troops. This was a major undertaking and it dominated squadron activities for the rest of the month, notwithstanding inspection visits by Air Chief Marshal Sir Robert Brooke-Popham and Wing Commander R.T. Leather AFC.

Twelve of the squadron's Harts, preceded by a ground party, operated from the landing ground at Qasaba deep in the Western Desert for the duration of the exercise, which culminated in a bombing raid by nine aircraft on Bir Fuad and Qattara Springs. Exercise over, adjudged a total success, they upped sticks and returned to Ismailia on 30 April. Once again Johnny had to miss out, remaining back at Ismailia where he spent his time ferrying air gunners around to practice their air-to-air firing. Worse yet, something had prompted F/L Luxmoore to suddenly start taking an unhealthy interest in how many hours of instrument flying Johnny had done. Instrument flying! Just what he needed.

Sandstorms were a regular feature of life in the desert and the bane of the ground crew's lives. Storms could sometimes last for days and the fine dust infiltrated everywhere, blocking oil filters, clogging gun mechanisms and choking engines. During one particularly bad squall on 4 May, gusts of up to 63mph were recorded and reduced visibility to 20yd, making all flying impossible. Several tents parted their tethers and were left flapping wildly in the wind, their contents scattered across the desert or buried by the driving sand, as the occupants staggered blindly away to seek shelter.

Then on 23 May 1936, after five days at Ramleh sharing facilities with the nomads of 'C' Flight, reconnoitring police posts and Jewish settlements in the area, Johnny and the rest of 'D' Flight were suddenly recalled to Ismailia. The situation in Palestine had worsened and the squadron was preparing for possible action. There was a purposeful air about the place, everyone scurrying about their business. There was also a good deal of excited chatter amongst the mechanics, which brought down torrents of highly colourful abuse from the redoubtable Warrant Officer Jenkyn DCM, the squadron disciplinarian.

Within the week, both 'B' Flight led by Flight Lieutenant Clarke and 'A' Flight under Flight Lieutenant Tighe left for Ramleh to join 'C' Flight, who were still there vainly attempting to maintain a permanent state of standby. Johnny and the rest of 'D' Flight soon joined them, along with the CO and a nucleus of the HQ Flight. They promptly set up an Operations Room. Nineteen Harts jostled for space on the already crowded airfield, so to accommodate the sudden influx of aircraft, a hangar was allocated for their use. Suddenly, things were moving fast.

By 29 May, No 6 Squadron at Ramleh were maintaining six Harts on permanent standby, ready to take off in thirty minutes, with an additional strike force of three aircraft ready to operate anywhere in the region within forty-five minutes of receiving the call. Every day from dawn to dusk was a constant procession of reconnaissance patrols, convoy escorts or interminable sitting around on standby waiting for the proverbial balloon to go up.

Despite the fact that they were now fully mobilised and officially 'on active service', one of Johnny's regrettably few letters to have survived from this period nevertheless captures the mood well. Sitting in the hangar waiting to take off at dawn, he wrote:

… the present conditions are somewhat prohibitive to letter writing. It is now 4.30 am on a nice summer morning & I have already been up quite an age. This early morning stunt is all very well but tends to get a trifle boring. We do little else but sit & wait which is infinitely more tiring than real hard work. The big idea is to leap into the sky when the Arabs get all het up & float around above them which seems to cool them off most effectively. It is surprising how the excitement dies down when aircraft appear over the blue.

I had a trip down to the frontier post where some of the more intelligent of the troublous faction are interned under the watchful eye of the Frontier Force. The compound is adjacent to the ruins of an old monastry & the shell of a wartime Turkish hospital. The dismantled railway built by the Turks & then destroyed by Lawrence & his tribes passes close by.

These 'operations' have been officially designated as 'active service' but you don't have to worry much about that! It looks, though, as if I shall be here for quite a few moons which isn't a very inspiring prospect. The weather here is much cooler than in Egypt & just like perpetual English August. Provided it gets no hotter it will be very nice indeed. As we can't go exploring to Jerusalem & Jaffa … life in camp gets somewhat humdrum & the waking day rather long. I shall be glad to get back to Egypt …

His boredom was to be short-lived. One morning soon after their move to Ramleh, S/L Massey brought the pilots and air gunners together and issued them orders that they could open fire, without previous authority, on openly hostile tribesmen, and return any ground fire that they may experience. Apparently all their practice firing at ground targets over the past few months would not be in vain. Then, and something of an anti-climax, he had bundles of propaganda leaflets handed out to be dropped on Arab villages exhorting them to keep the peace.

A new routine was established, squadron aircraft being mainly engaged in convoy escort duties. Roads and railways were prime targets for attack and communications had to be kept open. Regular armoured convoys patrolled most of the major routes, but it was simple enough for small bands of hostile Arabs to move a few boulders and barricade a road or railway line and attack passing traffic. During the first week in June, one squadron aircraft was placed on permanent standby to support the Cameron Highlanders who regularly patrolled the road from Ramleh to Jerusalem. A wireless tender accompanying these ground patrols could call up air support at short notice.

On 11 June, they received a call for support from a company of Seaforth Highlanders under attack by a band of thirty tribesmen south of Bala, on the Tulkarm–Nablus road. Three Harts took off in the usual cloud of dust and climbed away into the distance, but although they were off within eighteen minutes of receiving the call, when they reached the area the hostiles had dispersed into nearby caves. Two days later F/O Theed opened fire on a group of armed Arabs at Burqa. They scampered off and sheltered by crowding into a nearby tin hut.

Over the next few days, a flurry of practice emergency take-offs got response times down to about five minutes, but it became clear that standing patrols over most main routes in the area was necessary. This placed an immense burden on aircraft and mechanics, that could result in serviceability problems as time went on, but at this stage in the unrest it was considered more important to make a show of strength and put down any trouble quickly with ruthless efficiency. Consequently, a series of patrols was instituted over the Tulkarm–Nablus, Jerusalem–Jericho and Jaffa–Jerusalem roads, as well as the railway line to Lydda, where one train had already been attacked.

According to his logbook, Johnny spent most of this period searching for Bedouin tribes, flying reconnaissance sorties from an advanced landing ground at Tel Auja and returning to Ramleh each night. Between times he also flew his share of convoy escorts, and on the morning of 18 June provided air support during the demolition of hostile enclaves in Jaffa by ground troops.

On the evening of 20 June, a cipher signal from the local police warned of plans for an attack on a convoy between Qalqilya and Deir Sheraf the following day. Warnings like this were unusual, but with police informants being notoriously unreliable squadron preparations went ahead as normal.

So the next morning found a solitary Hart, piloted by F/L Clarke, escorting the convoy along the Tulkarm–Nablus road when the column of vehicles was brought to a sudden halt as it came under rifle fire from both sides of the road. Clarke immediately signalled base and a strike force of three Harts took off in support. Clarke then made attacks on the hostiles who were firing at the convoy from the cover of rocks flanking the road, before flying off to drop messages at both Tulkarm and Nablus to alert the local garrisons there. Meanwhile, the troops escorting the convoy were exchanging increasingly heavy fire with their attackers in what was clearly developing into a major engagement and not just another skirmish.

A total of nine Harts were engaged in almost continuous action over the convoy throughout the rest of the day, making front- and rear-gun attacks on rebel tribesmen, flying low over their positions. Return fire was fierce and disturbingly accurate, three aircraft making forced landings after being damaged by hostile fire. One was flown back from Tulkarm the next day but the other two were so badly damaged that they had to be dismantled and towed back to Ramleh by road. Of the crews, only F/L Reynolds suffered any serious injury and was packed off to the RAF General Hospital at Sarafand. The fighting lasted until well after dusk, when the firing petered out and the Arab tribesmen melted away into the surrounding countryside.

Throughout all of this, Johnny was engaged in message dropping. He seethed at missing the action but later consoled himself when cruising 1,000ft over Gaza on dusk patrol. It was pleasantly cool flying in shirt sleeves at this height and he spent a soothing couple of hours watching the brilliant red orb of the sun slowly sink into the ground haze below. Compared to Egypt, even the Nile Delta, Johnny found the fertile Palestinian countryside, over which he now flew daily, simply breathtaking.

Orange groves and green pasture encompassed every small town or village, the surrounding hillsides all terraced and under cultivation with luxuriant groves of vines, fig and almond trees. Scattered flocks of sheep and goats grazed the fields and roadsides, tended by shepherd boys wielding sticks. Johnny was mesmerised by the simple beauty of this holy land. Along with all the other pilots, he had got accustomed to the chill early morning starts at 4.30 a.m., the intense stifling heat throughout the day and the blessed relief of dusk when they all stood down for the day. He was enjoying every minute but simply bursting to see some action.

The following morning, as pilots and gunners took stock of events and regained some of their composure, Air Ministry approval was granted for the use of bombs against legitimate targets in future, provided they were dropped no closer than 500yd from any village. Within two days, even this restriction was lifted, and squadron aircraft carried four 20lb high-explosive bombs on operations over Palestine. This significant development finally brought home the growing seriousness of the situation they faced. Events were rapidly deteriorating into a full-blown Arab revolt.

Undoubtedly, from June 1936, they were operating on a war footing. The squadron diarist even introduced a significant addition to the monthly summary of activities in the Operations Record Book. For alongside the usual breakdown of sorties and total hours flown, a new statistic appeared – a record of the monthly tally of hostile casualties claimed. That month, it was a modest thirty-seven casualties for more than a thousand hours flown, but in coming months that ratio was to rise significantly, particularly with the use of bombs. But it would be another three weeks before bombs were dropped, during which the squadron carried on with its regular pamphlet drops, one or two aircraft exchanging fire with small groups of hostiles found in open country.

Mid-morning of 26 June, Johnny was sent off on an emergency call to the Nablus–Qalqilya area, but despite patrolling the area until he ran short of fuel he failed to spot any hostiles so, once again, saw no action. Excitement over, he returned to more pamphlet dropping and routine mail runs.

On 13 July, a squadron aircraft on routine patrol was fired on by a group of about a dozen Arabs hiding in a maize field south of Jenin. Attacking with guns and bombs, the first to be dropped during the current crisis, the pilot claimed four hostiles killed by machine-gun fire and six more probably killed in the bombing. Meanwhile, Johnny continued to fret at not seeing any action while reading newspaper accounts of an army rebellion in Spain where it seemed a civil war was about to erupt.

Finally, on 29 July, he opened his account. At 1045hrs he was sent off in K4477, with LAC Jane as his gunner, on an emergency call to 'Route G. Kilo 84'. Every squadron aircraft responding to emergency calls from ground forces was now fitted with a W/T set to call for assistance or relief as required. Crews carried code tables, every main road and railway in the region being given an individual code for easy identification.

Reaching the designated area, Johnny spotted a group of armed tribesmen and immediately attacked, using his front gun. A shallow dive kept the target in sight longer and he managed to get off a good few bursts before pulling out and giving the rear-gunner a chance. The Arabs simply melted into the landscape but he claimed at least two as possible casualties.

Meantime, Arab attacks on road convoys continued almost unabated. The territory was too large to cover adequately, and the terrain ideal for ambush with narrow roads often passing through rocky defiles and outcrops. Surrounding scrub also provided perfect cover for the small groups of armed tribesmen involved.

Forced to fly low to spot their targets, the squadron's Harts were exposed and vulnerable to ground fire which was becoming increasingly heavy and more accurate as the rebels gained experience of ground-to-air firing, their sporadic individual fire giving way to concentrated volley fire. Daily, aircraft would stagger back to land at Ramleh holed by rebel fire, though casualties among the crews remained mercifully low. But on 7 August, one pilot was hit in the left thigh and seriously wounded during an attack by five aircraft on Arabs attacking an army patrol on the Nablus–Deir Sheraf road. Despite his wound the pilot managed to bring his aircraft back to a safe landing at Ramleh, where, obviously in great pain, he had to be lifted from the cockpit, his overalls caked in blood.

Welcome reinforcements arrived early in August when the Hawker Harts of No 33 (B) Squadron flew into Gaza from Amman to take over duties covering the southern part of the region, which allowed No 6 Squadron at Ramleh to concentrate on patrolling northern Palestine. Also, to improve response times to emergency calls from the far north of the area beyond Jenin, three aircraft from 'B' Flight, under F/L Clarke, were detached to the advanced landing ground at Samakh, ground crews and equipment going by road escorted by a section of armoured cars.

Johnny's next chance of action came on 10 August. Mid-morning, an emergency call sent him careering off from Ramleh with two more Harts of the squadron's strike force heading for the Nablus–Turkarm road, where they spotted a group of about ten armed rebels a few miles north-west of

Bala. The hostile tribesmen were caught in the open, but made excellent use of what little cover they had and sent up spirited rifle fire every time any of the Harts ventured within range. Johnny, flying K4477 with LAC Findlay as gunner, fired a total of 200 rounds killing one tribesman for sure and possibly two others. The Arabs should have stood little chance against three aircraft, but the Harts' attacks were unco-ordinated and disrupted by the ground fire, and they soon departed leaving four hostile casualties to be dragged away by their companions. Johnny landed back at Ramleh after two hours and twenty minutes in the air.

Three days later, another emergency call for support sent Johnny, along with P/O Hunter and F/L Clarke, to the Jerusalem–Nablus road. There, the three aircraft made repeated attacks on a group of armed Arabs near Iskaka, leaving at least seven dead on the ground. Flying in K4474, Johnny and Aircraftman Norman fired 190 rounds between them and dropped eight bombs to good effect, later claiming two hostiles killed. It was a scene repeated on an almost daily basis throughout August, with squadron aircraft responding to a dozen emergency calls and fourteen immediate reconnaissance flights, on top of an already heavy schedule of standing patrols and escort sorties. Like most of the other pilots, Johnny was starting to feel the strain and would have welcomed a few days' rest.

Thankfully there was a slight lull towards the end of the month when the Foreign Minister of Iraq, Nuri Pasha, attempted to persuade the Arab leaders to call off their strike and restore order. To reduce tension, No 6 Squadron, along with every other military unit in Palestine, was ordered to avoid punitive action whenever possible during the few days of negotiation. It was a gesture doomed to failure so long as aircraft continued to come under fire, and the following day the squadron's Harts were back in action against twenty to thirty armed rebels found in a wadi north-east of Jaba. One aircraft was forced to abandon the fight and force-landed near Jenin, others returning with slight damage, but at least twelve more rebels became casualties.

After a few days transporting assorted spares, delivering mail and ferrying senior officers to and from Ismailia, Johnny was back in the thick of it again on 3 September. The day had started like any other, he and P/O Hunter going off mid-morning in response to an 'XX' emergency call. Finding the road between Nablus and Tulkarm barricaded, they flew down to investigate and were greeted by a sudden and intense barrage of fire from rebels hidden amongst the rocks. Hunter's aircraft K4473 was hit and sheered away to glide down under control to crash in a wadi south-west of Bala.

Flying low over the gently steaming wreck, Johnny could see no sign of movement from either Hunter or his gunner, Aircraftman Lincoln, when suddenly, before his horrified gaze, the whole thing exploded in a huge ball of flame. If either of the crew had still been alive, which was doubtful, they were almost certainly unconscious, and now stood no chance as the flames rapidly took hold.

Numb with fury, Johnny flew back to the main road. There, in a series of frenzied attacks with bombs and front and rear guns, he poured hate on any rebels he could find. He was oblivious to the heavy and accurate return fire and his aircraft was hit repeatedly, one bullet going clean through the gravity petrol tank but mercifully without exploding. Bombs and ammunition finally exhausted, Johnny was reluctantly forced to break off his attacks and returned to base leaving at least four tribesmen dead on the ground.

He and his gunner, Aircraftman White, were extremely lucky to make it back in one piece. At Ramleh they reported the grim news to the CO, S/L Massey, and a shocked group of waiting pilots. Everybody knew P/O Hunter well. He had joined the squadron back at Ismailia and had been flying operations since the start of the current troubles. More than once he had brought an aircraft back to Ramleh badly holed by hostile fire and would walk around the machine studiously inspecting the damage, quietly smiling to himself. He was a good pilot and, like his gunner, AC1 Lincoln, a popular member of the squadron. Johnny had crewed with Lincoln often. They had flown together from Helwan to Ismailia on first joining the squadron back in January. Everyone was devastated by their loss.

Follow-up attacks were immediately ordered and a total of nine aircraft dispatched to the scene to maintain attacks on the rebel-held barricade throughout the day. During one of these, S/L Massey, hit and badly wounded in the knee, managed a forced landing near Tulkarm. Johnny's aircraft, too badly damaged to fly, remained unserviceable for three weeks. There were no spare machines so he stayed grounded.

Later, back at Ramleh, a solemn group of pilots surveyed the day's dismal events. Ground troops had reached the site of P/O Hunter's crash and confirmed that there were no survivors. The CO, in hospital at Sarafand, was out of action for the rest of the month so F/L Tighe, OC 'A' Flight, assumed command of the squadron.

As well as Johnny's aircraft, many others had returned in tatters or varying degrees of damage, reducing serviceability even further. And as far as anyone could ascertain, they could lay claim to no more than six hostiles killed, which included the four claimed by Johnny during his initial attacks. With dusk, a sombre mood fell across the airfield. Only the occasional sound from the hangars, where the mechanics toiled long into the night, disturbed the eerie silence which settled on Ramleh like a shroud.

Next day, as the funerals of Hunter and Lincoln took place at Ramleh War Cemetery, six Harts of 'A' Flight No 33 Squadron arrived from Gaza to reinforce the depleted squadron. They would remain until No 6 Squadron could get back up to strength. Meanwhile, Johnny and Aircraftman Drake flew in search of the hostiles responsible for yesterday's outrage and provided air support for troops laying demolition charges at Bala. The Arab village was razed to the ground in reprisal.

Two days later, on the afternoon of 6 September, Johnny was one of four pilots responding to a request for support from the Nablus police who reported some Arabs digging trenches at Juneid. Light was already starting to fade when they arrived in the area and located what turned out to be a fairly large group of hostiles. There was obviously no time to lose so, dropping their bombs on the hostiles below, all four aircraft immediately went into the attack in pairs, taking full advantage of the confusion caused by the bombing and diving at both sides of the hostile group to split their fire.

Releasing his bombs, Johnny reefed K4477 over on one wing and wheeled into the attack. Attacking head on, he brought his front guns to bear on the rear of the hostile band before quickly switching to a medium bank along its entire length allowing his rear-gunner, Aircraftman Walkden, to rake the sides. Panic stricken men, boys and animals scattered and stampeded under their guns, seeking whatever cover they could. Others fled from the main group to make themselves less of a target while many simply lay down in the dust covering their heads. A brave few stood their ground and kept up a withering fire from the cover of the trenches.

As he flashed past overhead and started making his turn for the next attack, Johnny caught a brief glimpse of the effects of their attack. It was a picture that would remain with him for years. Through the smoke and dust, Johnny glimpsed terrified men and beasts jostling, colliding and stumbling over the rocky, thorny ground below. Mercifully, the screams of wounded men and animals were drowned by the noise of his engine and the clatter of machine guns. It was clearly bedlam down there. But it was what he had trained for and he had no moral qualms about that – just make a good and thorough job of it and get it over with as quickly as you could.

They found flank attacks at low level, the most effective with the rear gun blazing away. It also seemed to reduce the amount of ground fire which greeted their attacks, but this may well have been wishful thinking on Johnny's part. He spent most of the time keeping a very close eye on his opposite number, as in attacking from different directions every time, a mid-air collision would be all too easy in the rapidly failing light. It was exciting and exhilarating, but with the occasional ping and whine of bullets just outside the cockpit, it was also bloody dangerous. He kept his head well down.

After a few more attacks, the rebels broke and dispersed across the countryside. Fifteen figures lying prone on the ground below remained silent witnesses as the four Harts re-formed and headed back towards Ramleh, their pilots and gunners exchanging cheery grins and waves. On landing they formed an excited knot as they inspected each aircraft for damage and exchanged increasingly lurid accounts of the action. But for some time afterwards, Johnny could still recall those stumbling figures in the twilight and found himself wondering if any of the other pilots and gunners involved remembered Juneid in quite the same way.

Later that evening, F/L Tighe called Johnny and the rest of the crews involved together in the CO's office. They all crowded in expectantly. 'I've just received this signal as a result of your efforts at Juneid this afternoon,' Tighe said quietly, indicating a message slip in his hand. His gaze passed slowly over every face in the room and in the pause that followed Johnny felt the ground start to open up beneath him. He sensed one or two others drop their gaze and shift their feet and could swear that he heard some swift intakes of breath. Christ! They must have attacked a group of innocent farmers digging bloody irrigation ditches or something. What a shambles! There would have to be an inquiry – they could all be court-martialled or worse.

Clearing his throat, Tighe proceeded to read the signal aloud: 'To No 6 Squadron, Ramleh. Stop. All of Nablus congratulates you on your marksmanship. Stop.' Relief flooded through Johnny as Tighe was suddenly moving amongst them, shaking hands and slapping their shoulders. They had all felt that they had a score to settle and the Nablus police confirmed seven Arabs killed and another eight badly wounded in their attacks. Johnny was credited with three of them.

'Well done chaps – damned good show. And that's not all,' Tighe continued excitedly, voice raised in the sudden hubbub. 'Tomorrow we go back to finish the job with some 112 lb bombs on those trenches. I've just got the go-ahead from HQ.' Johnny's face creased with that inimitable grin, his eyes shining. What wouldn't he give for a chance to drop one of those big beauties – quite a change from the usual 20-pounders.

In the event he was to be disappointed, for he didn't fly at all the following day. He was one of the pilots forced to watch as two Harts, laden with 112lb bombs fitted with two-second delayed action fuses, clawed for height over the airfield before setting course for Juneid.

There, two direct hits ensured total obliteration of the offending trenches but was almost incidental compared to the devastating effect such huge explosions had on the local population. The villagers were thrown into turmoil as terrified animals reared and bolted in all directions amidst much wailing, screaming and general consternation. As a deliberate and potent demonstration of the weight of British air power, it undoubtedly had a significant effect on both the local populace and opinion in the region. Before the end of the month the squadron was authorised to use the heavier bombs whenever they deemed it necessary.

September dragged on with relentless routine patrols, occasional emergency calls and searches of the Tulkarm, Yabad and Saida areas. Convoys were still attacked and barricades thrown across roads; armed rebels continued to return fire, and aircraft limped back to Ramleh or Samakh with fresh damage, but there did seem to be a definite slackening in hostile activity throughout the region. Four replacement pilots, fresh from No 4 Flying Training School at Abu Sueir, arrived on the 12th, which suggested to the more optimistic amongst the weary squadron pilots that a leave roster may be in the offing at last. It wasn't.

Lieutenant General Dill, the new commander of British forces in Palestine, paid Ramleh a visit on 18 September, accompanied by Air Vice-Marshal Peirse, and this was followed within a matter of days by a visit from Air Chief Marshal Sir Robert Brooke-Popham, the AOC-in-C, who was keen to meet all the pilots and gunners.

There was a flurry of excitement on 24 September when a signal from Nablus reported that the rebel leader, Fawzi, and his gangs were all supposedly congregating at Jaba. A large force of troops and police were going to cordon the area next afternoon and attempt to round them up. No 6 Squadron was to provide air support as the rebels were expected to try to break out and move away east.

However, that same morning 'D' Flight had been ordered up to Samakh to join 'B' Flight and provide additional escorts for road convoys between Deir Sheraf and Jenin. Despite their wails of protest, Johnny and his chums would miss the action. Thoroughly disgusted, they all acted quite disgracefully but finally had to accept the inevitable. He spent the day checking out his old aircraft K4460, all damage now repaired, and contented himself with hearing about the Jaba 'do' later.

The story, as related by those involved, went something like this. At the appointed time a single Hart, piloted by P/O Rampling, cruised high above Jaba doing its very best to look as if it was going about its routine business. To have sent any more aircraft would have aroused the rebels' suspicion and Rampling could always wireless for support as the situation dictated. Spotting a group of mounted Arabs rapidly moving east through woods outside Jaba, Rampling sent off a call for support and dived to the attack.

Within seconds of opening fire on the riders below him, Rampling's aircraft was bracketed by ground fire and took several hits. His radiator exploded in clouds of steam, as bullets splintered the interplane struts just in front of his head and riddled the cockpit sides and floor. Hit in the left thigh and wrist, Rampling attempted a high-speed forced landing which resulted in a monumental crash. Picking his way out of the tangled pile of shattered spars and flying wires, which was all that remained of his Hart, Rampling was relieved to find his gunner sitting on the ground nearby, winded but otherwise unhurt. They stayed put for some time, nervously clutching their side arms, but fortunately they had managed to put some distance between themselves and the rebel band so the first people to reach them were friendly troops. Rampling was whisked off to the RAF General Hospital at Sarafand, which was rapidly becoming home from home for No 6 Squadron aircrew, whilst his gunner was sent on his way back to Ramleh for a thorough once-over from 'Doc' Ryder, the MO.

Five Harts had responded to Rampling's call for support and kept up continuous attacks against pockets of rebels in the area until dark, claiming over forty rebel casualties, almost half their tally for the entire month. The following day Johnny flew air cover for ground troops engaged in demolition at Jaba – another act of reprisal. He found himself wondering how long all this would have to go on. But the squadron's efforts at Jaba were clearly appreciated by the new AOC, Air Commodore Roderic Hill DFC, who arrived the next day in a Gordon to speak to those involved.

Behind the scenes, political pressure was being brought to bear on the Arab leaders to call off the strike which now seriously threatened the autumn citrus crop. If this harvest failed, thousands of Arab farmers and workers could starve. A public appeal by King Ghazi of Iraq, Ibn Saud of Saudi Arabia and the Emir Abdullah of Transjordan offered the Palestinian leaders an honourable means of ending the disturbances. A British Royal Commission was to be set up to investigate the whole issue.[*]

On 8 October, 'B' and 'D' Flights, both still operating from Samakh, used guns and bombs against rebels in a wadi south of Balad Ash Sheikh. It was to be Johnny's last sortie of the campaign, a three-hour flight in K4477 with LAC Smith, his gunner. They took off from Samakh and flew to the ALG at Haifa from where they made a low reconnaissance of the Carmel area in support of a drive by ground forces. Some suspected hostiles were flushed out into the open and received all eight of their bombs, together with 500 rounds from Johnny's front gun plus 300 rounds from LAC Smith in the rear. For once, the number of casualties they inflicted went unrecorded in Johnny's flying logbook for, at this stage, he was obviously beyond caring. It was to be No 6's final flourish for after this the fighting simply petered out.

---

[*] A year later, the British government's study of the Palestine problem, headed by Sir Robert Peel, would recommend partition of the mandated area: 'While neither race can justly rule all Palestine, we see no reason why if it were practicable, each race should not rule part of it.' Sixty-five years on, as this book was written, nothing has been resolved and bitter inter-racial strife continues to plague this troubled region.

Three days later the Arab strike was called off and general orders issued to military units to revert to defensive military action, and then only if strictly necessary. A semblance of normality slowly returned to the region; No 6 Squadron responded to one solitary emergency call after the strike was called off and was flying half the number of sorties they had done previously.

To relieve any danger of boredom setting in, the advanced landing ground at Samakh was visited by the GOC, Lieutenant General Dill, and the AOC, Air Commodore Hill, on 16 October. They chatted with the pilots and crews and discussed the very real possibility of an end to all the violence. There was a definite 'end of term' spirit abroad.

The GOC also took the salute at a parade of Nos 6 and 208 Squadrons taking place at Ramleh on 5 November. He spoke in glowing terms of their part in the recent actions and a small shower of awards was announced. S/L Massey, now released from hospital, got a DSO to add to his MC; F/L Clarke, 'B' Flight commander, and P/O Burns, another squadron stalwart, each received the DFC. Representing the lower orders, Sergeant Dale picked up a well-deserved DFM. It was congratulations all round.

There was nothing in squadron daily orders for Sergeant Pilot J.C. Wells, though this didn't prevent him from celebrating just as much as all the others. But as a permanent record, details of every major action in which he had taken part was entered in the squadron Operations Record Book. Rafidiya, Iskaka, Bala and Hill 772 at Juneid – his very own battle honours. They are there to this day.

On 12 November 1936, 'D' Flight returned to Ramleh. Four days later they flew to Ismailia where they disbanded; their six trusty Harts, more than a little patched and looking well worn, were flown to Aboukir for allotment to other squadrons. On the 27th, Johnny ferried K4477 to Aboukir on his last flight with the squadron and found his thoughts drifting back over his experiences since he arrived in Egypt: the inhospitable desert with its flies, dust and relentless heat; sudden sandstorms and choking hot winds; the glorious sunrises; the welcome relief of dusk ushering in deep velvet nights with myriad stars which covered the immense bowl of the sky. The memories flooded back like so many snapshots in an album: constantly boiling engines and burst tyres; brewing up thick, sweet tea in dixies on petrol and sand fires; clustering around the fire at night and sleeping under the wings; the camaraderie and companionship of squadron life – the trust between fellows.

More troubling pictures crowded in: the abrupt shock of casualties – losing friends to hostile fire somehow far more terrible and obscene than simple flying accidents; S/L Massey, F/L Reynolds, P/O Rampling and all the others; the oily black pyre at Bala which had been Hunter and Lincoln; the carnage and chaos they had wreaked at Rafidiya. Thank God it was over. Two days later, F/L

Luxmoore led the remnants of 'D' Flight No 6 (B) Squadron aboard a transport for England and a spell of Home Establishment. They were going home.

That evening, Johnny took a turn around deck smoking a cigarette and watched the sun slip below the horizon. With the ship's wake streaming back towards Port Said, he bade his own personal adieus. Beyond all the heat, the dust, the noise, and the poverty and squalor, there remained an indefinable something about Egypt and particularly Palestine that had struck a chord deep within him.

Despite all that had happened over the past few months, he felt a strange affinity with the country and the Arab people, whom he had found to be mainly gentle by nature, and both courteous and hospitable. It was an emotional tie which he didn't truly understand but couldn't deny and had no real desire to examine more closely. It simply existed and he accepted the truth of it. Yet he still felt that he was going without taking proper leave of them, with something unsaid, some debt unpaid, and he knew with absolute certainty that one day he would have to return.

7

TARGET TOWING

Back in England Johnny enjoyed a welcome spell of leave while catching up on all the news at home which was dominated by events in Spain and the abdication of King Edward VIII, who was to be succeeded by George VI. He also enjoyed his first family Christmas in over two years. But all too soon, with the New Year festivities over, he was again packing his kit before reporting for duty at No 4 Armament Training Camp, West Freugh, on 5 January 1937.

Wigtownshire is one of the southernmost counties in Scotland, but the interminable train journey to get there made him feel that it might as well be the North Pole. All he could see of the passing scenery through the grimy rain-swept carriage window was stark bare trees in snow-drenched fields or glistening wet rooftops of a uniform grey with dirty smoke whipped by the wind from a thousand chimneys. Nothing moved in this desolate landscape, apart from the occasional crow. It was all very depressing. Condensation trickled down the window to pool on the window frame, then dripped on to his sleeve forming a large damp patch. Johnny's spirits sank lower the further north they trundled.

After a pint and a snack at Carlisle, where he had to change trains, he stretched his legs and bought a newspaper. He started to feel a little better. But somewhere beyond Dumfries the compartment heating failed and he ran out of cigarettes. The last 20 miles or so were torture and Johnny was mighty glad to find transport waiting at Stranraer when they arrived.

West Freugh, a brand new camp a few miles south-east of Stranraer, on the west coast of Scotland, had just been completed, building and construction work having commenced the previous August. It had opened that very week, Johnny being among the first of the permanent staff to arrive. The CO, W/C Porter, put them in the picture.

The camp at West Freugh provided a bombing practice facility for visiting RAF squadrons who would fly in and stay on a monthly rotation. They were expecting their first visitors in April and preparations to receive them must be completed by then, static bombing targets still needing to be set up in nearby Luce Bay. The station commander was W/C C.S.V. Porter and the Station Flight, which Johnny joined, was commanded by F/L W.J.H. Lindley. There was also a marine section, comprising three launches and two armoured target boats, which operated from Drummore, a few miles down the coast. Any questions relating to armament were the responsibility of S/L H.L. Patch or his senior armament officer, S/L M.B. MacKay, and flying came under the jurisdiction of F/L W.H. Forbes-Mitchell.

West Freugh came as a bit of a shock. It was a distinct change from Egypt and Palestine, the driving rain and biting winds far worse than even Norfolk; Johnny sensed that he might have trouble re-acclimatising. But once the weather relented and flying got under way things would start to improve a little. Most of his time, Johnny gathered, would be spent target towing. And him with over a thousand flying hours logged!

Part of his responsibilities was to liaise with the visiting squadrons and act as general advisor on local flying conditions, recommended routes and authorised target areas. So he started to get to know the local terrain very well indeed. Thirty miles to the west, across the choppy waters of the North Channel, lay Belfast Lough; while eastward, across Luce Bay and beyond the Machars, lay Wigtown Bay and the broad waters of the Solway Firth. Over 40 miles north, beyond the Ailsa Craig light, was the Mull of Kintyre, the Isle of Arran and the Firth of Clyde. Due south lay the Isle of Man. Johnny learned to recognise every inlet and headland, revelling in the rugged coastline so unlike that of his native north Norfolk.

Much of Johnny's early time at West Freugh involved the positioning of static targets set up in the broad waters of Luce Bay, which sprawled between the Mull of Galloway and Burrow Head. Each target was to stand on immense wooden piles driven 17ft into the sand and filled with concrete to a depth of 17ft. Steel girders were then bolted on top of these piles to form three towers on which a superstructure was built of heavy steel plate. When completed the targets stood like behemoths, rising at least 30ft out of the water, and were designed to withstand several direct hits from practice bombs – always assuming the bomb aimers were that good, of course.

Johnny had not been getting much flying, partly due to inclement weather, but mainly due to his heavy involvement in preparations to receive the first squadrons. But, on 20 April 1937, with West Freugh finally in a good state of readiness, he snatched the opportunity of a short refresher course at No 4 FTS, Sealand, where F/L Stephens checked him out on Hawker Hart K4896.

It was his first flight in five months and it felt good to be back in the air again, particularly in the old familiar Hart. The following day he ferried Westland Wallace II K6064 back to West Freugh which within the week had officially opened its gates, and on 26 April the Hawker Hinds of Nos 107 and 218 Squadrons arrived to commence their training.

From then on it became a regular progression of squadrons flying in and out every month to pulverise the targets and then depart. Johnny lost track of the various units and multitude of aircraft types they had to accommodate: Boulton Paul Overstrands, Bristol Blenheims, Fairey Battles, Handley Page Harrows, Hawker Hectors, Vickers Wellesleys, even Saro London, Short Singapore and Supermarine Stranraer flying boats – every squadron in the Metropolitan Air Force seemed to come their way eventually.

Meanwhile, he was busy flying Wallaces over designated routes streaming either flag or sleeve targets behind him at the end of 1,200ft of cable while inexperienced pilots and gunners blasted away in his general direction with their machine guns. It was no job for a growing lad, but it was honest toil and somebody had to do it. As with all things in life, Johnny gave it his best.

On 29 May, Empire Air Day, the station threw open its gates to the public with a flurry of fresh paint and whitewash splashed everywhere. It was the station's first open day and the biggest gathering in the province since a Royal Garden Party at Castle Kennedy two years before. The public arrived in droves, an estimated 8,000 people attending. The local press reported 'West Freugh Invaded', and the newspaper cutting which Johnny sent home in a letter to the family carried his scribbled note in the margin, 'You telling me!'

All flying areas were roped off and helpful printed cards appeared everywhere directing people hither and thither. Ground crew had spent days cleaning aircraft with paraffin rags until the cowlings gleamed like jewels. And never one to let the side down, Johnny entrusted his favourite flying overalls to the laundry. They returned starched stiff as a plank and he had a real struggle forcing legs and arms back into them again.

Every available aircraft was wheeled outside with a ladder placed alongside to allow the curious to clamber up and gawp into the cockpit. Neatly printed placards festooned propellers giving technical details of each aircraft and obliging sergeant pilots were on hand to answer questions and prevent small boys unscrewing anything. On the ground, exhibitions of bombs, ammunition, and armoury in general were on display and an aircraft set up to demonstrate firing at the butts. But the crowds poured in to watch the aircraft taking off and landing, diving and soaring, looping and rolling high above the airfield.

An ambitious programme of flying had been organised. To start, three Gauntlets performed a 'breath-taking exhibition' of aerobatics which thrilled the crowds and these were followed by 'attacks on a towed target, an example of the training carried out at Freugh' which the local hack reporter deemed 'not quite so spectacular, though of considerable interest to the technical-minded visitors'. Thus damned with faint praise, it was Johnny who stooged around in Wallace K8688 towing the drogue target for these mock attacks by a No 98 (B) Squadron Hawker Hind which snarled and crackled aggressively around him. Meanwhile, a commentary over the airfield public address system kept the crowds below informed of what was going on. The indignity of towing a large canvas target flapping about at the end of 400yd of cable was a thankless enough chore for a service pilot and something which Johnny was starting to find exceedingly dull even on the best of days.

Next, a set-piece dummy attack on a tented Arab camp set up in sandhills adjacent to the airfield gave what the newspaper described as a 'grim indication of duties the RAF have to carry out in earnest'. Two flights of Hinds swooped over the tents dropping 'bombs' that appeared to reduce the camp to a smoking shambles amidst much smoke, flame and dramatic explosions, as a motley assortment of suitably attired 'Bedouin' scurried off into the dunes in search of cover. All very entertaining but a mite too close to home for Johnny's liking.

Later in the day a single Hawker Fury gave an impressive aerobatic display drawing gasps from the crowd, and the Fleet Air Arm made an appearance with three Blackburn Sharks from the carrier HMS *Courageous*, recently returned from the Mediterranean. And throughout the entire afternoon the Northern and Scottish Airways made a small fortune taking scores of people up for joyrides over Galloway.

Target-towing duties done for the day, Johnny took up a press photographer for the grand finale, the formation fly-past. Every available type on the station was put in the air for the occasion: Tutor, Fury, Vincent, Heyford, Anson, Shark and Hind. They formed up alongside Johnny, while he struggled to keep the Wallace straight and level as they filed past, the photographer clicked away happily. At the end of a most successful day, as the last visitor filed through the gates and the vast job of clearing up began, West Freugh again returned to something resembling normality.

For Johnny, now rapidly becoming ever more disenchanted with his daily lot, one of the only advantages of being stuck at West Freugh was the wide variety of aircraft passing through and the occasional opportunity to gain experience of new types. On 29 July, he got his hands on Hawker Fury K8299 for some local flying practice.

A sleek and rakish biplane, the Fury perched on a rather dainty-looking undercarriage which framed a huge box-like radiator slung under the belly. Armed with twin Vickers machine guns, fired through the propeller thanks to Constantinesco interrupter gear, it was by far the most potent RAF fighter in service at the time. It was Johnny's first flight in a Fury, or indeed any high-performance interceptor for that matter, so quite a test of his flying ability. He taxied out somewhat gingerly, using the toe-operated hydraulic brakes to swing the nose from side to side to see ahead. Crabbing his way forward, Johnny reached the end of the runway and let the aircraft roll forward a few yards to straighten up before applying the brakes and coming to rest. Pre-flight checks completed, he adjusted his straps and squinted down the runway beyond the highly polished engine cowling. He opened the throttle steadily, feeding in the power from the Rolls-Royce Kestrel which snarled and crackled away lustily through its stub exhausts. Correcting a slight swing with a touch of right rudder, Johnny was surprised to find himself suddenly off the ground after what seemed a very short take-off run. The Fury simply soared off the runway and climbed like an express, its rate of climb at 140mph, not far short of 2,000ft per minute. This is all rather exciting, he decided.

It handled like a dream, positive and responsive to his every movement on the controls. Johnny found that it cruised comfortably at 160mph and got it up to a top speed of around 215mph at 13,000ft, but the performance tailed off a bit above 20,000ft. Light and positive on aileron and rudder, the Fury was every inch the thoroughbred aerobatic fighter that it looked, and Johnny revelled in its manoeuvrability and overall performance. Slow rolls, loops and spins, split-arse turns and rolls off the top, it all seemed so effortless – he was at one with the aircraft and lost in the pure enjoyment of flying, entirely captivated by the machine.

Reluctantly he returned to West Freugh and touched down, deftly dropping the tail skid the merest fraction after the main wheels were well and truly down and keeping his feet well away from the brakes to avoid any embarrassing ground loops. He had just enjoyed some of his happiest moments since Palestine and was now more than ever convinced that, somehow, he had to return to a squadron and regular service flying – preferably on interceptor fighters.

Next month another new aircraft appeared in his log when, on 12 August, he took up No 601 Squadron Hawker Demon K5714 for a 'first solo on type', taking Aircraftman McIntyre as passenger. He had to work hard to persuade a very reluctant flight lieutenant to let him borrow his precious red and black liveried Demon, for 'They can be a bit tricky you know'.

Johnny eventually got his way but the flight lieutenant's evident relief when the Demon was later returned without a scratch was almost touching to behold. Ironically, on its very next flight the following day, the flight lieutenant hit a gang-mower on landing and the Demon was so badly damaged that it was only fit for use as an instructional airframe. Johnny hadn't had such a good laugh for months.

But such trifling incidents were seemingly commonplace in No 601 Squadron, a London auxiliary unit widely known throughout the service as 'The Millionaire's Squadron'. It had the reputation of being more of an exclusive flying club than an air force unit, numbering several wealthy, well-connected socialites amongst its pilots. They clearly made an impression on Johnny for he mentions them in one of his regular letters home to his mother. Almost disapproving in tone, this letter reveals a more serious, sober side to his nature:

> We have got two Territorial Squadrons up here from London. They have quite a number of big names amongst them and make a lot of noise, tearing round the country in large cars when they are not working. Lord Beaverbrook's son [the Hon. John William Maxwell Aitken] is here, and someone belonging to Cleavers of 'Robinson and Cleaver' [F/O G.W.S. 'Mouse' Cleaver]. All of them seem to have no end of money and some have their own aeroplanes as well. They seem to be having a good holiday and they are only here for two weeks.

It was whilst stationed at West Freugh that Johnny also got his first experience of night flying, usually only permitted after a requisite amount of instrument flying but, with Johnny's experience, his flight commander felt this formality could be waived. He had fourteen hours of instrument flying logged, most of which he had completed during his initial training at Sealand, but no actual night flying. It was an omission that his flight commander was keen to rectify.

Like so many embryo nighthawks before him Johnny was cautioned to ignore his own sensations when judging the aircraft's attitude in the air at night. F/L Lindley insisted: 'Trust your instruments, think fast, and when you need to, act decisively. But never ever panic, night flying is a lot to do with learning to control your emotions.' In Johnny's view, all much easier said than done, but night flying was a challenge he had somehow managed to avoid for too long and he resolved to master it. So, after a few practice night landings in the rear cockpit, his first night flight was scheduled for the evening of 4 March 1938 in Wallace K5071 with Lindley as passenger.

Spluttering paraffin flares stretched away into the distance marking the length of the runway. A fairly strong headwind was blowing, whipping the flames about. Somewhere in the darkness far ahead of him lay the end of the runway, where Johnny could just make out another dim line of flares laid at right angles, forming an elongated 'T'. He flashed his recognition lights and the duty pilot responded with a green light. He was cleared for take-off. This was straightforward and Johnny climbed steadily away from the airfield, his eyes glued to the instruments, before levelling off around 1,000ft and turning left on to circuit. It was a clear moonlit night and he was surprised at just how much of the ground could be made out at night. He made another left turn and checked his position relative to the airfield, which twinkled away below him under the port wing. Just a few more circuits and it would be time to put the Wallace back on the ground – the really tricky bit.

Flashing his signal lamps he requested permission to land and got an almost instant green light. His was the only aircraft up that night so the duty pilot must have been bored stiff. He turned gently to face the runway and straightened up. Throttling back carefully, Johnny kept one eye on the flickering lights below him as he watched his air speed slowly drop away. Approaching the runway, landing light on, he kept the Wallace heading straight down the middle, with a good margin of speed, before levelling off and cutting the throttle. All neat and tidy.

Holding back on the stick he hit the ground much sooner than expected and bounced several feet back into the air but managed to stay in control. There were a few more thumps, each one slightly less than before, until the main wheels trundled along the runway and the tail dropped gently. They were safely down.

They walked back across the grass together, Johnny's legs still a bit shaky. 'Sorry about that landing,' he explained to Lindley, who had stayed remarkably silent throughout the whole adventure, probably rendered speechless with terror. 'It's a bit tricky to judge your exact height at night.'

'Don't worry about it, nothing was broken,' Lindley replied airily. 'It comes with practice. You get a feel for it after a while. Besides, I've seen much heavier landings than that after a first night flight.' Johnny started to feel a bit better until, over his shoulder as he turned and headed back towards the flight office, Lindley added, 'But they all generally proved fatal!'

Johnny's night landings would improve as his confidence grew with more experience, although finding and holding the green light of the newfangled flight path indicator wasn't as easy as it sounded in the briefing room. It required strong nerves and a deft hand on the controls when approaching a runway at night, often shrouded by mist, whilst juggling the controls to adjust height: yellow light – too high; red light – too low. But he persevered and eventually got the hang of things. Half the secret of night flying, Johnny decided, was to keep a good lookout outside the cockpit when the conditions allowed. Many budding night hawks spent far too much time glued to the instruments on the blind-flying panel, with occasional disastrous results.

Late in January 1938, taking advantage of a sudden improvement in the weather, Johnny took an Avro Tutor on a cross-country flight from West Freugh to Abbotsinch, returning the following day. It was a welcome break from the routine, and kept his flying hours over the four hours a month required by regulations, but it only reinforced his growing frustration and boredom.

At first, Johnny had found the work at West Freugh stimulating and a welcome change from dodging ground fire from hostile Arabs. But once a familiar routine had been established and things settled down, it rapidly became more than a little tedious. Apart from exchanging gossip and news of old comrades and mutual friends in the squadrons which came and went, plus the occasional opportunity to fly a new type, it had to be said that target towing could be somewhat monotonous. He was starting to feel trapped in what he suspected could turn out to be a very quiet and turgid backwater. To add to his growing discomfort, he was being slowly eaten alive by a particularly voracious local breed of midges which descended on him every evening in droves, their bites becoming infected and requiring treatment by the MO. He was, first and last, an RAF pilot and craved more stimulus from his flying than seemed remotely possible given his current duties.

With the turn of the year a new station commander, W/C R.S. Sorley OBE DSC DFC, took over at West Freugh and Johnny determined to broach the subject with him through the proper channels. Ralph Sorley arrived fresh from a stint with the Operational Requirements Branch at the Air Ministry and it was due largely to his influence that the next generation of RAF fighters would be armed with eight machine guns, a decision that would have dramatic consequences barely two years later when the Battle of Britain would decide the fate of the nation. However, he seemed rather less than sympathetic and distinctly noncommittal when Johnny raised the subject of a possible transfer before expiry of his current tour of duty.

In September 1938, triggered by the Sudeten crisis, political events took an unexpected turn. Things in Europe had been going from bad to worse for some time. Six months before, Germany had marched into Austria and, despite French and British efforts to appease the situation, German demands over Czechoslovakia had finally come to a head. Prime Minister Chamberlain arrived back from meeting Hitler in Munich brandishing an agreement announcing 'peace in our time' which prompted mobilisation and the recall of squadrons to their home bases.

Simultaneously, there was an appeal throughout the entire service for experienced pilots, desperately needed as instructors in order to accelerate pilot training. Ink still wet, Johnny's formal application landed on the adjutant's desk the very day that the notice was posted. Far better a flying instructor than fret around here any longer in what was rumoured would soon become, horror of horrors, an Air Observers School!

To his delight his application was accepted and, with what seemed indecent haste, Johnny was away from No 4 ATC West Freugh on an immediate posting to No 1 Flying Training School at Netheravon. It was a welcome reprieve and a happy release. After 14 months and over 275 hours dragging acres of canvas around the sky, Johnny was not sorry to be on his way.

8

FLYING INSTRUCTOR

Its circuits and bumps from morning to noon
And instrument flying till tea
Hold her off, give her bank, put your undercart down
You're skidding, you're slipping, that's me.

The Instructor's Lament, A.P. Herbert

Johnny arrived at Netheravon, a few miles west of Andover, to discover that No 1 Flying Training School had only just settled in there, having moved from Leuchars the previous month. The chief flying instructor, F/L Willis, interviewed him soon after his arrival and set about giving him all the gen and explaining the set-up.

No 1 FTS was a flying training school for Fleet Air Arm pilots, but as the RAF retained responsibility for all basic flying training most of the instructors and staff were air force personnel. Some of the pupils were officers, mainly naval lieutenants, but most were ordinary seamen – either regular RN or reservists in the RNR or RNVR. They came to Netheravon direct from their Elementary Flying Training Schools where they had already learned basic flying on Tiger Moths or Avro Tutors. At No 1 FTS the aim was for them to learn to fly service machines.

The school, organised into two squadrons, was made up of three flights. There was an Initial Training Squadron, largely equipped with Hawker Harts but with one flight of Fairey Battles, where pupils completed a training programme lasting two to three months; depending on weather. Then, after a period of leave, they progressed to the Advanced Training Squadron for a month flying Battles and Hinds and learning something about combat flying.

On average, of the sixty or so pupils in each squadron, about one in five would fail to complete the programme – either assessed as unsuitable or, if unlucky, packed off home in a box. Of the survivors, the majority were potential FAA fighter pilots while the rest would be selected to pilot torpedo bombers or floatplanes.

The school could handle up to 120 pupil pilots at a time, spread across both squadrons, and the staff establishment was 40 officers, 68 NCOs and 500 air-craftmen; so the pupils were outnumbered almost five to one – a good ratio. Group Captain L.F. Forbes MC, the current CO of the school, was awaiting a posting to the Middle East; his successor, G/C W.B. Farrington DSO, took over in November and came from HQ Training Command.

Johnny was pleased to find himself assigned to 'F' Flight, part of the Advanced Training Squadron under Commander Dickens RN, and was intro-duced to F/O Sayers who would be his flight commander. Johnny busied himself settling into the school routine. With over 1,300 flying hours under his belt and assessed 'above the average' as both a tow and light-bomber pilot, Johnny felt ready for the inevitable challenges that instructing would bring.

He had always been a careful and methodical pilot, setting himself high standards in everything he did, and he expected no less of others. But his time at West Freugh had taught him patience, and it had also helped him come to understand that other people's standards could, despite their best efforts, fall far short of his own. So, in terms of both flying ability and temperament, he felt quite comfortable about taking on an instructor's role. After all, the best way to learn something really well was to teach it to others, and he was quite keen to learn more about this flying business.

Despite such high-minded principles, Johnny was rapidly brought back down to earth. For within days of arriving at Netheravon he found himself back in the all too familiar cockpit of a Hawker Hart dragging a drogue target for ground-to-air and air-to-air firing practice. He consoled himself with the fact that at least the scenery was different.

It was mid-October before he did any instructing with some cross-country flights, instrument flying, and formation practice. After this his logbook records regular dual flights, sometimes up to four a day, covering a variety of activities including formation take-offs and landings – always great fun with a ham-fisted pupil in control – to dive-bombing practice on the ranges at Porton, which were even worse and would put the wind up the most sanguine of veterans. He also put in some night-flying practice in a Hind with one of the more experienced instructors, F/Sgt Kean, checking him out on landing by floodlight. Johnny qualified as a first pilot (night) that same month.

In April 1939, after two weeks at Sutton Bridge on gunnery practice, Johnny returned to Netheravon to find the school had just started taking delivery of a new modern trainer, the North American Harvard. He first flew one of these aircraft on 20 April, taking the imperturbable F/Sgt Kean along to act as referee. After fifteen minutes' dual instruction, Johnny took over the controls for a further ten minutes of circuits and bumps before landing, feeling very happy with the new machines. Maybe he could say goodbye to the dear old Hart at long last?

A spate of accidents followed, no doubt due in part to unfamiliarity with the new Harvards. But with the prospect of war becoming more imminent by the day there was also a marked increase in activity and thus more accidents. In the five months from June 1939, nine pupils were lost in accidents – most of them at night. Johnny logged thirty-four landings with four different pupils on the night of 9/10 May, taking up five more pupils three nights later.

It was September before the last Hart went into storage. Johnny, having been flying them on and off for four years, wasn't sorry to see them go. It was a good aircraft but it had long had its day and there were now modern types available which could do a better job. However, his pleasure was short-lived for, within six months, the Admiralty decided that pilots destined to fly Swordfish or Walrus aircraft didn't need to fathom the mysteries of retractable undercarriages, landing flaps or variable pitch airscrews. Consequently, a few Harts and Hinds were dragged back out of store and returned to the fray but, mercifully, Johnny seems to have avoided them, sticking with his preferred Harvard.

In the meantime, with the German invasion of Poland and the inevitable outbreak of war, there was a sudden spate of postings so Johnny prudently set about quietly putting his affairs in order. A letter written to his mother within a month of war being declared seems to dwell on routine domestic affairs and simple financial arrangements. It appears surprisingly devoid of any emotion or the reassuring phrases one might expect from a son writing to his mother at such a time, until you read between the lines:

> The pal I have been sharing the car with is posted away so we have had to re-organise things. I don't expect to have to go but have made all arrangements in case. The trouble about these postings is that they are a bit sudden & there isn't much time to spare for making arrangements for private property. It's far better to have it all cut & dried. Not much been happening here. Everything going on as usual.

Christmas came and went in a delirium of flying, weather permitting, one week's leave only being granted to those who could be spared. Johnny, evidently one of them, welcomed the break. Since joining No 1 FTS he had done close to 300 hours' flying, 25 of them at night, and probably felt that he deserved a breather.

Accidents continued to mar events and threaten progress. On 23 February 1940, Acting Sub-Lt Skinner RN was killed when his Harvard crashed at Lower Clatford after flying in low cloud. A fortnight later, two Battles collided during formation practice and a disastrous outcome was only avoided by some very competent flying by both pilots involved. Leading Airman Wines RN kept his head and managed a forced landing with a badly bent propeller, while Corporal Beeston RM put up a particularly good show. With his rudder torn away and both elevators out of action, Beeston stayed with the aircraft and brought it all the way back to Netheravon making aileron turns – no mean feat for a relatively inexperienced pilot. He put down just outside the airfield perimeter, wiping out the undercarriage in the process. Johnny was nonetheless most impressed.

Then on 10 May 1940, after months of the so-called phoney war, Germany unleashed its long-awaited assault in the west with a devastating attack through Holland and Belgium into France. Reports from the Continent were at first encouraging, but as more news began to filter through it was apparent that things were not going well. Allied forces were being driven back everywhere by German armour operating in close co-operation with overwhelming local air support, while so-called defensive strong points were simply bypassed or overrun by parachute or glider troops. A new word appeared in the press to describe it – *blitzkrieg*.

At Netheravon flying training carried on as usual although with a degree of greater urgency, 'training comes first' being the watchword of the day. But essentially the training programme remained much the same as always, and little if anything of real consequence changed from earlier practices. Yet within days it became clear that there was little hope of stopping the German advance and the awful prospect of an invasion of Britain started to look like a distinct possibility. Every available aircraft would be needed to counter this threat so, to bolster numbers, HQ Training Command called for lists of experienced pilots 'with aircraft suitably equipped for bombing and gunnery' who would be available for future emergency operations in the UK.

This chilling request brought home the dire state of our defences and introduced a sobering dash of reality to the situation. And although, if he were to be totally honest, Johnny would have no doubt admitted that he didn't much relish the prospect of diving a Harvard through intense flak and swarms of angry Messerschmitts to drop bombs on German paratroops dressed as nuns (according to the more lurid newspaper accounts), he nevertheless put his name forward.

Under this so-called 'Banquet Plan', No 1 FTS kept twelve Harvards and nine Battles fully equipped to operate against enemy troops landing in this country. The two flights of six Harvards were made ready to deploy, at only four hours' notice, to Scampton; while the Battles, also organised in two flights, were originally intended to operate from Mildenhall, but this was later changed to Benson.

In addition, three Hawker Hinds were wheeled out to form Netheravon's 'Offensive Battle Flight' and readied to attack any enemy troop carriers which might care to land on the airfield. At best, and despite their appropriately aggressive title, a single sortie was all the antiquated Hinds were expected to achieve before any that survived buggered off and put down wherever they could.

There were also other, more obvious, signs that the war had taken a turn for the worse. Everybody now sported an anti-gas respirator and those entitled to side-arms had, rather self-consciously, strapped canvas holsters about their person. Walking across a dew-drenched airfield towards dispersal early one morning Johnny glimpsed, through the mist, groups of airmen formed into rifle parties for instruction in bayonet fighting. This struck him as being a bit late in the day, besides which there were only fifty rifles on the entire station. Elsewhere trenches were being dug, making life hazardous after dark. Additional machine-gun posts sprouted up at vantage points and guards were doubled – woe betide anyone found without their pass. Around the perimeter, acres of fresh barbed wire appeared and plans to destroy the airfield before evacuating were dusted off and revised. Come what may, Netheravon was as ready as it would ever be to repel the invader.

Across the English Channel, over in France, the evacuation of Allied troops from northern ports began. Calais finally fell on 27 May and the Dunkirk evacuation ended on 4 June, the day on which Churchill, who had replaced Chamberlain as prime minister on 10 May, told the House of Commons: 'We shall not flag or fail. We shall fight on the beaches, we shall fight on the landing ground, we shall fight in the fields and in the streets, we shall fight in the hills. We shall never surrender.' Along with the rest of the nation, Johnny, who heard the BBC broadcast of the speech that evening, was stirred to the marrow.

Two weeks later a strange gaggle of French aircraft unexpectedly appeared in the circuit and came in to land at Netheravon. Four Blochs and a Caudron created quite a lot of interest amongst pupils and instructors alike. Flown by five Polish pilots who had been serving with the French air force, they had flown in from Tangmere and Andover, where they had first landed in this country after escaping from France ahead of the German advance.

Despite the almost constant disruption to night-training flights due to air raid warnings, another advanced course was completed at the end of June 1940, its pilots leaving on posting to Fleet Air Arm units all over the country. There, they would complete their training and convert on to the aircraft with which their squadron was equipped before being deemed fully operational.

But now, for the first time, many of these young men, who had all been earmarked as FAA fighter pilots, were being sent on to Operational Training Units for a quick conversion course on Hurricanes or Spitfires. After which they were to be posted to RAF fighter squadrons to make up the serious pilot shortfall in Fighter Command due to severe losses over the south coast and the English Channel in recent weeks. Over fifty Fleet Air Arm pilots served with Fighter Command during the Battle of Britain, and nine of them died.

Johnny realised then just how hard our backs were to the wall and how close we were to irrevocable defeat. Scores of our pilots had already been lost in France and over Dunkirk, and many others were out of action wounded, but it was clear that the worst of the fighting was yet to come. He applied for an immediate posting to an operational squadron but his application was turned down flat, not even getting beyond the CO's desk.

In August 1940, as the Battle of Britain raged over southern England, HQ No 23 (Training) Group issued instructions that training aircraft were not to be used for offensive or defensive operations although the threat of imminent invasion remained very real. There were still several incidents involving train-ing aircraft attempting to take on the Luftwaffe, all very heroic but, inevitably, usually ending in disaster. And only two weeks before, on 21 July 1940, an Me110 engaged on a photo-reconnaissance sortie attacked two aircraft from No 1 FTS within ten minutes of each other.

One of them was a Fairey Battle blithely flying along on instruments with the pupil pilot under the blind-flying hood, totally oblivious to all that hap-pened. Fortunately the instructor, F/L John Wray, OC of 'E' Flight, had the presence of mind to grab control as the 110 suddenly slid alongside and the rear-gunner raked them with machine gun fire at point-blank range. Wray wrenched the Battle away and plunged into some nearby cloud, informing a thoroughly bewildered pupil just how close they had come to 'collecting their tickets'. They made a forced landing on Salisbury Plain, the Battle's smoking engine riddled with bullets.

The second incident a few minutes later had a less fortunate outcome. On a practice solo in a Hart over Old Sarum, a pupil pilot of the Initial Training Squadron was attacked by the same enemy aircraft. The Hart immediately burst into flames and the badly wounded pilot, Acting Leading Airman J.A. Seed RN, bailed out but his parachute failed. Everyone on the station was stunned. They were used to casualties, of course – fatal accidents were common enough on any flying training establishment – but to lose unarmed aircraft to enemy action was particularly bitter pill to swallow. Enemy fighters were not expected to be operating that far west; meeting the Luftwaffe during a routine training flight was a chilling prospect.

Later in the day, they learned that the Messerschmitt 110 responsible had been forced down near Chichester by a section of Hurricanes from Middle Wallop. They were less pleased to learn that both of the crew had survived and were taken prisoner. Johnny had been flying that day and could easily have been one of those attacked. It was simply a matter of luck. But this incident prompted him to again approach his flight commander, F/L Younghusband, and broach the subject of a transfer to an operational squadron.

The response was sympathetic but as expected: 'You are doing a damned good job, Johnny, and an important one.' Younghusband explained:

You are needed right here. Instructors with your sort of experience are bloody hard to find. Besides, by the time you got enough hours on Spits or Hurricanes to be of any use other than to provide some target practice for Gerry, it will all be over. Stick with it, your turn will come.

Johnny shrugged and nodded, recognising the good sense of it all.

Younghusband went on:

Don't you think I feel just the same way? I would like nothing better than to get into the action, but our job is to get as many of these youngsters through the programme just as quickly as we can. And if you, or I, or any of the other instructors fail in that, then we might as well pack up and go home because it will all be over for good. Think about it.

Which Johnny did.

It was difficult to do otherwise as the weekly casualty lists of the pilots missing, killed or wounded grew longer and included too many familiar names. Some Johnny had known for years, but more recently there had also been some of his ex-pupils: Blake, Patterson, Smith – familiar names from his logbook. However, it wasn't always bad news for others seemed to be doing quite well: Bramah and Jeram, both flying Hurricanes with No 213 Squadron at Exeter, and Dicky Cork, making something of a name for himself with the Canadians of No 242 Squadron at Duxford. How desperately Johnny must have wished he could join them.

Part of the training in the Advanced Squadron involved teaching Tyro 'naviators' how to land on an aircraft carrier at night, putting a Hind down within the tight confines of a carrier flight deck. For this, a dummy deck was laid out on the airfield complete with pillar lights and all the other usual snags to the unwary and paraphernalia to be found on a carrier. When lit up it resembled an enormous fairground attraction and could be seen for miles, illuminating most of the surrounding countryside. Obviously, it would attract the Luftwaffe like moths to a flame.

So late in July 1940, to avoid potential attacks on Netheravon which could render the whole airfield inoperable, this 'carrier' flare path was moved to a relief landing ground at Shrewton, on nearby Salisbury Plain. It was an opportune move for, within a matter of weeks, the night-landing ground at Shrewton was attacked twice, one stick of incendiaries landing barely 500yd off the flare path. But nothing was allowed to interfere with training.

The Luftwaffe assault on Britain raged throughout those glorious summer weeks. The enemy was met, matched and bested by the Spitfires and Hurricanes of RAF Fighter Command, fighting implacably and resolutely in defence of their country. But as the weeks passed and the threat of German invasion slowly receded, relief in Britain was tempered with the growing real-isation that it would be a long and difficult war.

In October, the number of pupils under training at Netheravon was increased to 200, putting considerable pressure on facilities already operating at full stretch. Another relief landing ground was set up at nearby High Post, an ex-Army Co-operation airfield, and the following month an additional emergency runway opened at Winterbourne Stoke. All Christmas leave was cancelled, although Johnny did manage to avoid flying on Christmas Day itself. He was spending a lot of time on Hinds doing night flying at Shrewton RLG and at High Post, where the newly extended runway could now handle night landings.

Months passed and, with the approach of spring 1941 and an improve-ment in the weather which had curtailed flying, training resumed in earnest. Instructors were working flat out in an effort to keep on top of the growing number of pupils coming through the school, but a serious backlog of candi-dates had built up over the winter months. Any prospect of leave was shelved indefinitely. Over 300 pupils were already 'in the system' awaiting vacancies at service flying training schools in Britain, which were already bulging at the seams and simply couldn't cope with demand. As a result, many pupils were being sent overseas for training.

Shortly before 0100hrs on 12 May 1941, the dummy deck at Shrewton received another visit from the Luftwaffe. A Heinkel He111, which had obvi-ously been stooging around biding its time, deposited a neat stick of bombs slap down the middle of the flare path. Johnny wasn't flying that night but a Battle was caught on the runway and was burned out. Fortunately, the pilot, who was more than a little discomforted by the sight of a line of explosions coming towards him at high speed, escaped with slight injuries. Night flying was scrubbed for the rest of the night but all was cleared by morning when training resumed as usual.

Two weeks later, Johnny, formally discharged as a flight sergeant, was granted an emergency commission as a pilot officer in the General Duties Branch. Admittedly there was a war on, but still not so bad for a Trenchard Brat. In the meantime, he continued to call for a transfer to an operational squadron.

On 22 June, in the greatest military attack in history, Germany launched an invasion of the Soviet Union opening a second front covering 1,800 miles from the Arctic to the Black Sea. And the following December, Japanese naval aircraft operating from carriers attacked the American Pacific Fleet in Pearl Harbor, so bringing the USA into the world war.

That month G/C J. Noakes AFC MM arrived to take over as CO, everyone knowing that his appointment was likely to be short term, as arrangements were already in hand to transfer control of the station to the army which wanted its own flying training facility. In addition to which, further RAF flying training was to become the responsibility of the new Operational Training Units so, along with the other instructors, Johnny was already prepared for another move and was still plugging away at that transfer to an operational unit.

It was the worst winter weather for years. Heavy falls of snow brought all flying to a halt and very severe weather continued well into the New Year. Despite these delays, fifty-one pupils still managed to complete No 27 Course, which wound up on 14 February. It was the last FAA training programme at Netheravon, and Johnny was one the few remaining RAF instructors left on the strength. Now deputy OC night flying at Shrewton, he would, as usual, have to see things through to the bitter end.

On 23 February 1942 another new CO arrived, W/C G.P. Marvin, whose brief included the transfer of Netheravon over to the control of Army Co-operation Command. This was effected on 7 March but Johnny was still there doing dual instruction for some days to come. He must have been one of the very last RAF instructors at No 1 SFTS, for his service record confirms that he was on the strength until 11 March, when he was assessed as 'above the average' as a pilot by the chief flying instructor, S/L Marcus Robinson.

Johnny's next posting was to No 52 Operational Training Unit, but unlike some of the other displaced instructors at Netheravon, it was not to join the training staff. Finally, after months of badgering, his long-awaited posting had come through and he was returning to mainstream service flying at long last. After three and a half years as an instructor, Johnny was switching roles. He would join the OTU as a pupil, but on a real fighter aircraft. He would be flying Spitfires.

9

SPITFIRE PILOT

Johnny joined No 15 Course at No 52 OTU, Aston Down, with seventeen other officers and eighteen flight sergeants. Most of them were British, but the Commonwealth and Dominions were well represented, with nine Canadians, six New Zealanders, a couple of Australian flight sergeants and a Rhodesian. Completing this 'league of nations', five Belgian officers were also on the programme. The course would make up 'C' and 'D' Squadrons, and there were two other courses also under training, making a total of just fewer than 100 trainees on the station, all told. Johnny was interested to find several ex-FTS instructors like himself among them and was soon busy swapping news and experiences. The training would last nine weeks, the first six being spent at Aston Down, deep in the Cotswolds not too far from Stroud, with the final three at nearby Chedworth. In all, each of them could expect to complete fifty-eight hours' flying.

Although itching to get on to operations, Johnny curbed any frustration with the knowledge that this was an important and very necessary posting. Pre-war he might have gone straight from Elementary Flying Training School to a squadron where he would have simply gained more experience by constant flying. But in wartime he knew, only too well, that he must be ready to play a full and active role as soon as he joined his unit, and must be able to do so with a better than reasonable chance of survival. Investment in a pilot's training was considerable and the RAF could ill afford to squander it by pitting its new pilots against the Luftwaffe without giving them some extra polish. Time spent at an Operational Training Unit gave them this edge, as well as the benefit of their instructors' own recent combat experience, before they were thrust into the cauldron of operational flying.

On 14 March 1942, after an hour solo in a Miles Master, Johnny clambered into his first Spitfire (AR227) and set off for a joyous ninety minutes of 'experience on type & R/T'. Many have waxed lyrical over the almost legendary qualities of this great aircraft so we can be sure that, with Johnny's flying experience, he would surely have been equally ecstatic and in his true element. After this he spent as much time in the air as possible, clocking up valuable experience of the Spitfire or practising cross-country flights in a Master with one of the instructors as passenger. 'Aerobatics, cloud flying, battle climbs, low flying, section attacks and gunnery.'

It soon became fairly obvious that all was not well at Aston Down. The previous month's training had been curtailed on a total of twenty days with weather unfit for flying. This was discouraging enough but there had also been sixteen flying accidents, five of them involving the Canadians and all of them fatal. To further aggravate things, the station was badly overcrowded and accommodation in the barracks poor by any standards. Discipline began to suffer and there was a general slackness about the place, which four inspections in the space of three weeks did nothing to improve. Morale was at rock bottom and the atmosphere in the sergeants' mess was appalling; friction between staff pilots and pupils was barely disguised.

An attack exercise and gas exercise on two consecutive days within the week of their arrival brought many pilots in the other squadrons to boiling point. Walking into this situation, Johnny and the rest of the pilots on his course had a pow-wow and decided to keep their heads down and concentrate on their training. They would ignore the petty squabbles going on around them and put up with things for the nine weeks that it would take to complete the programme.

No 52 OTU was commanded by Group Captain F.F. Argyle Robinson DFC, and the chief flying instructor was S/L Tony Rook, who had won a DFC for his work in Russia. On Johnny's course, 'C' Squadron was commanded by F/L W.M. 'Bill' Sizer DFC and 'D' Squadron by F/L 'Neddy' Nelson-Edwards, who, like all COs of the six squadrons in the unit, were both very experienced fighter types that had fought in the Battle of Britain. Normally, after completing at least one full tour of operations, these seasoned combat veterans would spend six months 'resting' from operations in the OTUs, where they could pass on their hard-won experience to the next generation of fighter pilots. After which they would return to operations, usually leading a flight or their own squadron.

Barely three weeks into the course, the CO of 'C' Squadron, Bill Sizer, was posted and left in a bit of a hurry. He had been poached by S/L Harold Bird-Wilson DFC, who had commanded 'A' Squadron at Aston Down, and had just been promoted CO of No 152 'Hyderabad' Squadron, based at Eglington in Northern Ireland. He took Sizer with him to be one of his flight commanders. It was two full weeks before S/L A.F. Sunderland Cooper arrived to take over 'C' Squadron and things settled down again.

Johnny was now well into the programme, studying fighting tactics and air combat, and clocking up over thirty-three hours flying during April alone. It was a particularly good month for flying with long spells of fine weather, although a fairly strong easterly wind was instrumental in causing several taxiing and landing accidents. The worst accident occurred on 7 April, when a Master crashed soon after take-off, killing both occupants. The funerals of F/O H.K. Smith and Sgt L.N. Brown took place at Chalford chapel three days later.

Then on the 16th, Sergeant Charron, seemingly oblivious to the intricacies of the variable pitch airscrew, tried to take off with the propeller in coarse pitch. The inevitable result was that he failed to leave the ground at the appointed time and steamed on until he eventually ploughed into another aircraft. This caused much hilarity amongst his fellow pilots, a notoriously unsympathetic lot, who found his subsequent report of the accident an absolute hoot. Part of it read: 'I crashed into another Spitfire which I had not seen and came to an abrupt stop. Relieved at being safe, and shocked, I sat in the aircraft pulling and pushing levers. I cannot say why or which.' Succinct but honest was the general view.

At this stage in the course, every pilot was brim full of confidence in the performance of the aircraft and their own flying abilities. Their tails were well and truly up, and there was an occasional sign that some were in danger of going beyond taking an acceptable risk and becoming rash bordering on the foolhardy. Sometimes it was difficult for instructors to make the distinction so, in the main, they tended to turn a blind eye to anything other than serious infringements of flying discipline.

Nevertheless, two pilots did actually manage to get themselves placed under close arrest for low flying. One, a pilot officer on No 16 Course, clobbered a telegraph pole, leaving tell-tale chunks of Spitfire behind, before managing a forced landing at Kingscote. The other, F/Sgt J.N. Miller, a Canadian on the same course as Johnny, was carpeted for flying too low over the air-firing range at Bedwin Sands. Another officer, flying a Spitfire II in formation low over the River Severn towards the Severn Bridge, misjudged his height and struck the water a glancing blow. Somehow, the story went on, he managed to regain control and flew under the bridge but wrote off the aircraft in a crash at Lidley, surviving with nothing worse than severe shock and a few bruises. And so it went on.

Then on 1 May 1942, and quite literally out of the blue, a Defiant flew into Aston Down carrying two fighter types on the lookout for new talent for their unit, No 609 Squadron based at Duxford. One was the CO, S/L George 'Sheep' Gilroy DFC, whose broad Scottish accent Johnny found almost impossible to understand, but who was rumoured to have the best eyesight in

Fighter Command. The other was a F/O Roger Malengrau, one of the many Belgian pilots serving in the unit.

Johnny had just landed his Spitfire after an hour aloft doing formation flying in cloud. He noticed the two visitors spending a lot of time in confab with the instructors before they joined a few of the pilots, including himself, for a chat and to swap yarns. During all of this they ear-marked three bodies as likely looking cannon fodder. They eventually selected two of the Belgians, Jean Creteur and Raymond Dopere, No 609 Squadron already having quite a strong Belgian contingent, along with P/O Johnny Wells.

Johnny could barely contain himself at the prospect of an operational posting at last. But the best of it was that No 609 Squadron was in the process of re-equipping with the Hawker Typhoon, Britain's latest fighter and the fastest single-engined fighter the RAF had. He was about to realise an ambition he had held since his first flight in a Hawker Fury back at West Freugh five years before. He was almost delirious with excitement at this extraordinary turn of events; suddenly things seemed to be looking up.

Of course, Johnny had heard all about the Typhoon, the latest Hawker design coming into RAF service. Talk in the mess was that it owed its origins to the ill-fated Hawker Tornado project. Apparently, when the Rolls-Royce Vulture engine in the Tornado failed to live up to expectations it had been replaced by the Napier Sabre and so the Typhoon was born. Rumour had it that it could be a bitch to fly but its performance was remarkable and it went 'like a dingbat'. Other pilots on No 15 Course, most of whom were awaiting posting to Spitfire units, would have none of this, of course, and invariably dismissed the suggestion that the Typhoon's performance was in any way superior to that of a Spitfire: 'Pure line-shoot, dear boy. Absolute bollocks.'

Within two weeks, every pilot had received a squadron posting and prepared to disperse. According to the Operations Record Book of No 52 OTU, No 15 Course was 'above average in all respects. It has given no trouble and all pupils were keen to fly and learn all they could.' In avoiding the general malaise which had greeted them on their arrival at Aston Down, Johnny and his mates had chosen to immerse themselves in work and avoid petty distractions – a tactic which had clearly worked in their favour. Even their accident rate had been lower than the average for all previous courses, there being only three avoidable accidents during the entire course. The flying skills of seven were assessed as 'exceptional' and Johnny was one of them.

So, following a riotous dance held on the station on 12 May 1942, attended by a hand-picked contingent of gorgeous WAAFs, everybody bade each other 'happy landings' and went their separate ways. Those who, like Johnny, stayed on a few days longer saw yet another funeral party leave for Chalford, where P/O O.A. Noah, an American on No 17 Course, was buried after his Spitfire II shed a wing over Yatesbury. How many funerals had he attended since he joined the service? And how many more friends and comrades would be lost before this rotten war was over?

10

DUXFORD TYPHOON WING

Duxford, just south of Cambridge, was traditional home of the Spitfire; the first RAF squadron to receive the legendary fighter being based there back in 1938. It was also famed as the station from which Douglas Bader's 'Big Wing' had operated during the Battle of Britain. It was a grass airfield straddling the main road to Royston, with Belfast hangars and sheds ranged along one side of the road and the officers' mess and domestic quarters facing them on the opposite side.

No 609 Squadron formed in 1936 as an Auxiliary Air Force unit under the RAF expansion scheme. When a territorial unit it owed its origins and allegiance to Yorkshire, proudly bearing the title 'West Riding', though this was by no means truly representative of the mix of nationalities amongst its pilots after more than two years of war.

Equipped with Spitfires, it had fought over Dunkirk and throughout the Battle of Britain and for the past year had been flying gruelling offensive sweeps across the Channel. If the hunting horns and the motto 'Tally Ho' emblazoned on the squadron badge were anything to go by, then Johnny judged himself lucky to be joining such a 'bang-on' crowd. The squadron had moved to Duxford towards the end of March 1942 and in May were temporarily suspended from operations to convert from Spitfire Vbs to the new Typhoon IAs and IBs.

The previous autumn, the air war over southern England had entered a critical phase with the introduction of the latest Luftwaffe radial-engined fighter, the Focke-Wulf Fw190A. This highly manoeuvrable and heavily armed machine immediately showed itself to be a formidable adversary. After it entered service on the Channel coast, in September 1941, incredulous RAF pilots were warned to 'avoid combat' with it until its measure was gauged. One experienced pilot had even been heard to admit that when he first met one in combat: 'it was enough to make anyone pass blue lights! It could walk away from a Spitfire with no trouble at all.'

Introduction of the new German fighter had not been without difficulties for the Luftwaffe. Its early service record was a strangely prophetic chronicle of the sort of problems which were to dog the Typhoon during its own introduction some three months later. Like its future adversary, the Fw190 came close to being shelved due to the poor reliability of its radical new engine, and was only saved by the persistence of service pilots responsible for its operational development. But, unlike the Typhoon, problems with the Fw190's BMW 801 radial power plant were never fully resolved and it remained unreliable.

Following the introduction of the new German fighter, and in an effort to redress some balance, various modifications were made to the Spitfire V, the best front-line fighter in RAF service at that time. All of them proved useless. And in the past few months, it had become increasingly obvious to hard-pressed RAF pilots in action over the Channel coast that even the Bf109F had the edge for speed and climb on the Spitfire V. With the arrival of the new Fw190A the Luftwaffe had successfully raised the stakes, and RAF Fighter Command was caught seriously wanting.

In an effort to counter this threat, the Typhoon was rushed into service before all the problems with its engine and airframe had been properly ironed out. There had already been some serious accidents, mainly due to engine failure, both the induction and lubrication systems causing problems. But on-going development of the aircraft was to be continued based on operational experience, a risk with service pilots' lives considered well worth taking.

The first squadron to re-equip with the Typhoon had been No 56 commanded by Hugh 'Cocky' Dundas DFC. They started taking delivery of their new aircraft the previous September and had experienced nothing but trouble since. More than once their Typhoons had to be grounded while major problems were rectified.

In March 1942, to share their misery, the newly formed No 266 (Rhodesia) Squadron under S/L Charles Green DFC arrived at Duxford, who were soon followed by No 609 (West Riding) Squadron, the third unit selected to convert to the Typhoon. All three squadrons came together under G/C John Grandy DSO to form the first Typhoon Wing, although No 56 was deployed to the satellite airfield at Snailwell, near Newmarket, where they enjoyed primitive accommodation and basic facilities, but were fairly self-sufficient.

In April 1942, W/C Denys Gillam DSO DFC AFC arrived on appointment as wing commander (flying), and the three squadrons began serious training as a wing whenever they could put enough serviceable aircraft together. 'Kill 'em' Gillam was something of an RAF legend. Having survived the Battle of Britain, during which he claimed six enemy aircraft destroyed and another ten probables, he had led a Hurricane squadron on anti-shipping attacks in the English Channel. Under his leadership, they perfected skip-bombing techniques, borrowing from Luftwaffe tactics which Gillam had studied in depth. These operations were so hazardous that an operational tour with the squadron was limited to one month. Gillam had personally destroyed thirty-two ships but lost thirteen wingmen in the process. He seemed to lead a charmed life.

Fresh from OTU, the recently promoted F/O Johnny Wells and the two Belgians, P/Os Jean Creteur and Raymond Dopere, joined No 609 Squadron on 12 May 1942. Each averaged over 1,500 flying hours, so brought useful experience with them. Although just starting his first real tour of operations, Johnny's length of service didn't escape notice. With his prematurely balding hair and sporting a medal ribbon for service abroad, he must have seemed ancient compared to some of the others. As 'Joe' Atkinson, a pilot in 'A' Flight, recalls:

> Johnny seemed rather older than most of his fellow pilots when he joined 609 Squadron and had much longer experience of the RAF than most of us. He was a cheerful and utterly reliable comrade; and when asked whether he was married would reply in the negative but add that he was driving without a licence.

Johnny joined 'B' Flight under F/L Digby Cotes-Preedy, known as 'Digger', an enigmatic type occasionally met in RAF circles. Having come through the fighting during the early stages of the war when the RAF, as often as not, was out-classed, out-gunned and certainly out-numbered, Digger had not only survived the experience but laid claim to a number of enemy aircraft destroyed – and this while flying Coastal Command Blenheims miles out to sea off the Cornish coast, where claims could seldom be verified. Not that this ever worried Digger – not a jot. He was far too laid back to attach any consequence to such trifles. Essentially a modest man, he never gained the reputation or sought the recognition often lavished upon lesser mortals, although Johnny did spot an unfamiliar medal ribbon adorning his tunic.

Later, Johnny learned that this was not some petty gong, it was the George Medal. Apparently, one morning late in January 1941, Cotes-Preedy had just taken off from St Eval on reconnaissance to Brest when he suffered engine failure. His Blenheim, crashing near St Columb, burst into flames. Despite serious injuries, including a suspected broken back which would have kept any normal individual in traction for a year, Digger somehow managed to fight his way clear of what was left of the cockpit. Stumbling around outside the aircraft he realised that his crew were still inside the blazing wreck. Twice, he fought his way back inside to drag the two sergeants to safety. 'But don't let on that I told you so, dear boy,' muttered Johnny's confidant, 'he doesn't like to talk about it.'

When he recovered from his injuries, Cotes-Preedy had done the rounds of the OTUs and converted on to Spitfires before returning to operations with No 610 Squadron at Hutton Cranswick. He had arrived on No 609 Squadron as a flight commander the previous March, just prior to their conversion on to Typhoons.

It was only in the weeks immediately prior to Johnny's arrival that the squadron had started taking delivery of its first few Typhoons, and they were still trying to come to terms with them. Much of the daily routine consisted of practice flying to get in as many hours as possible on the new type. Talking to some of the pilots in the officers' mess that first evening, Johnny learned that some of them held a fairly jaundiced view of the new aircraft. Many would have preferred to stick with their reliable old Spitfires than risk their necks on this untried monster, which 'Joe' Atkinson described as 'A great lumbering thing, but never a source of any real anxiety'.

But one of the many Belgian pilots in the squadron, Sgt Raymond 'Cheval' Lallemant, held very different views based on some recent experiences of his fellow countrymen:

> Bob Wilmet, who had lost a wheel on take-off, had to make a belly landing – his third. Mony van Lierde, pushing in vain on his rudder bar – which had become blocked after leaving the ground – managed to survive thanks to a highly aerobatic landing. Raymond Dopere fortunately noticed he had lost his tail unit before leaving the ground. Joseph Renier's very first Typhoon flight ended in a wheels-up pancake. Jean Creteur managed to damage the maintenance hangar with his guns without even pressing the trigger. And finally, Jean de Selys had to leave his Typhoon by parachute because it was on fire. After such experiences it was scarcely surprising that they regarded the Typhoon as a killer, and called to be put back on Spitfires.

Such accounts must have been rather unnerving for recently arrived pilots like Johnny, but he no doubt kept his thoughts to himself and sensibly decided to form his own judgement of the Typhoon after he had flown one.

After all, so far there had been no serious accidents involving Typhoons in the West Riding Squadron, but, it had to be said, reports from the other two units were worrying. Several aircraft had lost their tails in vertical dives and no one seemed to know why. At the time, engine or structural failure was costing the Typhoon squadrons an average of one aircraft for every squadron operation flown, a casualty rate far higher than that expected from enemy action.

While most pilots were philosophical about their lot, the reputation of the Typhoon was becoming more than a little tarnished.

Johnny's new CO, S/L 'Sheep' Gilroy, had no such qualms and his confidence in the aircraft was infectious. Once, as he was fond of confiding to all new arrivals, he had been surprised to find that he still had 30 gallons of petrol left after an hour and a half of flying, until he discovered that he had left his flaps down the whole time. 'Settle yourselves in and meet the rest of the chaps, then get yourselves down to dispersal and take a good look over a Typhoon,' he told them in his rich Scottish brogue. 'We've got busy times ahead and you'll need to be fit for operations when we get the call.' Johnny, needing no second invitation, headed for the nearest hangar.

This was the first time he had ever got really close to one. The Typhoon stood there, sturdy and purposeful, its enormous radiator gaping at him from under the nose. That looks a bit vulnerable, was the first thought to flash through his mind. Good, rugged undercarriage though, nice wide track must spread over 13ft, so good and stable on the ground. He walked around it giving it the 'once-over', passing a hand across its streamlined finish, letting his first impressions sink in. It was certainly large and heavy for a single-engine fighter, thick wings spanning well over 40ft with four bloody great cannon poking out of them. Lovely! The earlier Mark IA models were armed with six machine guns in each wing but the Typhoon IB came equipped with four 20mm Hispano cannon, each carrying 145 rounds apiece, on top of which it could carry a 1,000lb bomb load.

The tail fin seemed about the size of a hangar door, so it must be true about its performance – that huge tail was for stability at high speeds. Fabric-covered rudder, he noted with surprise, everything else being flush metal. Inspection over, Johnny stood back arms folded across his chest. Clearly, this was no dainty aerobatic fighter, and there was no denying that it lacked the graceful looks of the Spitfire. It was massive, an assault plane, a battle wagon, a real warplane in every sense. Johnny could well understand young 'Babe' Haddon telling the CO that he had no intention of flying in 'such a big bastard'. But his overall impression of the Typhoon was of immense power and ruggedness. He would cheerfully go to war in that big bugger, he decided. But how long would he have to wait before he got his hands on one?

Three days later, Johnny needed help to clamber up into the Typhoon's cockpit, which stood some 9ft off the ground. There were a multitude of unfamiliar hand- and foot-holds, cunningly buried in the fuselage hidden under sprung trapdoors, and they took some finding. The cockpit door was also a curious arrangement reminiscent of an Austin tourer and Johnny found himself fervently hoping that he would never have to vacate the aircraft in anything approaching a hurry. With a final effort, he hoisted himself over the sill and settled himself inside 'T for Tommy'. The squadron engineer officer, P/O Tom Yates, squatted on the wing outside, ready to check him out on the cockpit controls and the procedures for take-off and landing.

At first glance the 'office' seemed quite complicated with lots of extra knobs, levers and switches. But it seemed fairly familiar as a result of a couple of flights in the squadron Hurricane, a sole example kept on strength to help familiarise pilots to the cockpit layout and assist their conversion from Spitfires. Also, the time he had spent poring over the Typhoon pilot's notes booklet over the past two days hadn't been wasted.

There was the standard blind-flying panel, with all the usual 'gubbins': air speed indicator, altimeter, gyro direction indicator, rate-of-climb, artificial horizon and turn-and-bank indicator. Everything where it should be. Above this, dimmer switches for the reflector gun-sight, the compass and the cockpit lamp. Off to the left were the flap and undercarriage controls, oxygen regulator, ignition switch and pressure gauges. To the right sat all the fuel and oil gauges along with the engine speed indicator. Down the left-hand side of the cockpit were the usual engine controls, flaps, radiator and undercarriage levers. On the right-hand side, carburettor and cylinder priming pumps, fuel cocks and starter. His hands ranged across them all as they checked things off together, until Yates was finally satisfied. With a cheery, 'She's all yours. Try not to bend it', he slid back off the wing leaving Johnny alone deep in the bowels of the monster.

What now? Of course! He had been told to wear his oxygen mask at all times because of the carbon monoxide which leaked into the cockpit from the engine. So he carefully set the oxygen regulator and checked the flow into his mask before clipping it in place over his mouth. Next he set the rudder trim full port to counter the massive swing he had been told to expect on take-off. Everything seemed to be falling neatly to hand as he went through the prescribed checklist prior to take-off, only this time it was for real.

Mixture to rich, propeller control fully forward then back slightly to avoid the constant speed unit running away with itself, check fuel tanks are over half full and open main fuel cocks, select 15 degrees of flap for take-off, set supercharger to moderate and open the radiator wide. He ran through it all once more, just to be sure, until finally he was ready.

His mind raced to remember everything he had been told. What was it that F/Sgt 'Darkie' Hanson, the squadron's senior engine fitter, had said? 'It can be a bit tricky to start,' a masterly under-statement, 'because 80 degrees of overlap of valve timing means it's not actually designed to start. But once you've got it running there's bags of power.' For all his years of RAF engineering experience, Darkie had recently returned from a month at Napier's factory in Luton where he, and a few selected fitters, had learned all about the remarkable new Sabre engine. Few on the squadron, if anyone, knew more about it.

To prod this monster into life, a Coffman starter unit, bolted to the back end of the engine, had to be triggered from the cockpit. This little 'gizmo' fired a cartridge causing a violent expansion of explosive gases in the engine which duly turned over and burst into life or, occasionally, burst into flames. Johnny glanced across at the mechanic outside who dutifully stood off to one side armed with a fire extinguisher. Obviously, in the event of an engine fire, he was the brave soul elected to rapidly advance and stuff the business end of the extinguisher up the Sabre's chuff. Most reassuring.

Johnny set the starting lever and gently opened the throttle to the start position. What next? Prime the carburettor. Just under 2lb/sq in – that should do it. He screwed the priming pump down and checked there was a cartridge already loaded in the starter. Ignition switch on. Finally, he gave the cylinder priming pump a few good hard strokes before, taking a deep breath, he stabbed down both starter and coil booster buttons on the dashboard to fire the cartridge.

Christ, what a racket! He managed to catch it with a couple more strokes of the priming pump, resisting the temptation to juggle the throttle. This, he had been reliably informed, would only flood the air intake, resulting in a guaranteed engine fire. After a few seconds the engine settled down to a steady if deafening roar, throwing small gouts of black oil back on to the windscreen. Almost reluctantly, the mechanic moved slowly away from his extinguisher, no 'Brock's benefit' for you today Johnny thought. He released the coil boost button, screwed down the cylinder primer and reset the starting lever.

Another grinning mechanic, with a mouthful of teeth like Highgate cemetery, stood outside on the wing root and wiped fresh gouts of oil from the windscreen with a handful of cotton waste. His leering countenance seemed to imply, 'Rather you than me mate'. Johnny smiled back weakly under his mask and gave him a thumbs-up.

Signalling 'chocks away' he taxied slowly towards the runway ahead of him beyond that pulsating lump of engine obscuring his forward view. It felt like driving a steamroller. The brakes were responsive, but he had to use them sparingly because they were useless if they got too hot. Gingerly ruddering his way forward, Johnny finally reached the end of the perimeter track and turned on to the runway which stretched away into the distance ahead of him. He was sweating.

Opening the throttle to give 2,500rpm to clear the plugs, he switched on the R/T and called control for permission to take off. He closed and locked the hood tight shut, a thin film of oil spreading across the windscreen fanned by the slipstream from the propeller. Control responding by flashing him a green light, Johnny gave a final glance over the instruments and tightened his straps. Releasing the brakes he opened the throttle slowly but firmly, his left foot jammed hard down on the rudder-bar pedal. Given his engineering background, Johnny was possibly more familiar than most with the technical specifications of the Napier Sabre, but nothing could have prepared him for the extraordinary surge of power. Developing 2,200bhp at 3,700rpm for take-off, the 24-cylinder engine with its 2-speed supercharger was clearly a very formidable lump indeed.

Thundering down the runway, Johnny had his work cut out to keep the aircraft in a straight line; the pull to the right felt as if the starboard main wheel had punctured. The tail came up easily but he had been warned about this and caught it before it got too high, clearance between the ground and the propeller blades allowing no margin for error. Then as he lifted off, the Typhoon swung viciously to starboard and despite full left rudder he had to cautiously feed in more power to keep the brute even more or less straight.

Strewth! They were actually off the ground and in one piece. He selected wheels up and even remembered to give the brake lever a squeeze to stop the wheels revolving before they arrived in their wing wells. A dull thump under each wing and two red lights on the dashboard flicking off confirmed that both main wheels were safely locked. At 250ft he raised the flaps and increased his rate of climb – this was more like it.

Soon he began to relax a bit and enjoy himself; exploring the aircraft's performance and handling characteristics. He found it a trifle unstable at anything other than high speed, the ailerons only really effective over 100mph, and it had a slight tendency to skid in turns. Also, he had to keep adjusting the rudder trim which seemed a mite over-sensitive for his liking. Elevator control was quite light and obviously needed to be used with equal care. But in spite of this, the Typhoon's performance was truly astonishing with a considerable margin of excess power. It might be less agile than a Spitfire but it was certainly faster, no doubt about it, and particularly at low level where it cruised along comfortably at just under 300mph. What was it those Spitfire pundits had told him at Aston Down? 'Absolute bollocks indeed!'

Checking that the radiator shutter was up, Johnny climbed to a safe height and tried a few shallow dives to get a feel for things before attempting his first steep dive. It turned out to be quite a sobering experience as over 5 tons of aircraft accelerated downhill at an impressive rate of knots. It was incredibly noisy in the cockpit with the Sabre howling away up front, and everything around him seemed to be clattering and rattling as he wrestled with the controls. It felt as if the tail wanted to come up all the time which made the dive seem steeper than it actually was. Apparently, as speed in the dive increased, the Typhoon tended to yaw to port causing the nose to drop further. He corrected this with a small movement of the rudder trimming tab, but could see that it would be very easy to go over the vertical in a dive.

There was an awful lot of vibration and Johnny was being shaken around. Terrifying at first, it was at the same time intoxicating to feel the power and noise building all the time until you thought the aircraft couldn't possibly take any more and was on the brink of blowing itself to smithereens. The vibration had been worse on early models, later variants having sprung seats fitted to reduce pilot discomfort.

Close to 450mph, he had to exert considerable pressure on the controls to pull out, which caused him to black out momentarily as gravity forced the blood from his brain. To counter this effect, the Typhoon had two-tier rudder-bar pedals, the upper pedals allowing pilots to put their feet higher to reduce the effect of gravity on the body. It certainly helped, but a degree of blacking out was inevitable and it could not be eliminated altogether. All too soon, Johnny realised he had been up for almost an hour and it was time to land. He located the airfield and joined the circuit, doing one fast orbit of the field to clear the plugs before throttling back to start his landing ritual. He adjusted the fuel mixture to rich and set the propeller to fine pitch.

Selecting flaps and wheels down, he watched the undercarriage indicator lights on the instrument panel change from red to green and then back to red again. Hell! Surely not undercarriage failure on his first flight. The Typhoon was yawing from side to side and feeling horribly unstable as the speed dropped away. He concentrated on keeping the runway dead ahead as the aircraft rapidly lost height, those huge flaps assisting his rate of descent. Speed was now down to about 175mph and still dropping, but with enough height to go around again if need be. Green lights, thank God! No, they were back to red again. No one had told him anything about this. His mind raced through emergency landing procedures.

His left hand groped for the hand pump at the side of his seat which would lower the main wheels in the event of hydraulics failure; the tail wheel should come down automatically. He also vaguely remembered that somewhere on the cockpit floor were two emergency foot pedals, one each side of the rudder bar, which released the catches holding the main wheels up. Theory was, once you released these catches the wheels simply dropped by gravity. Fat chance! Wait a second: green lights! Three beautiful, shining, emerald lights – wheels down and locked. Hallelujah!

The nose dropped slightly as the wheels came down, but he crossed over the boundary hedge bordering the runway spot on 100mph. There still seemed to be plenty of lift from the wings but it was deceiving and the Typhoon finally dropped the last few feet like a brick and bounced once or twice before trundling down the runway as if nothing had happened. Johnny was careful on the brakes but there was still a distinct whiff of smouldering linings and burnt rubber when he finally turned in, gave the engine a last burst before switching off and unclipped his oxygen mask.

He wound back the hood and sat there for a few seconds, collecting his thoughts as he listened to the metallic clicks from the hot engine. The ever-friendly mechanic 'Highgate', he of the permanent leer, appeared at the side of the cockpit, leaned across him and turned off the fuel cock. 'Everything go all right, sir?' he enquired. 'Sure,' Johnny replied with a weak grin. 'Piece of cake.'

With his first flight out of the way, and without incident, Johnny had good reason to feel pleased with himself. Even more so, for that very day S/L Gilroy suffered the ignominy of the first Typhoon accident in the squadron when one of his brakes locked on, causing an oleo leg to collapse, thus damaging the aircraft. He stumped away from the scene muttering strange, inarticulate Gaelic curses and, as the squadron diarist later recorded, 'According to standing instructions he put himself under open arrest, interviewed himself sternly, found himself not guilty of neglect, and released himself.' Maybe not such a dour Scot after all.

Johnny rapidly fell in with the routine of the squadron, local flying and practice formations being the main order of the day, with occasional co-operation flights and bomber affiliation thrown in for good measure. The weather stayed generally fine and they got a lot of useful flying in whenever there were sufficient aircraft serviceable. On 19 May 1942, he was subjected to a practice scramble to 30,000ft and managed to get airborne in a respectably short time, anything under four minutes being considered reasonable.

When the weather prevented flying, pilots were kept busy viewing the latest batch of Fighter Command combat films, attending lectures or doing aircraft recognition tests organised by the squadron intelligence officer, F/L Frank 'Ziggy' Ziegler. These tests were universally hated by pilots, who went to extraordinary lengths to avoid them.

By the middle of May 1942, as pilots gained more experience of the Typhoon, formation flying and frequent practice scrambles continued, and air firing off Blakeney Point on the north Norfolk coast commenced. They were all growing in proficiency and confidence with their new aircraft, despite the occasional engine failure or irritating minor accident to dog progress.

Practice interceptions, usually on neighbouring Spitfire squadrons, also did much to instil further confidence in the Typhoon's performance. One evening, P/O Christian Ortmans surprised a vic of three Spitfires on which he made practice attacks, discourteously making V signs at each of the startled pilots as he flashed past them. On another occasion, fourteen Typhoons caught the Spitfires of No 616 Squadron stooging around and in dummy attacks by sections they inflicted 'casualties' to most of them according to Denys Gillam, who counted it the most successful Typhoon interception to date. At this rate, they would soon be ready for wing operations, although some diehards in the squadron still lamented the loss of their beloved Spitfires, carping on about the Typhoon's lack of manoeuvrability.

These and other practice interceptions, which tended to dominate squadron activities at the time, prompted much discussion on flying tactics. Such debates, universally beloved by all flying men, often continued into the small hours. Since converting on to Typhoons, the squadron had reverted to flying in vics of three aircraft rather than the usual line astern formation favoured by most Spitfire squadrons and they were still trying to get to grips with things.

After one wing practice interception of some Spitfires, No 609 Squadron was well and truly 'bounced' on the inside of a turn and flying far too slow. Later that evening, with everyone enjoying a few jars in the mess, F/L de Spirlet was witnessed vigorously poking the wingco flying in the chest whilst extolling the virtues of adopting crossover turns. Hiding their mirth, Johnny and the other pilots maintained a discreet distance.

Tactics aside, major accidents dogged the Typhoon squadrons and so serious were the problems that aircraft were grounded while a full investigation took place. Jerry Sayer, from Gloster's, took up semi-permanent residence with No 56 Squadron at Snailwell, while Philip Lucas, Hawker's chief test pilot, spent a fortnight with No 609 Squadron at Duxford. These two did everything but turn the aircraft inside out to try to find an answer as to why tails should suddenly shake loose. And Johnny and the other pilots would stand agog watching Lucas diving, climbing and throwing one of their Typhoons around high above Duxford with great elan.

There was a lot of talk in the bar most evenings about something called 'compressibility', an effect sometimes experienced in high-speed dives. But 'if you don't want the wind-up, don't let your tail up' seemed to be the best, and only, practical advice to follow. One potential reason for the accidents, elevator flutter, was another theory Johnny heard bandied around, but the cause was never properly identified and flying eventually resumed as before – albeit with strengthened rear fuselages.

It was only much later, after a Typhoon actually shed its tail taxiing, that the true cause was discovered. Apparently the mass balance weight in the tail was mounted on a pivoting arm with a bush at the pivot. Under certain flying conditions this would vibrate until it eventually snapped, which caused the elevators to come up violently, placing impossible strain on the rear fuselage and breaking off the tail. This could occur when pulling up after a half roll and a dive, when heavy loading was put on the elevators. In Paul Richey's view, it was a disgrace to put the Typhoon into service with these problems unresolved.

Squadron Leader Richey had arrived at Duxford on supernumerary attachment to the squadron on 25 May 1942, while Johnny was away for a couple of days attending a combat film assessment course. During the previous summer, Richey had completed a gruelling tour of fighter sweeps as a flight commander with the squadron before taking over as acting squadron leader of No 74 Squadron at Acklington. He was a familiar figure around dispersal and a celebrated author, his book *Fighter Pilot* recounting his experiences flying Hurricanes with No 1 Squadron in France during the early part of the war being a best-seller.

More recently, he had done a spell at HQ Fighter Command where, amongst other things, he had been largely responsible for selecting the first three squadrons to be equipped with the Hawker Typhoon. Not surprisingly, given his knowledge of their experience and standard of flying, he had included his old squadron, No 609, in the selection. But, itching to get back on operations and knowing that 'Sheep' Gilroy was due to be rested, he got the ear of the C-in-C, Air Marshal Sir William Sholto-Douglas KCB DSO MC and had himself put firmly 'in the frame' as Gilroy's eventual successor.

It was the end of May 1942 when S/L Gilroy learned that he was appointed squadron leader (tactics) at No 12 Group. The traditional squadron farewell party ensued, during which he was cajoled into autographing the mess ceiling from atop a precarious human pyramid that collapsed causing several minor injuries. His protests about surviving so many sweeps over enemy territory only to meet an inglorious end on the floor of Duxford officers' mess fell on deaf ears.

The loss of such a popular CO was tempered by the news that his successor was to be Paul Richey, who had left the previous day on posting to Snailwell to take over a flight in No 56 Squadron. Richey's return as CO of No 609 promised further festivities, but on the night he arrived at Duxford to take over it was a sadly depleted crowd of pilots that greeted him. A large contingent had gone off to rescue one of the Belgians, P/O Baron Jean de Selys Longchamps, from the hospitable clutches of the Cambridgeshire Home Guard. Earlier in the day, he had the unenviable distinction of becoming the first pilot in the squadron to bail out of a Typhoon when his engine had suddenly caught fire south-east of March, near Ely. So when the already boisterous rescue party arrived back at Duxford, and long after the bar had closed, they found another thirty-two pints of beer waiting for them, courtesy of the new CO, all tastefully arranged on a table to spell out '609'.

The following morning, both Duxford squadrons simulated a low-level 'tip-and-run' attack on King's Lynn for the benefit of Spitfires scrambled to intercept them. During the course of this exercise the Typhoons picked up an R/T message from the Spitfire leader who trumpeted, 'Objective sighted ahead'. At which, the Typhoons simply opened their taps and pulled away into the distance feeling distinctly smug – just like real Fw190s. However, the next day the proverbial boot was on the other foot when the Typhoons attempted to intercept some low-flying Spitfires, one formation of which turned out to be brand new Spitfire IXs. As the Typhoon pilots would later agree, these proved far too fast to be hostile.

For some months past, the Luftwaffe had maintained a limited daylight offensive campaign by launching series of 'tip-and-run' raids against targets of opportunity along the south coast. Streaking in low under British radar, and often using indifferent weather for additional cover, small formations or pairs of German fighter-bombers would attack gasometers or rail traffic, bombing and strafing coastal towns with seeming impunity, before scuttling back across the Channel at wave-top height. So unpredictable and fleeting were the attacks that they were often over before local air-raid warnings sounded.

Several ports and south-coast towns had been hit quite hard resulting in civilian casualties and damage to property. Something needed to be done and questions were already being raised in parliament. Unfortunately, it was difficult to see what could be done when the enemy arrived without warning and retired almost as quickly. Standing patrols along such a wide front were costly to maintain and were proving ineffective. Even when our fighters were lucky enough to sight enemy aircraft, it was usually after an attack when they were already hot-footing it back to France too fast for our Spitfires to catch them.

In the main, the aircraft employed by the Luftwaffe for these 'tip-and-run' attacks was the formidable Focke-Wulf Fw190A fighter-bomber which, once relieved of its bomb load, became a superlative fighting machine with a performance far beyond that of the Spitfire V then opposing it on the Channel coast. Only the Typhoon stood any real chance of matching it. So, at the end of May 1942, No 56 Squadron was ordered down to the south coast, one flight of four Typhoons under S/L Dundas going to West Hampnett and another four led by W/C Gillam going to Manston. The Duxford Wing buzzed with excitement. At last the Typhoon was to be tried against enemy fighters. Everyone, pilots and ground crew alike, was confident that it would give the Germans a nasty surprise.

Within a week No 56 Squadron were back at Snailwell, an angry, frustrated and demoralised bunch. The whole thing had been a fiasco. Despite non-stop patrols the Luftwaffe had failed to put in an appearance so nobody had even got a sniff at a Fw190. Worse still, they had lost two aircraft on the same patrol, with one pilot killed, having been mistaken for Fw190s and shot down by a pair of Spitfires off Dover. It was time to smooth some ruffled feathers and reconsider strategy.

Meanwhile, in their absence, both Duxford squadrons had been engaged in Army Co-operation work in the shape of Exercise 'Blitz', involving low-level attacks on ground targets that were not to everyone's liking. As the squadron diary put it, 'Blitz in Spits is well enough, but in Typhoons is rather tough'. Apart from this diversion, formation practice continued to feature regularly in pilots' logbooks, Paul Richey having instituted a regime of two flights in formation before lunch every day.

These were not the only changes introduced by Richey. He was determined to get all the gremlins ironed out of the Typhoon to achieve fully operational status. Practice flights of bewildering variety increased that no one was allowed to duck. Sheaves of written orders on revised flying practices and operating procedures emanated from his office, as the squadron gained more and more experience. But unlike the bumph which circulated in most other squadrons, this stuff was actually useful.

One instruction, helping to counter the Typhoon's tendency to swing viciously on take-off, was welcomed. Conventional wisdom at the time was to get the tail up quickly and accelerate fast. But, due to engine torque, the Typhoon would start to swing long before enough speed was attained to gain proper rudder control, resulting in some hair-raising formation take-offs and a few accidents. The knack, according to the latest squadron written orders, was to take off with the control column more or less central, so the tail didn't come up straight away. Then, with enough speed to keep the aircraft straight, simply fly it off the ground.

On the afternoon of 9 June 1942, the squadron was paid a visit by Air Commodore the Duke of Kent, who spoke to the pilots. This was occasion for the first ever fly-past by the entire Duxford Wing, and for a first effort was not too bad; so all that formation practice paid off. It was also a good dry run for a visit the following morning by the C-in-C, Air Marshal Sir Sholto Douglas, and AOC, Air Vice-Marshal Saul, during which it was announced that they hoped to have the wing operational within the next five days. Once the pilots got over the shock it was smiles all around.

After the VIPs departed, while everyone was congratulating themselves on yet another successful fly-past, F/L de Spirlet brought the party down to earth by pointing out that putting thirty-five Typhoons in the air at one time must have given the C-in-C a mistakenly optimistic view of their serviceability. As they all pondered this gem, and by way of proving the point, P/O 'Mony' van Lierde made a spectacular belly landing right outside, his Typhoon careering across the airfield with a jammed rudder pedal, gouging up great clods of earth, shedding wing panels and sundry debris, to come to rest in a huge cloud of dust. For surviving this, he subsequently received congratulations from the AOC, although Paul Richey insisted that the commendation was actually for not abandoning the aircraft.

The following day, Johnny and another pilot went off to Newmarket for a couple of days' liaison with the 9th Armoured Brigade during which they got to try their hands at driving a tank. Afterwards, Johnny was forced to agree that the ground-handling characteristics of the Typhoon were not so bad after all.

As it had been raining heavily during their absence, they missed out on very little, apart from lots more recognition training and a Ladies' Night Dance. But probably the most exciting thing to have happened while they were away was that the CO's Typhoon now sported a complete rear fuselage and tail unit painted a fetching shade of duck-egg blue. This desperate effort to distinguish it from a Fw190 was considered a complete waste of time by most of the pilots, but meanwhile Flying Officer Giovanni Dieu took his Typhoon on a 'Cook's Tour' of airfields in No 10 Group, in the fond hope that close inspection might help them recognise a Typhoon when they saw one.

On 20 June 1942, with an improvement in the weather, the first sortie by the Duxford Typhoon Wing was flown by aircraft of Nos 56 and 266 Squadrons. They were to sweep the French coast to support the withdrawal of returning Spitfires. Led by W/C Gillam and accompanied by G/C Grandy, the station commander, they took off from Duxford at 1512hrs and flew to Mardyck, where they crossed the French coast, returning via Calais and Boulogne without incident. All the time they were in the air, Johnny and other frustrated No 609 Squadron pilots were forced to kick their heels back at Duxford, all crowding into the operations room to follow events with anxious expectation. A similar sortie took place three days later, a sweep of the French coast from Dunkirk to Cap Gris Nez, during which some Fw190s were actually sighted but kept their distance, and again 609 was not involved.

There was considerable excitement on 24 June, with the startling news that an Fw190 had landed intact at Pembrey the previous evening. Denys Gillam, Paul Richey and Philip Lucas all dashed off to inspect this bête noire at close quarters. On return the somewhat chastened pilots admitted to being considerably impressed by the design and finish of what Paul Richey would later admit 'must have been the best fighter of the war'. The captured German pilot, Oberleutnant Arnim Faber, Gruppenadjutant of I/JG2 Richthofen Geschwader, was shown over one of their vulgar Typhoons, but his opinions were unfortunately not recorded.

Two days later tragedy struck. Early in the morning of 26 June 1942, shortly after the squadron had stood down from dawn readiness, F/L de Spirlet decided to take two of his pilots, Christian Ortmans and Raymond Lallemant, up for some formation practice before breakfast. Bob Wilmet joined them as No 4 and as the four Typhoons thundered down the runway together, just as they were about to lift off, de Spirlet suffered a burst tyre, sending his aircraft careering to the left directly in front of Cheval Lallemant. They tangled. With starboard wingtip lodged firmly between the port wing and tail unit of de Spirlet's aircraft, Lallemant had no lateral control. There was obviously going to be a horrendous crash so in a desperate attempt to disengage, Lallemant had the presence of mind to stick his nose down deliberately. His aircraft sliced clean through de Spirlet's Typhoon, cutting off the tail, and the aircraft reared up and plunged into the middle of the airfield, exploding on impact. A thick plume of oily black smoke marred the air, a ghastly beacon to the fire truck and ambulance which lurched off towards it with bells clanging.

Miraculously, Lallemant survived. His engine, torn clean off its mounts, bounced down the runway to come to rest 50yd away. He was pulled from the wreckage with no serious physical injury but was severely traumatised. It was only Paul Richey's prompt and sympathetic handling that eventually restored the young Belgian's shattered confidence and got him back in the air again.

The death of Francois de Spirlet was a severe blow, casting a pall over the entire squadron; his Belgian comrades were particularly inconsolable. He had been among the first Belgian pilots to arrive on the squadron back in April 1941 and had taken over 'A' Flight from Paul Richey the following August. Most of the squadron threw themselves into particularly hectic activity and some very serious parties in an effort to shrug off the gloom. But this didn't even begin to lift until two days later when, with due ceremony and respect, de Spirlet's cortege was escorted to Whittlesford railway station where the squadron took their leave of him. He would be very hard to replace.

Fortunately for the squadron, there were some outstanding candidates. And, in a sudden flurry of changes, 'Joe' Atkinson, who had flown with the squadron since November 1940 and, as a result of administrative oversights would continue to do so until April 1943, was promoted to take over 'A' Flight. Simultaneously, Johnny's flight commander, 'Digger' Cotes-Preedy GM, announced his own imminent departure from the squadron on appointment to the Directorate of Fighter Operations at the Air Ministry.

Raising himself to his full height, which was considerable, Digger apologised to the assembled troops: 'Can't tell you anything about it chaps. All frightfully hush-hush I'm afraid. I expect I shall be put in charge of paper clips or something.' Johnny was sorry to see him go, but they were to cross paths again two years later when Digger was CO of Tempest squadron based at Volkel and giving the new German jet fighters a tough time. Thus, in a move which was later to prove of immense significance to the squadron and secure the future of the Typhoon, Digger relinquished command of 'B' Flight to F/L Roland Beamont DFC.

'Bea' Beamont was vastly experienced and eminently well qualified. He had flown Hurricanes throughout the Battle of France and the Battle of Britain with No 87 Squadron and, on completion of his first tour of operations, was engaged as a production test pilot with Hawkers at their Langley works. There he had been involved in intensive flight testing of the Typhoon so knew the aircraft well. But after six months with Hawkers, he had engineered his return to operations on Typhoons and for the past week had been flying as a super-numerary flight lieutenant with No 56 Squadron at Snailwell. Attending a party at Duxford the night before de Spirlet's tragic accident, he had stayed overnight and so became sad witness to events. After a brief conversation with Paul Richey that same morning, his appointment as 'B' Flight commander of No 609 Squadron was confirmed three days later.

Beamont duly arrived at 'B' Flight dispersal early one morning in his MG sports and almost gave Darkie Hanson a fit, for it sported tyres obviously 'acquired' from two of His Majesty's trolley accumulators. Incriminating RAF serial numbers were still prominently stamped on each tyre. This evidence was swiftly removed by the judicious application of a hot soldering iron – the prospect of their new flight commander being dragged off for misappropria-tion of government property being too awful to contemplate.

At 1105hrs on 30 June 1942, the West Riding Squadron recorded its first Typhoon scramble. The readiness section of two Typhoons was airborne in less than six minutes; the pilots involved being Johnny Wells and Sgt Blackwell. With engine and heart rates at full boost, they orbited base await-ing instructions, frantically checking gun-sights and engine temperatures. After twenty-five minutes, and still requesting a vector from control, Johnny was instructed to pancake which made him suspect that it was merely a prac-tice 'flap' laid on by the wing commander flying, Denys Gillam. Nothing was ever said, so presumably the wingco was well satisfied with their performance.

The constant routine was somewhat relieved on 3 July 1942 with the news that the squadron was officially operational once more, after more than two months in the doldrums. This made precious little difference to day-to-day activities but did mean that they spent more time at readiness, though their services were rarely called upon. Meanwhile, wing practice, formation flying and air firing continued to occupy their time while Tom Yates' engineering team continued to struggle with engine problems and serviceability.

So far Johnny had been lucky. Unlike other pilots in the squadron he had avoided engine trouble, mid-air fires, lost wheels, undercarriage failure, locked controls and the host of inconveniences then so familiar to many Typhoon pilots. Methodical by nature, he always tried to anticipate potential problems and worked hard to develop safe flying habits. Some may have thought him a mite too pernickety, over-cautious, even lacking sufficient 'dash' for a fighter pilot; but if ever taunted Johnny would invariably smile broadly and simply point to his spotless flying record. But on 8 July 1942 this changed when he suffered engine failure during camera-gun practice.

The Sabre had been running a bit rough for some time before it finally gave what could only be described as a violent sneeze and gave up the ghost, grinding to an abrupt halt. Johnny called up Duxford Control and started switching everything off. He wasn't unduly worried for Cambridgeshire, being relatively flat, was generously sprinkled with airfields.

Taking a quick look around, Johnny found himself a little west of Waterbeach, home to Short Stirling bombers – that would do nicely. Everything was under control and the airfield had a good long concrete runway, so he decided to turn the situation to some advantage and practice a glide approach landing without flaps; the engine-driven hydraulic pump was no use anyway and it would save pumping them down manually. It was something that he had practised often enough, but never without engine power for real.

Pre-landing checks were simplicity itself. With no engine or flaps to consider all he had to do was get the undercarriage down. He pumped away vigorously at the emergency lever until the wing indicators and green lights on the dashboard confirmed that the wheels were down and locked in position. Good, no problems. Flying wheels down the Typhoon tended to yaw a bit and Johnny had to concentrate to keep PR★U for Uncle in line with the runway which was now looming up ahead of him. Fortunately there were no other aircraft in the circuit.

With engine off and no flaps, his final approach speed needed to be at least 20mph higher than normal so, watching this carefully, he waffled in towards the runway cautiously fish-tailing to take off as much speed as he could. He still managed to come in over the boundary fence at an indicated air speed of 160mph – far too fast. No sweat: there was plenty of runway ahead – that is, there had been the last time he saw it; for you couldn't see much beyond the Typhoon's engine when landing without flaps because of the nose-up attitude of the aircraft.

With a hefty thump, he touched down a lot further down the runway than planned and still travelling at a fair rate of knots. But there was still be plenty of room to stop. Then, gently squeezing the brake lever on the control column, Johnny suddenly realised he was in deep trouble. It felt spongy, with very little resistance. Too late, he flicked a glance at the pneumatic pressure gauge. There was a reading of sorts, but far too low for the brakes to be effective. What now? He couldn't go around again, he had no engine. Cautiously, he tried the brakes again. There was something there but precious little. What the hell! Better some brakes than none at all. Johnny grabbed the brake lever and clamped it hard against the spade grip.

Hanging on for dear life, Johnny was now front-seat passenger in 5 tons of metal as the Typhoon thundered down the runway. Out of the corner of his eye, he glimpsed hangars and buildings going by at what seemed far too rapid a pace. But he sensed the aircraft gradually starting to slow. His hand hovered over the undercarriage selector ready to retract the wheels – a last resort, but still the most effective way of stopping. How much longer could the runway be? Then, suddenly, the aircraft was bucking and shuddering as the brakes, or what was left of them, started to bite and the speed dropped away. Please God – no ground loop! He rocketed past a perimeter track, a small tractor towing a trolley accumulator flashing past under his wing. Obviously the driver had seen him coming and got out of the way. Johnny made a mental note to buy him a drink later – if he survived.

Then, he was taxiing, admittedly far too fast, and straight towards a couple of stationary Stirlings starting to fill the windscreen at an alarming rate. They looked much bigger than the ones at Bourn and appeared to be in the process of loading up with bombs – how bloody marvellous! Small groups of mechanics scattered ahead of him like the parting of the Red Sea. Much too fast for comfort, he risked a turn and swung off the runway. His luck held. Miraculously, the long-suffering oleo legs stood this final abuse and, with what felt distinctly like a couple of small hops, the Typhoon came neatly to a stop, both main wheels smoking ominously.

Johnny slid back the hood and took a few deep breaths. He was furious with himself for making such an elementary mistake. He knew that he was lucky to get away with it in one piece and was content to sit there for a while in quiet gratitude as the tension drained away. Slowly he became aware of sounds from outside; the excited chatter of a small crowd of airmen as they neared the aircraft and somewhere in the distance an alarm bell started clanging. Probably the crash tender – late as usual.

The first official operation by Typhoons of No 609 Squadron took place on 30 June 1942. Other squadrons in the wing had taken part in sweeps but never engaged the enemy, although there had been several combats – but all with Spitfires. But you couldn't altogether blame the Spits. The sad truth was that, in silhouette, the unfamiliar Typhoon I, with its huge under-slung radiator, bore a more than passing resemblance to the radial-engined Fw190A. Up against such a superior opponent, and in the heat of combat where the difference between life and death was often measured in the blink of an eye, Spitfire pilots tended to shoot first and ask questions later, sometimes with tragic results. And while most Typhoon pilots might grudgingly concede the point, to lose friends in such a way inevitably resulted in a certain amount of rancour and bitterness.

The irritations and frustrations of the past months began to take their toll. Everybody was working flat-out to make things go right for the Typhoon and such setbacks were acutely demoralising. Many pilots released pent-up emotions by throwing themselves into increasingly wild parties but even these paled and morale had slumped to an all time low. Finally, on the afternoon of 19 July 1942, No 609 Squadron joined the rest of the Duxford Wing in a low-level sweep of the French coast from Berck to Hardelot, while Spitfires operated further inland. It was the first time that all three Typhoon squadrons had flown an operation together, but Johnny was not amongst them.

After briefing, Denys Gillam led the formation of thirty-five aircraft taking off at 1455hrs, three of them returning almost immediately with engine trouble, including that of Paul Richey. The untidy wing formation flew out over Pevensey, crossing the Channel at zero feet to Berck, where they turned sharply and followed the French coast to north of Hardelot before returning via Dungeness. Apart from a solitary Spitfire taking a brief squirt at one air-craft of No 56 Squadron it was uneventful.

Two days later, the pilots of No 609 were officially released and set forth to London where they were invited to join in festivities celebrating the national day of Belgium. As almost half the squadron originated from there, this was viewed as a wholly appropriate exercise and an occasion to be celebrated in time-honoured squadron tradition. Even a blistering lecture and dire threats from the CO on their abysmal lack of discipline, both in the air and on the ground, did little to quell the general enthusiasm for what promised to be an epic day out.

Congregating at Chelsea barracks at 1000hrs next morning to wit-ness a parade and speeches, the squadron then attended midday service at Westminster Cathedral, followed by lunch at the Rembrandt Hotel, before an evening reception at Grosvenor House. Between times they visited several favourite haunts, including the Royal Court Hotel, the Antelope in Sloane Square, Ritz Rivoli Bar, Shepherds, the Wellington, the Ambassadors and Embassy Club. Not surprisingly, there were a few non-starters the following day, though the majority of pilots were back at Duxford in time for readiness at 1300hrs. Notable by their absence, the CO and Johnny were posted 'miss-ing believed drunk'. As the squadron ORB records:

> P/O Wells has apparently been shot down in flames. At any rate he is found in his hotel bedroom, apparently dead and lying amidst a heap of charred pyjamas, silk eiderdowns and bits of wick. On the command, 'Blue section scramble!' he does however stir, but relapses on remembering he is on leave.

Early on 30 July 1942, the Duxford Wing decamped to West Malling where all three squadrons congregated in eager anticipation of an offensive sortie against the Luftwaffe airfield at Abbeville; a sortie which had been a long-held ambition of Denys Gillam's. But after waiting around the entire morning, the mission was scrubbed by No 11 Group who decided that the Typhoons would be better employed supporting Circus 200. They were eventually ordered off shortly after midday, with only half an hour's notice and a very sketchy understanding of what was required of them. With No 609 leading, they flew out across the Channel at 18,000ft until some 20 miles east of the North Foreland. Crossing the enemy coast at Gravelines, they turned towards Cap Gris Nez before heading back across the Channel to Dungeness.

Given the doubtful reliability of the Sabre engine at the time, these sweeps over the Channel were no picnics. Hours spent high above the Channel, eyes glued to oil pressure gauges, every sinew taut straining to detect a fault or mis-beat from the engine, were a constant nervous strain. And all this without interference from the Luftwaffe.

10 miles off Dungeness Johnny's engine started cutting out. He radioed control and turned back towards the English coast, maintaining as much height as possible to prolong the glide if the engine decided to pack up alto-gether. Like every other pilot, Johnny knew only too well that attempting to ditch a Typhoon in the sea would invariably end in disaster for, even in calm conditions, that enormous bucket radiator under the nose would scoop up hundreds of gallons of sea water sending the aircraft down to the bottom. No 609 Squadron lost four pilots this way during the first month of patrols over the Channel, so Johnny prepared to bail out if it became necessary. Mercifully his engine settled into an irregular rhythm and he managed to nurse it all the way back to Duxford.

Flying Officer Haabjoern, one of No 56 Squadron's Norwegian pilots, was not so lucky. Also nursing a failing engine off the English coast, he was clob-bered by a Spitfire and shot down. He managed to bail out at around 2,000ft, his parachute opening just before he hit the water, and was picked up from his dinghy by an Air-Sea Rescue launch within fifteen minutes of landing in the briny and deposited safely at Dover. To the amazement of his CO, 'Cocky' Dundas, he returned to Snailwell the following day without a scratch and seemingly none the worse for his experience. A spate of dinghy drills at Royston swimming baths ensued across all three squadrons, which was not thought to be entirely coincidental.

During the first week of August 1942, No 266 Squadron left Duxford on detachment to Matlaske in Norfolk. Johnny must have had more than a few pangs of jealousy at the thought of them enjoying their off-duty hours in some of the local hostelries around Sheringham. But to cap it all, within a week of taking up residence there, a routine patrol of two Typhoons inter-cepted a lone Ju88 flying low some 50 miles off Cromer and shot it down in flames. It was the first recorded victory for the Typhoon and was just cause of great excitement and jubilation, a flurry of congratulatory messages and signals passing back and forth amidst celebration and clinking of ale jugs.

Having successfully opened the scoring for the Typhoon Wing, No 266 Squadron returned to Duxford. Their run of luck continued for, on the evening of 13 August 1942, a patrol of four aircraft intercepted what they took to be another Ju88 which one of them tipped into the North Sea 30 miles off Lowestoft.* Hopeful of getting in on the action, No 609 mounted dusk and dawn operations aimed at intercepting German weather and shipping recce aircraft. At 1900hrs on the 16th, Johnny took off with F/O Roelandt and Sgt Blanco, F/L Beamont leading, for a low-level sweep over the east coast. They got back just before dark having seen nothing but No 137 Squadron Whirlwinds and a floating mine. Beamont deemed that they had taken off too early.

Then, on 19 August 1942, the Duxford Wing finally got involved in the real shooting war. They had Denys Gillam to thank for the opportunity. Two days earlier, at an HQ Fighter Command briefing, plans for Operation Jubilee were revealed. This combined operation planned to put Canadian troops and British commandos ashore on the French coast at Dieppe as a 'reconnaissance in force'. It would provide useful 'gen' and important experience to help any future invasion of the Continent.

The attack was to be supported by the largest force of RAF aircraft ever assembled, but there were no plans to involve Typhoons. Incensed, Gillam argued strongly that they should be allowed to take part, and Leigh-Mallory had to intercede; consequently the Duxford Wing was scheduled to cover the beachhead area at low level during the landings.

That something big was brewing became increasingly clear at Duxford days prior to the event. For a start, flying was limited which was usually a sign that full serviceability was required for something special. Then, all three squadron leaders were frequently to be found closeted together with the wingco having hurried conferences. Finally, on 18 August, a disgruntled 'Bea' Beamont was recalled from a day's leave at Predannock so everyone knew that, whatever it was, it was imminent.

A pilot briefing was scheduled for 2200hrs that evening but postponed at the last moment until the following morning. This added considerably to the growing air of secrecy and anticipation, but also had the desired effect of ensuring that all the pilots were back on the base at a reasonably early hour. Most of them had already decided that they were about to fly in support of an invasion or, possibly, to repel one.

Next morning, while most of the pilots were still at breakfast, the BBC broadcast news of 'combined operations' on the coast of France. His piercing blue eyes flashing, W/C Gillam then gave them a briefing, outlining plans for

---

*   It was later established to be an Me210, one of the Luftwaffe's latest fighter-bombers, on a reconnaissance sortie from Soesterberg. The gunner bailed out and spent six days and nights adrift in his dinghy, without food and water, before being picked up by the British 'somewhat the worse for wear'.

the day. Johnny was scheduled to fly wingman to 'Bea' Beamont, with the Belgians, P/O Roelandt and Sgt Blanco, making up Blue Section. Push buttons was scheduled at 1100hrs.

The weather was fine and hot, and visibility good, as they lifted off from Duxford and flew south-east to rendezvous with nine Defiants over Clacton. The plan was to escort the Defiants to within 10 miles of the Belgian coast at Ostend before breaking away to sweep the enemy coast as far as Mardyk in a diversionary feint aimed at drawing enemy aircraft away from Dieppe. Hopefully German radar would be fooled into thinking that the formation was an approaching bomber raid and send up fighters to investigate. Unfortunately, the Luftwaffe didn't oblige, so after an uneventful trip the Typhoons landed at West Malling to refuel, with the exception of Paul Richey who returned to Duxford with a dud aircraft.

Like every other airfield across southern England that morning, West Malling was teeming with aircraft. A Spitfire Wing was also operating from there and Johnny had never seen so much activity. They squeezed themselves into the circuit and landed, and had just enough time to park their aircraft, organise refuelling and grab a quick cuppa before a hurried briefing prior to the next sorties. Then, climbing back into their sweltering cockpits, they sat there waiting for the order to take off. A couple of tattered Bostons sat alongside the runway, riddled with bullets and looking decidedly second hand, mute testimony to the bitter fighting which had been going on across the Channel since dawn.

Orders came through at 1400hrs, this time a sweep along the French coast from Le Treport to Le Touquet to cover the withdrawal of the invasion force from Dieppe. Johnny, stifling in his cockpit, checked his controls and instruments, adjusted the tension on the throttle nut, clipped on his oxygen mask and checked that the R/T was live. All around the airfield Sabre engines coughed, spluttered and exploded into life, filling the air with thunder, as the leading Typhoons taxied out to take off.

Johnny ruddered his way around the taxi track, keeping close behind 'Bea' Beamont. One aircraft refused to start and the forlorn pilot, Paul Richey's wingman Christian Ortmans, was forced to watch as the rest of the wing took off in a rising cloud of dust and disappear south, flying low until they were lost in the distant haze.

They crossed the English coast at Beachy Head, climbing to 10,000ft over mid-Channel before turning west away from the Somme estuary. Gillam took No 609 up to 15,000ft, with No 266 maintaining station above them, while 'Cocky' Dundas and his boys flew top-cover around 17,000ft. Conditions over the French coast were far from ideal with broken cloud between 2,000 and 4,000ft. The harbour and seafront at Dieppe were wreathed in smoke from several fires while, off-shore, naval vessels and retreating assault craft weaved their way through a welter of exploding shells and bombs. There was a lot of radio traffic and obviously plenty of aircraft about.

Ten miles off Le Treport, they were warned by control that radar had detected enemy bombers approaching from the direction of Douai and, almost immediately, No 266 Squadron reported three Dornier Do217s at 5,000ft. Gillam ordered them to engage. The Rhodesians dived to the attack and three Typhoons managed to close on the bombers, claiming one destroyed and one probable before streams of tracer from behind heralded the arrival of an escort of Fw190s. Then the rest of No 266 Squadron arrived and took on the Fw190s, claiming one probably destroyed before having to break off their attack.

Bursting to get into the action, and with 'Cocky' Dundas holding No 56 Squadron above them as top-cover, Denys Gillam led No 609 down on four more Fw190s which had suddenly popped out of the clag below them. Surprised, the enemy fighters dived away with the Typhoons in hot pursuit. Emerging through cloud at 1,000ft Gillam closed to within 400yd of one and managed to knock some bits off it, later claiming it as 'damaged', before they both had to pull out of their dives. Elusive as ever, the enemy fighters slipped back into the murk.

During this encounter, F/O Wilmet, one of No 609's Belgians, had an interesting experience which proved it wasn't only Spitfire pilots who failed to recognise a Typhoon when they saw one. In the dive he unwittingly over-hauled and drew alongside an Fw190 which started to take up formation on him line abreast. Sgt 'Fifi' de Saxce, who was behind them, spotted what was happening and shouted a warning in French which Wilmet didn't under-stand. De Saxce finally managed to flush the Fw190 away from the Belgian's tail as Typhoon and Fw190 pulled out of the dive in perfect formation before going their separate ways.

A little later, Wilmet, now quite alone having become separated from his Fw190 wingman as well as the rest of the squadron, was returning back across the Channel at zero feet when he was well and truly bounced by a Spitfire IX. He was a sitting duck but, fortunately, the over-eager Spitfire pilot allowed insufficient deflection and missed him by a mile. More than a little shaken by the afternoon's events, Wilmet returned to base soberly reflecting on life's many ironies.

But he had been lucky. For, scuttling back across the Channel at zero feet after their attack on the three Dornier 217s over Le Treport, two of No 266 Squadron's Typhoons ran slap-bang into the Spitfires of 331 and 332 (Norwegian) Squadrons who had just taken off from Manston. There were a nervous few seconds as some of the Spitfires closed on the Typhoons before recognising them and breaking away, while the Typhoons went to full boost and started weaving frantically. In all the confusion, one No 332 Spitfire suddenly found itself head-on to another aircraft which the pilot took for an Fw190 and instinctively opened fire. The 'Tiffie' staggered, shed some bits and half-rolled into the sea from 100ft, exploding on impact.

Back at West Malling there was a hurried debriefing after which Denys Gillam stomped off to wring someone's neck. The Spitfires seemed to be totally oblivious to the presence of Typhoons in the battle area and there had been several aggressive moves on aircraft in the wing. A greater margin of height between them was needed or a potential disaster was on the cards. Meanwhile, armourers and mechanics swarmed over the Typhoons readying them for further sorties, while pilots swapped experiences over a welcome cup of tea and a wad.

They lifted off from West Malling at exactly 1700hrs for their third and final operation of the day – a sweep of the area from the Somme Estuary to Cap Gris Nez. Denys Gillam was once again leading but over mid-Channel a gun panel in his port wing worked loose, forcing him to turn back. Due to a cock up with radio frequencies there was more confusion which resulted in eight of No 609 Squadron's Typhoons also breaking away and accompanying him back to England.

Squadron Leader Green of No 266 Squadron took the rest of the wing over the French coast at 12,000ft but meeting 10/10 cloud he scrubbed the mission and led them back to Duxford. It was a distinct anti-climax to a very hectic day; though 'Joe' Atkinson later voiced the opinion that it had been a comparatively uneventful trip. Most of the pilots were completely drained after nearly four hours over the Channel and pleased to finally switch off their engines. Johnny heard that most of the Spitfire boys had flown four missions since dawn. How must they be feeling?

Once again, it had fallen to the Rhodesians to chalk up the only successes for the wing, claiming one Do217 destroyed and two Fw190s damaged. But at what cost? Any celebration that evening was clouded by the sobering fact that on this, their first day of operations as a wing, they had lost two Typhoons and pilots, one a flight commander. Worse still, this had not been due to enemy action, one Typhoon clobbered by a Spitfire and the other reportedly losing its tail during that high-speed dive. It all seemed so depressingly familiar. 'Bea' Beamont summed it all up neatly: 'The enemy may have been as frightened by the Typhoons as we were … though I doubt it.'

On 26 August 1942, in a practice emergency move, No 609 Squadron took up temporary residence at Bourn, a satellite field to Oakington situated on a plateau north of Cambridge, where they took over the rather basic facilities recently vacated by the Wellingtons of No 101 Squadron. While this could hardly be described as a Romany existence, it was certainly no pastoral idyll.

The sparse accommodation of four wooden huts was stiflingly hot at night and daily ablutions had to be completed using an outside standpipe for cold water and a battered old bucket. At least dawn readiness was comparatively easy to achieve as the dormitory and dispersal hut were one and the same.

When off duty, the pilots sat about in the sweltering sun in various stages of nudity, and evenings were spent cooling off swimming in the river at Cambridge until late at night. Also, unless otherwise occupied, most evenings the pilots would watch the Stirlings that shared the airfield take off for targets deep in Germany, the huge four-engined aircraft lumbering aloft and staggering over the hangars with what seemed like inches to spare. Not all of them returned.

Between dawn and dusk sorties from Bourn, wing sweeps over France and maintaining constant readiness, pilots would occasionally nip back to Duxford to change aircraft, replenish kit or take a welcome bath. The mess at Bourn, it must be said, was not what they were accustomed to; the food was at best 'indifferent' and stocks of drink perilously low by squadron standards. One day 'Bea' Beamont took the entire stock of seventy-two pints of beer, draining the bar dry and causing much distress to the mess president who reportedly commented, 'It is impossible for 12 officers to have drunk so much beer!' Clearly he didn't know much about Fighter Command or the West Riding Squadron, but he was in fact quite right, for the ale was shared with the parched and very grateful ground crews.

The glorious summer weather did much to compensate for such trifling domestic inconveniences. It even reminded some in the squadron, particularly those with Auxiliary Air Force backgrounds, of halcyon days of pre-war summer camps. So not everyone was too aghast when, after two days, the CO cheerfully announced that he had decided to extend their stay another two days in order to allow the rest of the ground crews, who had yet to experience these rigours of operating in 'an emergency'.

On 29 August the squadron spent the day practising air firing at drogue targets over at Matlaske, while Johnny and 'Joe' Atkinson lounged around at Bourn to maintain a section of two aircraft at constant readiness. At 1300hrs, amidst much ringing of bells, scattering of furniture and firing of green flares, they were scrambled.

Both Typhoons were off the ground in less than four minutes, an excellent response time, and gained height waiting for a vector from control. But they stood no chance whatsoever of engaging the aircraft they could see leaving condensation trails at well over 30,000ft, the cause of the excitement – obviously a pressurised Ju86P reconnaissance aircraft. Thoroughly disgruntled at this unwelcome interruption, F/L Atkinson took the opportunity to land back at Duxford and take a welcome bath.

Later that same evening, 'Bea' Beamont, flushed with success at scoring by far the highest results in the air-firing practice, suffered a serious fall whilst exercising on parallel bars in Cambridge and was admitted to hospital with what was initially thought to be a broken pelvis. Fortunately, his injury was not that severe, but he was obviously going to be unfit to fly for some considerable time and was forced to quit the squadron. In his absence, P/O Jean de Selys took over 'B' Flight as acting flight commander. So after four days at Bourn, and still picking the straw from their hair and clothes, a depleted No 609 Squadron returned to the comparative luxury of Duxford, announcing their return by thundering low over the officers' mess in close formation and fine style, landing just in time for afternoon tea.

On 30 September, Johnny and F/O Solak flew an uneventful evening patrol from Hawkinge and had just landed when enemy fighters appeared. No 91 Squadron, having an aircraft up on an air test, managed to intercept and damage two Fw190s, one directly over the airfield within earshot of the dumb-founded 609 pilots. General feeling within the squadron was 'it's only a question of time' – or divine intervention by the goat.

About this time, all three squadron leaders at Duxford were reluctantly forced to conclude that offensive operations by the Typhoon Wing were not proving the success that had been hoped. Ominously, G/C Harry Broadhurst, then group captain operations at Fighter Command, also shared this view. In his opinion, the Typhoon was unsuitable for close escort work and, due to its lack of performance at anything over 18,000ft, was no good in a high-cover role either. The Typhoon's performance simply didn't fit RAF strategy on offensive fighter sweeps. It must find a different role if it was to remain in service.

Conferences at Fighter Command and No 12 Group failed to reach any agreement, some of the debates getting quite heated. Both John Grandy and Denys Gillam tried to defend the wing concept and a spate of reports on the subject were submitted to HQ Fighter Command. One such report, dated 12 September 1942, written by Paul Richey, was severely critical of current policy.

In Richey's view, the Typhoon had exceptional qualities which were not being properly exploited. It was very fast below 20,000ft, had a good rate of climb to that height and it was heavily armed. Employing it in wing strength on conventional fighter sweeps was, he argued, a seriously flawed policy which should be abandoned forthwith. He recommended that Typhoons be employed on sweeps in squadron strength, possibly in a rear-support role, where its superior low-level performance could be used to better effect. Actually, No 609 Squadron had been operating this way for some time, developing and perfecting such tactics under Richey's energetic guidance. Flying loose line abreast at ground level over northern France they had been shooting up or bringing down any worthwhile target they came across. But Denys

Gillam was unconvinced and remained cool to the idea. He preferred to stick to the original wing concept.

Richey's report went as far as to suggest that the Typhoon squadrons be dispersed to coastal areas where they could be deployed against recce aircraft and low-flying fighter-bombers, and concluded by detailing the precise areas in which the Typhoon should operate. This succinct document obviously struck a major chord at HQ Fighter Command for, within three weeks, the Duxford Typhoon Wing was disbanded, the entire concept abandoned and the three squadrons dispersed almost exactly as Richey had suggested. The mandarins at HQ Fighter Command were giving the Typhoon one last chance.

Some post-war accounts suggest that all three squadron leaders at Duxford had come to the same conclusion: that the Typhoon's speed and firepower would be best directed against the 'tip-and-run' raids along the south and east coasts, where separate squadrons operating independently could cover a wide area. It is suggested that, after thrashing it out between themselves and consulting Denys Gillam, the wing commander flying, Paul Richey drafted a report outlining their joint views, a copy of which eventually reached the C-in-C. But this version of events is unlikely.

First, in addition to the report submitted by Paul Richey, separate reports on the tactical deployment of the Typhoon are known to have been made, quite independently, by Denys Gillam, Cocky Dundas and his predecessor, Prosser Hanks – amongst others. Second, Paul Richey's report of 12 September 1942 is signed by him alone and not countersigned by any others. A report such as that suggested, expressing the joint views of the commanding officers of the Duxford Wing, would have undoubtedly gone out over the signature of the wing commander (flying), Denys Gillam, or possibly even the station commander, G/C John Grandy.

Richey would also have appreciated only too well that a report from himself, possibly above others, would carry greater weight with the C-in-C. It was Sholto Douglas himself who had Richey posted to the staff at Fighter Command HQ on the strength of his analytical approach, tactical nous and writing skills, in order to draft just such reports. So, while he may well have had the full support and total agreement of both fellow squadron leaders on the subject of the future deployment of the Typhoon, it is almost equally certain that this view was not entirely shared by their superior officer, Denys Gillam. So it would seem that it was Paul Richey alone who finally put the ailing beast out of its misery and killed the Duxford Typhoon Wing concept stone dead.

Clearly disappointed, Denys Gillam moved on to RAF Staff College, the squadrons in his command dispersed to strategic points around the south and east coasts. First to leave Duxford, at the end of September, No 609 flew back to its old haunt at Biggin Hill. Much to his disappointment, No 56 moved to Matlaske on the east coast, near Johnny's family home in Sheringham, while No 266 Squadron went to Warmwell to cover the south-west coast. Rumour had it that this move came just in time for the Rhodesians. They were so thoroughly browned off that they had all been on the point of resigning their commissions en masse.

No doubt sorry to have missed the chance to move nearer home, Johnny was nevertheless pleased that while based at Biggin Hill they would be operating from Manston or Hawkinge, both forward airfields on the south coast no more than ten minutes' flying time from the enemy. Talk about closer to the action. This gave the Typhoon a better than decent chance of tackling any 'tip-and-run' raiders who might venture across the Channel and finding out what it could really do when pitted against low-flying Fw190s. They would be the first and only Typhoon unit operating in No 11 Group and it remained to be seen if someone had straightened out all those trigger-happy Spitfires.

11

FRONTLINE MANSTON

Thou shalt not be afraid for the terror by night;
Nor the arrow that flieth by day

Psalm 91

On arrival at Biggin Hill the squadron found that Spitfires were the very least of their problems. The south coast of England, to a depth of 5 miles inland, was bristling with light AA and the gunners would fire at any single-engined aircraft flying under 1,000ft with its undercarriage up. And if that wasn't enough, there were hundreds of barrage balloons waiting for an unwary pilot to chance by, and they certainly didn't distinguish between British and German aircraft. So, whilst welcoming the move south and a chance to see more action, Johnny and the other pilots all agreed that they could be in for some fun and games.

Dashing their hopes, they found themselves settling into a daily routine of section standing patrols off the coast between Dungeness and Beachy Head with the prospect of an occasional freelance patrol over the Channel thrown in to relieve the boredom. Repeated requests for permission to mount offensive 'Rhubarbs' over enemy territory fell on deaf ears at Group HQ. Consequently, throughout the entire month of October the squadron didn't fire a shot in anger.

On 2 October, Johnny became one of the very few pilots in the squadron to even see an enemy aircraft during this period. They were returning from Circus 221, an uneventful operation in support of Bostons bombing Le Havre, about 5 miles south of Selsey Bill, when a solitary Fw190 flashed past below them at low level going flat out for France. Even with boost plugs pulled and the advantage of height there was not a hope in hell of catching it.

Along with the move south, there were some other significant changes. Early in October, S/L Richey received news of his imminent promotion and posting to India to command a Hurricane wing. Despite the Herculean celebrations which resulted, the prospect of losing such a popular leader plunged the entire squadron into something approaching deep gloom. 'Joe' Atkinson took over the reins pending arrival of a new CO. Adding to the general malaise, some clot at HQ decided that, in the event of a renewed night offensive by the Luftwaffe, Typhoons could adopt the role of night fighters. As nobody on the squadron was night operational on type, this prompted a spate of dusk/dawn landing practices doing little to improve the prevailing mood.

Then on 17 October, when No 486 Squadron at West Malling were grounded due to weather, No 609 were obliged to fly their patrols as well as their own. Ever sympathetic to the plight of his hard-worked pilots, when he had this pointed out to him the C-in-C was rumoured to have said, 'They can work till their engines drop out'. Adding considerable insult to this injury, after a gruelling series of fruitless section patrols of the south coast throughout the entire morning and early afternoon, in atrocious weather conditions, No 609 were incensed to learn that no sooner had No 486 finally got a section airborne than they had shot down a Fw190 off Hastings. Johnny's views of this, or those that were printable, were recorded in the Squadron Operations Book as representing the feelings of the entire squadron: 'There is no bloody justice in this world!'

Then in a move which delighted everyone, 'Bea' Beamont returned and took over command on 19 October. Now fully fit after his accident the previous August, his appointment at this stage in the Typhoon's changing fortunes proved most opportune. He believed in the aircraft and was totally committed to proving it in action; the Typhoon could have no better exponent or protagonist. Things were looking up again.

Within a matter of weeks of taking over, Beamont was summoned to attend a meeting at HQ Fighter Command where, to his astonishment, he learned that the main item on the agenda was to discuss the future of the Typhoon and the question of its continued production. The RAF were on the point of scrapping it. The AOC 11 Group, Air Vice-Marshal 'Dingbat' Saunders, and the new C-in-C, Air Marshal Sir Trafford Leigh-Mallory, were in attendance with an assortment of other exalted ranks. Then there was Beamont, a 22-year-old, newly promoted squadron leader and the most junior officer present. But he was never someone who was easily intimidated. In the teeth of vehement opposition from some Engineering Branch officers loudly supported by a strong Spitfire lobby, Beamont dug in his heels, argued the Typhoon's case and won it a reprieve.

Beamont knew full well that this was a pivotal moment in the Typhoon's already chequered history and he returned to Manston to address his pilots with a zeal and fervour remarkable even by his standards. A real sense of purpose permeated the entire squadron. It was infectious and soon spread across every Typhoon unit in Fighter Command. Now they were all left in no doubt, they had to prove the Typhoon in battle and do so quickly.

Within the week they were given their chance. A pair of Fw190s were intercepted en route for Dover which, when spotted, immediately turned for home. No doubt they were relying, as usual, on their superior speed to beat it back to France unmolested. But to their undoubted surprise, the standing patrol of RAF fighters they encountered turned out to be two Typhoons and they were rapidly overhauled. Both Fw190s went into the drink.

On the last day of the month, the Luftwaffe mounted a large-scale fighter-bomber attack on Canterbury, catching the defences unaware. In the resulting confusion, two of 609's Typhoons, managing to get off from Hawkinge, came under concentrated AA fire between Dover and Deal. With so many bandits reported in the area the gunners were taking no chances by firing at anything that moved. Unfortunately, their aim was all too good. P/O Payne was forced to vacate his blazing Typhoon over the coast and dragged himself ashore suffering second-degree burns to his hands and face, while P/O Amor managed an emergency landing at Hawkinge with serious damage.

This did little to improve the already strained relationships with AA Command and was particularly galling as the Typhoons had been prevented from making an interception when there were more enemy aircraft around than at any time since the Battle of Britain. Despite flashing navigation lights, firing colours of the day and generally doing all they possibly could to avoid disaster, ground fire continued to dog the Typhoon. Many pilots openly admitting that the temptation to return fire was fast becoming very difficult to control.

After yet another similar incident during an air raid, but this time mercifully without casualty, two separate sections of Typhoons were fired on by the same Bofors gun sited on the North Foreland. To the astonishment of the pilots concerned, the AA duty officer later telephoned the squadron to enquire, 'and I'm afraid it will have to be very tactfully – did we get anywhere near them?' The squadron's reply was unrecorded.

Within days of the attack on Canterbury No 609 Squadron moved from Biggin Hill to Manston where they remained 'on attachment'. Hangar accommodation and storage space were almost entirely lacking and their temporary mess infested by cockroaches, but they were now closer to the enemy than any other squadron in Fighter Command so just let 'Jerry' try that one on again – please. Defensive standing patrols were intensified and they flew in all weathers. Meanwhile, night-flying practice continued until, by the end of November, nearly every pilot was moonlight operational.

Shortly before midday on 5 November, Johnny and his wingman, a Canadian flight sergeant named Spallin relatively new to the squadron, were scrambled after a Dornier was reported to be bombing Deal. The weather was frightful; 10/10 cloud at 600ft and raining hard. They took off and clawed for height through the clag. As they approached Deal, Biggin Hill Control ordered them to follow the coast to Dungeness. Flying just offshore, Johnny skirted Dover and patrolled up and down in the murk being vectored hither and thither by a controller whom Johnny began to suspect was giving him his own radar plots to chase. There was no sign of Spallin, which worried him, and Johnny's repeated calls to 'Fetter Blue Two' brought no other response than heavy static.

On return to Manston Johnny learned that Spallin had hit a balloon cable and crashed into the sea at Dover. Evidently he had tried to cross over the harbour and hadn't been aware of the balloons aloft in thick cloud which veiled the area. Nothing was found but a miserable patch of oil on the water. As acting flight commander, Johnny felt this loss keenly. The young Canadian had been a cheerful, obliging and a reliable, enterprising pilot. A damned shame and a stupid waste.

Within the week, they were treated to a visit to Manston by the Secretary of State, Sir Archibald Sinclair, no less. The station commander, Desmond Sheen, ushered him around and introduced him to the CO and some of the pilots, who stood around somewhat self-consciously, desperately trying to look as if they weren't enjoying the attention. Clearly, the Typhoon was still high on somebody's agenda.

Around the same time, in an effort to avoid confusion with the Fw190 and any further losses to friendly ground fire, the squadron's Typhoons emerged from the hangars one morning sporting dazzling white noses and radiators, and with dramatic black and white stripes adorning the under-surface of the wings. On with the motley!

Apparently, Mustangs had experienced similar problems with AA Command when they were first introduced into RAF service, so some months earlier they had adopted conspicuous yellow stripes which seemed to do the trick. Along with other pilots, Johnny was happy to try anything to avoid being shot at by his own side, but as the squadron diarist recorded, 'Though the white fronts look most bridal, it is doubtful whether any scheme short of pink all over with amber spots will make much difference in the eyes of the ground defences'. God knows what the Germans would make of it all.

Now Beamont had always argued most forcibly that the Typhoon should adopt a more offensive role and seek out more opportunities for action. Having shown it could handle itself against the Fw190, he warmed to his theme. Surely, he maintained, the Typhoon possessed all the necessary characteristics of a perfect ground-attack aircraft. It was high time to initiate Typhoon intruder sorties over France. Beamont, no stranger to intruder operations, had flown them on Hurricanes. But to his pilots' great surprise, even consternation, he was not just suggesting that the Typhoon be used to fly intruder sorties over France – he was advocating they do so at night. He argued, and Johnny saw the logic of it, that daylight attacks by Spitfires on enemy transport and communications across France and the low countries, 'Rhubarbs' as they were known, simply caused the Germans to move more of their rail and road transport after dark. That created a real opportunity for the Typhoon to carry on the good work with intruder sorties over occupied Europe by night.

In November 1942 the AOC, 'Dingbat' Saunders, finally capitulated and Beamont got the go ahead. Beamont had got his way at last. He could pro-gramme a few trial night intruder sorties during the coming full moon period just so long as he maintained the squadron's defence of the south coast against further enemy Jabo attacks.

So, at 2020hrs on 17 November, Beamont took off alone on the first Typhoon night intruder sortie. Keeping above a useful blanket of cloud, he crossed the French coast near Berck. Spotting tell-tale steam from a goods train on the line between Port-le-Grand and Noyelles-sur-Mer, he carried out five attacks and left the engine wreathed in steam, with intermittent dull red explosions coming from the trucks. He returned to Manston after just over an hour in the air. It was the first damage inflicted on the enemy since the squadron equipped with Typhoons.

That same night, Johnny and 'Joe' Atkinson put in extra night-flying practice, both anxious to get in on the act. After a couple more solo efforts during which he damaged more trains, Beamont was satisfied that his tactics were sound and called all the pilots together. Their on-going responsibility was the defence of the south coast against the Fw190, he explained, and this alone was more than enough to justify their flying pay. Night intruder sor-ties would be an extra assignment beyond their normal duties and entirely voluntary. In any event, no pilot would even be considered for such a mis-sion until he had gained sufficient night-flying experience, and this was to include a series of cross-country flights without radio aid and more low-level flying practice in moonlight.

'Night Rhubarbs' were not greeted with universal enthusiasm. 'I wasn't very enthralled at the idea of flying around at nought feet at night,' Pinky Stark admitted, recalling one particular sortie:

I'd gone fairly deep into France around the Somme area and then came more or less due north aiming to come out between Calais and Dunkirk.

But I obviously picked up a wrong landmark at some point and came out slap over the middle of Dunkirk dodging church spires and searchlights. But 'Bea' was ace at this, he would be off every night and get several trains. I think he had the train timetable from Boulogne to Paris. He used to trap them at a particular point.

Beamont also recalls Johnny at dispersal one day, expounding a philosophy based on his years of service experience. 'Never volunteer for anything,' Johnny was saying. 'Why tempt fate? If your number's going to come up, let it come up later rather than sooner.'

'Fair enough, Johnny,' Beamont retorted. 'But in that case how come you always seem to be in the thick of it when there's any fighting going on?'

'That's easy,' Johnny replied, flashing that wide grin of his. 'I simply follow you around.'

Which, of course, is what they all did. Over the coming weeks practically every pilot in the squadron completed the necessary night-flying experience in time for the December moon phase. While they readied themselves, the CO was busy making sure that the aircraft were equally well prepared.

Thanks to his previous experience of night intruder operations, he got the squadron armourer and ground crews to make some interesting modifications to improve the Typhoon's night-flying capabilities. Cockpit instrument lighting was dimmed right down to reduce glare inside the cockpit and, thanks to the squadron workshop, the reflector gun-sight had a neat little slide fitted to obscure all but the sighting bead which now reflected directly on to the windscreen, the de-misting panel having been removed to help improve downward vision. As a final touch, tracer ammunition was forbidden on night sorties as it would help enemy gunners.

The tedious programme of standing patrols, with the French coast under constant surveillance by at least one section of two aircraft during every hour of daylight, finally paid dividends. On 5 December 1942, a *Schwarm* of four Fw190s jumped the western boundary hedge at Manston and swept across the airfield strafing everything in sight but only managing to damage a stone building close to No 3 Squadron's Hurricanes. Somewhat optimistically, four Typhoons took off in pursuit but the 190s were caught off Deal by a section already airborne and one of the raiders was tipped into the Channel by F/S Haddon.

At 0840hrs the following morning and in a flurry of red Very pistol flares to clear the circuit of all traffic, Johnny and F/O Nankivell scrambled against Fw190s attacking Lympne but made no contact. Enemy activity was certainly on the increase.

The squadron flew their first daylight offensive Rhubarbs on 13 December when two pairs of Typhoons ranged across Belgium and northern France attacking trains. Between them, they claimed four engines probably destroyed, F/L Jean de Selys Longchamps returning slightly damaged and with several yards of telegraph wire trailing from his radiator scoop – a souvenir of his trip to Ostend.

One of the busiest days for the squadron in well over a year turned out to be 15 December 1942, which started quietly enough with the inevitable routine standing patrols. But early in the afternoon, two sections mounted successful Rhubarbs over Belgium and northern France; a third section sent off to Belgium returned early, cloud base being 'on the deck' when they made landfall near Furnes.

The first two pairs had better luck clobbering five railway engines and a tug between them. Sergeant Turek returned minus his cockpit door and hood, having flown through a tree outside Roulers whilst avoiding light flak. His badly damaged aircraft, testimony to the ruggedness of the Typhoon, was the focus of much attention by squadron pilots, but the Pole seemed singularly unmoved by his experience.

In the meantime, several Typhoons had taken off independently as a number of Fw190s had been sighted in the vicinity. In a series of fleeting and sporadic engagements they would later claim one Fw190 destroyed and two damaged, but P/O Amor failed to return. He was last seen off Ramsgate at 900ft, his aircraft totally enveloped in flames, pumping shells into the Fw190 which had set him alight but then overshot him. He was the first pilot lost due to enemy action since the squadron re-equipped with Typhoons. Rounding off a very busy day, two solo intruder sorties were sent off that evening but, for once, finding no worthwhile targets they returned without further incident.

Early the following afternoon, Jean de Selys Longchamps and the irrepressible Pole, Turek, meeting a couple of Fw190s off Dungeness, chased them back across the Channel to Boulogne, claiming one destroyed and the other damaged. Things were definitely heating up but Johnny was still yet to see any action. Even a Rhubarb to the railway complex south of Cayeux on the 18th proved a total washout when Johnny, accompanied by 'Joe' Atkinson, found no cloud cover under 4,500ft in the target area, which made them somewhat conspicuous and forced their return.

It was a similar story two nights later when Johnny was the last Typhoon away from Manston, taking off at 2024hrs on an intruder mission to the area Le Treport–Abancourt–Le Havre. It was cloudy but ground visibility was still fair, despite the usual haze over the Somme Valley. He made landfall at Berck, crossing the coast at 9,000ft and descending to 3,500ft as he approached Abbeville.

Off to his right, somewhere west of Amiens, a blue searchlight swept the sky but it wasn't seeking him. Desultory light flak rose into the night sky behind and below him, the vivid red tracers reaching up but failing to find him.

609 ready for take-off from Manston, 1943.

'A' Flight No 35 Squadron, Bircham Newton, 1931. Johnny stands fourth right, back row.

No 609 Squadron, early 1944. Johnny far left.

Avro Tutor basic trainer, 1934. 'A real peach'.

'Bea' Beamont with personal tally of locomotives destroyed.

'Bea' Beamont's Typhoon.

Bircham Newton, 24 May 1934.
Wing Commander Raymond
Collishaw escorts King George V
on his tour of inspection.

Bristol Bulldog TM two-seat trainer, 1935. 'After the tutor it felt decidedly skittish.'

'C' Flight No 35 Squadron in front of a Fairey Gordon I. Johnny stands fifth left, back row.

'D' Flight No 6 Squadron, Ismailia, February 1936. Sgt Wells seated second left, front row.

'D' Flight No 6 Squadron over Wadi Rum, 1936.

Fairey Gordon I that re-equipped No 35 Squadron from July 1932.

Fairey IIIF J9822. Johnny's first flight was made in this aircraft on 30 April 1931.

Fairey IIIFs of No 45 Squadron Helwan in Egypt 1935.

First prang. South Creake, 9 March 1932.

First prang. South Creake, 9 March 1932. Johnny leans against the wing far left. His pilot, Sgt Fox, stands fourth right.

Hawker Hart K4472 No 6 Squadron at Ismailia, 1936.

Hawker Hart K4473 of 'D' Flight No 45 Squadron at Helwan and later No 6 Squadron at Ismailia, 1935–36.

Hawker Hart trainer of No 1 SFTS. Used for night landings on the dummy flight deck at Shrewton, December 1941.

Hawker Hind L7175 in pre-war livery. Flown by Johnny as a target tug at No 1 SFTS, November 1940.

Johnny Baldwin, Johnny Wells and 'Moose' Evans, Manston, 1943.

Johnny with Wing Commander de Goat, Manston, 1943.

Johnny, Manston, 1943.

Leading Aircraftman Wells on
completion of his Halton training, 1930.

Leaflets ready to be dropped on Arab villages. Ramleh, April 1936.

Manston, 20 May 1943. Johnny and Uffz Ehrhardt of 2.SKG210 with FO Treweeks (IO) centre.

No 609 Squadron, Llanbedr, April 1944.

No 609 Squadron Typhoon sporting under-wing recognition stripes.

Mayfly constructed at Halton, 1927, prior to conversion.

Bircham Newton, 24 May 1934. No 35 Squadron ready for inspection by HM King
George V. Johnny, in flying boots, stands in front of the first aircraft.

RAF Halton, 1927.

The rakish Harts of 'D' Flight No 6 Squadron at dispersal, Ismailia, 1936.

Westland Wallace IIs of No 4 Armament Training School, West Freugh, 1938.

Westland Wapiti IIA K2260 Air Armament School, Eastchurch, 1932.

It seemed odd stooging around miles over enemy territory at night looking for likely targets of which, it had to be said, there was a noticeable absence. He scoured the Forges to Dieppe railway line looking for traffic but without success. Then his cockpit lights decided to give up. He had no option but to fly blind back to Manston, crossing back over the French coast near Fecamp at 6,000ft. Yet another uneventful trip chalked up, but how many more would he have to endure before he finally got something to shoot at?

The ever-present dangers and nervous strain of operational flying were again evident the following afternoon, when Johnny was flying yet another Rhubarb with 'Joe' Atkinson; this time to the railways south of Le Treport. Without warning, Atkinson's oil pressure dropped to zero when they were only 10 miles from the French coast. There was some broken cloud over the Channel at 500ft and they were flying through slight rain, but irrespective of weather, this close to the enemy coastline with an ailing engine was obviously dangerous. Atkinson sent out a preliminary Mayday as they both turned for home, Johnny closing up alongside him in support. It was a tense few minutes haring back across the Channel, both of them rubbernecking like mad on the lookout for enemy fighters but, perversely, Joe's Typhoon kept on flying and they got back without incident. Yet another abortive sortie notched up in Johnny's logbook.

His patience and persistence finally paid off next day. With F/O Renier, he went on a Rhubarb hunting rail targets in the Le Treport–Formerie area, but they got separated in cloud mid-Channel Johnny crossing the French coast alone near Cayeux. About 6 miles inland, he broke through the rain and cloud at 1,800ft and found perfect conditions below. He was determined to score but there simply wasn't a single locomotive to be seen. Frustrated, he eventually made three attacks on some rolling stock at Blangy and followed the line to the next station, Gamaches, where he made two further attacks on more wagons. With the satisfaction of at least seeing some strikes on both targets he reluctantly set course for the coast and home.

Recrossing the French coast at Cayeux, Johnny let down slowly and emerged from cloud over the Channel, when he saw a Junkers Ju88 1,000ft below him to starboard and heading in the opposite direction. Just what the doctor ordered. Johnny stood PR★V Victor on one wing and reefed around, closing to attack the Ju88 from the starboard quarter, opening fire at 500yd range. He was closing fast and deflection was down to about 10 degrees as he fired another short burst closing to 200yd, his incendiary shells twinkling along the enemy's wings and fuselage. Barely conscious of return fire from a heavy calibre gun, which in any event was passing him too low and off to starboard, Johnny kept up his attack until, with a last gasp of compressed air, his ammunition ran out. Helpless, he sat and watched as that beautiful fat sitting duck of a Ju88 slipped into the rain cloud shrouding the French coast and vanished in the mist.

Seething, Johnny turned about and set course for home, calling up Renier to warn him of the presence of a Ju88 near the Somme estuary. But his message was not received due to poor reception. Bugger all that bloody useless rolling stock! On return to Manston, Johnny made his report to the squadron intelligence officer, Frank Ziegler, who, after viewing his camera gun film, credited him with '1 Ju88 and rolling stock damaged'. Delighted to have opened his personal score at long last, Johnny was nonetheless annoyed at missing what should have been a relatively easy victory. But his mood improved a little later when the CO read them all a letter received earlier in the day from the C-in-C, Air Marshal Leigh-Mallory, congratulating the squadron on recent successes. At least Johnny now felt he had made some degree of personal contribution.

The following morning he lost another wingman, picked off by Fw190s over the Channel. It started as another routine standing patrol with Johnny and Sgt Davis stooging up and down between Dungeness and North Foreland. Towards the end of their stint, with Johnny bored almost witless and hoping that the relief section would show up soon, out of the blue Swingate Control ordered them to give cover for two anti-submarine vessels sailing 15 miles off the South Foreland. As they approached the designated area, the controller called them again: 'Hello Vaccine Black, Vaccine Black. Watch out for bandits east of you at fifteen thousand feet. Bandits, east, fifteen thousand. Over.' The Typhoons immediately went into a steady climb to gain height. Johnny had made 1,500ft when Davis, flying a little below him, reported a dinghy in the water. Visibility was tricky owing to haze and reflection of the sun on the water, so Johnny ordered Davis to maintain height and orbit to provide cover while he went down to investigate.

'Roger, Black One,' Davis acknowledged, as Johnny hauled his Typhoon on to one wing and dived for sea level. He dropped away south in order to come back at the dinghy from up sun. But before he even reached sea level there was a huge splash in the water away to port. Fearing the worst, he called up Davis but got no reply.

Reaching the area, Johnny searched back and forth across the water in vain, only a sickly smudge of oil slowly spreading across the waves marked the end of another aircraft. It must have been all over in seconds. The buggers must have started their dives as soon as the Typhoons had split up. Grimly, Johnny gained height over the spot and transmitted for a fix. Maybe air-sea rescue would find something. Hornchurch Control later confirmed that Davis had fallen victim to a prowling Fw190 and no parachute had been observed. Johnny was left pondering just how easily it could have been him sitting strapped in his cockpit at the bottom of the Channel. He added a bitter 'Happy Christmas!!!' in the margin against details of this flight in his logbook.

Fortunately he had little time to dwell upon such tragedies. It was the last night of the current phase of the moon, heralding the end of night intruder sorties for a while. Consequently, the squadron planned to send six Typhoons over Belgium and northern France that night, and Johnny was scheduled to do some trainspotting in the Forges area. Crossing the French coast at 8,000ft near his favourite spot, Cayeux, at 2134hrs he turned south to pick up the Le Treport–Aumale line. Conditions were perfect but for a slight mist hugging the folds of the valleys. In the moonlight, roads and railways stood out and were clearly visible even from 4,000ft. More importantly, the steam from a train could be seen up to 5 miles away, so travelling 'without a ticket' Johnny followed the track for a few minutes until he spotted a train heading north near Cramaches.

Attacking from the port quarter, he gave it a ten-second burst, seeing hits on the engine. Then suddenly the whole sky lit up as vicious light flak opened up on him from behind forcing him to break away east. The defences were certainly alert and, to make matters worse, they were obviously talking to each other, for he was engaged by two more flak posts as he flew between Chepy and Moyenville. Deciding to let things quieten down a little, Johnny swung away south-east and, throttling back to make less noise, flew in a wide arc to come back at the train he had attacked earlier.

It was stationary on the track with steam pouring from every orifice. There was no sign of movement; the crew and guards probably well away by now, or dead and wounded. It was quite eerie. Everything was clear as day. It was so tempting to go down and finish it off. The train stood there inviting him to come. But it was all too neat and perfect. Only a few minutes earlier every gunner for miles had been hammering on the cockpit door and you could be damned sure that they hadn't all suddenly run out of ammunition. So not tonight, thank you!

Somewhat reluctantly, although he was sure it was the right decision, Johnny turned away south towards Aubancourt Junction where he picked up the track heading west towards Dieppe. This brought him to the St Valery line which snaked north ahead of him all the way to the coast which he reached without meeting any more traffic. Dropping through a slight cloud layer between 2,000 and 3,000ft, he landed back at base at 2222hrs claiming '1 engine damaged' to add to two others clobbered by the CO earlier.

The year drew to a close with the traditional round of festivities, a gamut of wild parties and a general letting off of steam; although most pilots preferred to achieve this with the reluctant assistance of enemy locomotives. Indeed, pilots were keen to fly Rhubarbs and intruder sorties, and competition was so intense that a roster had to be posted at dispersal to avoid pilots doing more than their fair share. Morale had never been higher.

The New Year started quietly enough, thanks to the weather, although Johnny had an exciting few moments on 3 January when a Bofors gun opened up on him when he was minding his own business patrolling off Hastings. He was forced to take evasive action out to sea. His comments, unfortunately, went unrecorded but a few days later he got something of his own back by beating up the gun positions at Sandwich in an exercise designed to help improve the gunners' aircraft recognition. Being a meticulous type, he first phoned up to make sure that they were expecting him and took great care to arrive bang on the appointed time.

On 10 January, another great character, F/Sgt 'Pinky' Stark, joined the squadron. Like Johnny, he had been a staff pilot at a gunnery school but managed to get himself out of that and, with some fifty hours on Hurricanes at No 56 OTU, he had been posted on to Typhoons. But, as he recalls, his route to No 609 Squadron was by no means direct:

> When I got to No.182 Squadron and reported for duty, I was smartly interviewed by the CO who said, 'Now look, this is no reflection on you, but I have 18 Typhoons and 24 pilots and only two of the bloody Typhoons are serviceable. Quite honestly, no matter how I try I can't see you getting your hands on a Typhoon inside three or four months, so I've got to get you posted.' That was the biggest favour he ever did me because he posted me to 609. I'd been sitting in the crew room at Sawbridgeworth reading Intelligence reports and practically all of 11 Group's Intelligence reports were about 609 at the time. So, of course, when I got this posting I was delighted.

Pinky, initially allocated to 'A' Flight, was soon doing the rounds being introduced to everyone:

> My earliest recollections of Johnny Wells was his language. I wouldn't call it flowery by any means, but it was very colourful – colourful in the extreme. One might say that he called a spade a bloody shovel and, by jove, more than that! He was a very outspoken chap in many respects, but he never spoke about himself.

After a couple of familiarisation flights in the squadron Hurricane to get the lie of the land, Pinky's flight commander, 'Joe' Atkinson, introduced him to a Typhoon, and four days after his first flight in one he was flying sorties over the Channel:

It was absolutely marvellous – lots of power. I was tickled pink. I didn't really know of any problems (with engines) before I got there, but I did over 600 hours behind a Napier engine and I never had a failure. They needed careful handling mind you. But no-one had any problems unless they were running them at far too high revs … and Beamont was largely responsible for teaching everyone that.

The weather that January was truly awful, grounded pilots enjoying a daily diet of gale-force winds, horizontal driving rain and freezing fog. QBI, the international code for bad weather, was freely interpreted as '*Quel Brouillard Intense*' by the Belgian pilots, and 'Quite Bloody Impossible' by the English. Conditions were so appalling that one pilot taxiing across the airfield to take off in thick mist was forced to steer by compass bearing. To his disgust, Flying Control refused to give him a green light, deciding that, even by 609 stand-ards, this was rash bordering on foolhardy.

But 15 January heralded the opening night of a new moon phase, so intruding was on again. Beamont, off first at 2137hrs, heading for the Bethune/Lille area, was back within the hour, reporting ideal conditions and with yet another loco-motive to his credit. Johnny took off at 2304, heading for his usual hunting ground and sniffing out rail traffic in the Abbeville–Amiens–Abancourt sector. He found a train heading north near Gamaches. Conscious that he had been here once or twice before, and well aware of some very dangerous flak in the area, Johnny held off and shadowed the train until it entered a convenient valley at Beauchamps, well out of the danger zone and almost at the outskirts of Le Treport.

Obligingly, the stoker had left the furnace doors open making aiming a doddle, so Johnny's initial attack was delivered from dead astern in a shallow dive. He watched his ammunition exploding up the length of the train, gently easing the stick forward as the sights came on the engine. Veering off to one side, Johnny skirted the gouts of steam and smoke which erupted from the exploding boiler as the train ground to a shuddering halt in great plumes of steam. Belatedly, light inaccurate flak drifted up from a nearby village. He flew in a wide arc surveying the turmoil below. Then, coming in low and fast in a beam attack, he gave the engine another long burst for good measure, before returning to Manston well satisfied with his night's work.

Another intruder foray in pretty marginal visibility four nights later over the Bethune–Arras–St Pol area brought forth no targets and Johnny was again forced to return with his ammunition intact. A sorry waste of effort, he thought. But he made up for it the following day which turned out to be something of an epic in the squadron's history.

It started promisingly enough with an early morning Rhubarb to Belgium, when Jean de Selys made a long-planned but unauthorised visit to Brussels where he shot up the Gestapo HQ in the Avenue Louise before dropping a Union Jack and Belgian flag on his capital city. While this was going on, Cheval Lallemand and Peter Raw, on standing patrol, intercepted a pair of Fw190s off Dymchurch, putting one into the sea and damaging the other. An excellent start to the day.

Then, early in the afternoon, Johnny was on a section standing patrol off Dover–Dungeness with Mony van Lierde when more bandits were reported approaching base at 14,000ft. Climbing hard, they had reached 9,000ft when van Lierde spotted twelve bogeys 3 miles behind them which he took for the reported bandits. Breaking formation, he headed for Dover alone but lost the suspected enemy formation in cloud. He eventually reached a layer of high cloud at 27,000ft where the controller told him to stay put as there was a great deal of enemy activity in the area.

Meanwhile, Johnny had continued climbing. His R/T was alive with traffic – clearly something big developing. He saw an aircraft splash into the sea 2 miles north-east of Deal, after which a Messerschmit 109G suddenly appeared, crossing ahead of him. Johnny curved into the attack, opening fire with a three-second burst from 150yd astern, but saw no results before the 109 ducked back into cloud. Livid at having seemingly missed what should have been an absolute 'sitter', Johnny landed back at Manston to find he wasn't the only one to have seen action.

That afternoon the Luftwaffe had launched their biggest daylight effort against Britain since 1940, with an audacious raid on south London by Fw190A fighter-bombers of 10./JG26 escorted by Messerschmitt Bf109G fighters of 6./JG26. Catching the defences unawares, they crossed the English coast at zero feet between Beachy Head and Rye, splitting into two formations, one being a diversionary feint in the Maidstone area. The other formation, penetrating to London, inflicted considerable damage and casualties before withdrawing back out over Dover. It was during this withdrawal phase that No 609 Squadron Typhoons encountered scattered elements of the returning raiders and their escort.

Back at Manston, apart from Johnny, there were at least six other pilots clamouring to file claims. The resulting bumph threatened the squadron IO, F/O Ziegler, with a severe migraine just trying to make sense of it all. But eventually, and to Johnny's immense satisfaction and delight, he was credited with half a Me109 destroyed, shared with his arch rival, Johnny Baldwin, who was credited with two more thus almost equalling the squadron record of three destroyed in a single sortie. Between them, the squadron was reckoned to have accounted for six enemy aircraft destroyed and another damaged for the loss of a single Typhoon, Baldwin having returned with tyres, flaps and petrol tank shot through. That night everyone turned out to celebrate at the

Old Charles, agreeing that, one way or another, it had been quite an eventful day. The fun was far from over.

On leaving the Old Charles, one of their taxi drivers was missing, so Jean de Selys, ably aided and abetted by Nankivell and Johnny, decide to 'take off' without him. Commandeering the taxi, they drove themselves back to the mess. Within a remarkably short time of their arrival, Doone House was invaded by the local constabulary who promptly marched the three miscreants off to the local police station for questioning. The ORB takes up the story:

> The attempts of the (Police) Inspector to come the heavy father fail dismally to extract the slightest filial sorrow from the accused, and in the small hours the police give it up, and after a day or two they are taken by the Station Commander to see the Chief Constable.

What the family made of Johnny's criminal record is not known. It is highly likely that he kept it very quiet.

Two days later, a German pilot fished out of the Channel was whisked off to be interrogated by RAF Intelligence. After breaking down his first story, it was determined that he was one of those shot down by Johnny Baldwin on the 20th and his information allowed the squadron IO to reassess every claim submitted by the squadron on that day. The upshot was that Johnny Wells' share in the Me109G was rescinded, the entire credit going to Johnny Baldwin who thus equalled the squadron record of three victories in one sortie.

Johnny, understandably miffed at having his share of this victory denied, gave his old adversary considerable stick on the subject. It provoked much good-natured banter, particularly when it emerged that Baldwin had 'helped' interview the German pilot concerned. Vile threats and foul calumnies were heaped upon him, along with much drowning of sorrows, until Ziegler revealed that the German pilot had expressed surprise that he and his pal should have been shot down by 'a worm like Baldwin'. Once the laughter subsided, everyone agreed this was a high price to pay for lifting the squadron record and so the matter was put to rest.

On 22 January 1943, the Typhoon was at last allowed to go public and its veil of secrecy finally lifted. It was a remarkable reversal of fortunes, from pariah to 'Britain's new high-speed fighter', as the austere *Aeroplane* magazine described it. The popular press descended on the squadron, but some of their more lurid accounts of its exploits caused the pilots acute embarrassment and much good-natured leg-pulling for weeks to follow. One wag was even heard to suggest that they should all start practising signing their autographs.

Despite all the publicity and lurid paint schemes, the Typhoon continued to draw fire from coastal gunners, the Royal Navy (so no change there) and friendly fighters alike. Yet morale in the squadron was now sky high. The Typhoon was proving itself more than capable against the best the Luftwaffe had to offer and even the most hardened, dyed-in-the-wool, Spitfire pilots grudgingly had to admit to being just a tad impressed. Even the Under Secretary of State for Air, Captain Balfour, asked to meet the CO, who flew over to Hornchurch on 7 February 1943 and, at the instigation of G/C Adnam, gave a blistering display of the Typhoon's performance which prompted Balfour to write, in a subsequent note of thanks: 'I wished you could have heard the comments of the Spitfire experts. They said they did not realize the Typhoon could be handled like that ...'

February 1943 saw No 609 Squadron again the top scorers in Fighter Command, Johnny adding two more locomotives and another Me109G to his tally. He was also unexpectedly promoted to acting flight lieutenant and OC 'B' Flight on the 5th, when Jean de Selys was admonished and demoted as a result of his unauthorised sortie to Brussels. Not wishing to leave the squadron, the Belgian elected to move over to 'A' Flight as deputy flight commander, which everyone thought most creditable in the circumstances.

On 10 February Johnny spent some time mucking out the squadron mascot, W/C William de Goat DFC, a chore generally accepted in the squadron as a good omen, before taking off on a defensive patrol with F/Sgt 'Pinky' Stark as wingman. There was 7/10 cloud down to 800ft and it was raining hard, as Stark would recall over fifty years later:

We were going (west) down the coast somewhere off Dungeness. I was nearest the coast and Johnny was about a mile out from me, when this 109 went the opposite way between us. I shouted and turned after it, and Johnny looked round and turned almost away from it but managed to cut it off. We only just had the legs on it and caught it just south of Folkestone but we couldn't really get close enough. Johnny was having a go at long range but whether he actually hit it or not I don't know. I didn't see any strikes.

Johnny's own account, dictated shortly after landing, survives in the Public Record Office as follows:

I took off as Black 1 at 1555 – 10/2/43 on routine Dungeness patrol. At 1655 when off Folkestone I was told that 2 E/A were going south from Deal. As I reached S. Foreland I saw 2 Me109s between my No.2 and the coast. I warned him and did a tight turn to the left to come in behind them. They apparently saw me as I finished the turn as first one and then the other went down from my level (300–400 ft.) to about 50 feet, and began to stream black exhaust smoke. One E/A was about 400 yds. behind the other, and they both heading for Gris Nez. I was about 800–1000 yds. behind the second E/A, and my No.2 was about 800 yds behind me. Owing to heavy rain I could not see E/A through my front windscreen panel, but could just keep him in sight through the quarter panels. I closed on E/A quickly, but as I knew I had only about 3 minutes to catch E/A before we had crossed the Straits, I fired a few rounds to make him weave. He did, and I closed very rapidly.

Attempting to close the gap more quickly by forcing the 109 to take avoiding action, Johnny fired a short one-second burst from dead astern at 800yd, during which one of the cannon in his port wing suffered a stoppage. He was down to three guns:

The E/A was too low to do any violent weaving. I had closed to about 200 yds. before I could see E/A clearly enough in my sight. I fired at 200 closing to 100 yds. I immediately saw HE strikes on wings, and white smoke pouring from his starboard radiator. He stopped weaving, I closed to 80 yds. and fired. The cockpit of E/A became one big glow (seen by my No.2 about ½ mile behind me), and E/A went straight into the sea.

His first four-second burst was clearly dead on target and was probably more than enough to have caused the 109 terminal damage. His subsequent three-second burst from 80yd removed all doubt:

The remaining E/A had increased his lead (owing to the second weaving) and was just visible about 800 yds. ahead. I chased him, closing all the time down to 400 yds. As we reached Gris Nez I fired a few rounds to make him weave, which he did, and I closed further. When he became just visible in my sight I fired, but one of my port cannons had stopped and I had difficulty in keeping the sight on. The E/A turned sharply under the lee of the cliffs and I followed, firing on the turn. He then pulled up over the cliffs and I followed. I gave one final burst and dived down back over the cliffs to seaward, thus losing sight of E/A. The time was then 1700 hrs. I returned to Manston and landed at 1708.

Five days later he was hopeful of a repeat performance when he spotted a couple of unidentified aircraft heading south at sea level over Sandwich Bay and going like dingbats. Despite the Typhoon's edge in speed, he was unable to catch them before they pulled up and vanished into cloud off Calais. But later that same night he met with more success during another night intruder sortie. He and Beamont went off independent about 2030hrs,

Beamont heading for rail targets in the St Omer area while Johnny scoured the Hazebrouck–Ghent network. Johnny crossed the French coast near Gravelines at 7,000ft and, reaching Hazebrouck, turned east scanning the railway tracks for traffic. Before too long he found a goods train heading east between Wevricq and Menin was left in clouds of steam after two attacks.

It was to be a fruitful night, for he went on to attack another train just west of Ingelmunster Junction. This particular target was nearly his undoing. Close to the end of his first attack, just as he was on the point of breaking away, the target suddenly blew up in front of him. There was no warning; no preliminary smoke, no licks of flame, just an enormous livid explosion which filled the night sky flinging debris high into the air. He must have hit an ammunition wagon. Temporarily blinded, Johnny was forced to fly straight through it, instinctively ducking his head below the instrument panel and gritting his teeth as fragments rained down on his wings and fuselage.

A mite rattled, Johnny emerged from the explosion faintly amazed to find his aircraft apparently still in one piece. But suspecting that it could well be damaged, he headed straight for home, crossing out over the coast at Mardyck. It was a long trip back across the Channel, eyes glued to his instruments and ears pricked for any suspect sound from the engine. But his luck was really in that night, for a close inspection of the Typhoon back at Manston revealed no damage beyond a few minor dents and blistered paintwork. Best of all, he had one locomotive destroyed and another probably destroyed against Beamont's claim of one locomotive probably destroyed and some rolling stock damaged; plus a car destroyed – the occupants of which had been dumb enough to drive around using full headlights. It was nice to outscore the CO once in a while.

On 18 February, Johnny and one of his Belgians, Sergeant Blanco, drew the short straw and were first off on the early morning patrol shortly after dawn. There had been a particularly successful squadron party at the West Cliff Theatre in Ramsgate the night before, during which squadron records reveal 'something like' 100 gallons of beer being consumed. Lifting his head off the pillow was hard that morning, but it was wonderful what a whiff of oxygen could do for a hangover.

Whatever their fitness state, the situation was not improved when, during the patrol, thick mist rolled in blanketing Manston. For once, Swingate Control was caught napping and failed to recall them. With the weather 'clamped', they were suddenly faced with a highly dangerous situation but, more by sheer luck than judgement, somehow managed to grope their way back to base and get down safely. As the ORB recorded, they 'only get in, shaken men, thanks to skill and friendly gremlin activity'.

A spate of bad weather with heavy mist covering the south coast prevented most flying for a few days, so the opportunity was taken for the pilots to practise evasion techniques. As the IO explained, in the event of them being shot down behind enemy lines, it would prove 'useful if you find yourselves having to cross hostile territory some day'. So wearing an odd assortment of nondescript clothing they were taken by lorry to various points in the surrounding countryside and dropped off about 7 miles from camp. The idea was for each pilot, equipped with a small compass and limited to using only basic English phrases, to reach the Intelligence Office at Manston without getting arrested. To add realism to the exercise, the local police and Home Guard were not advised, as a result of which, many an adventure was had. Johnny was the last man home, arriving just before search parties were sent off to find him. But, as squadron records acknowledge, he was 'a very thorough pilot'.

'Joe' Atkinson, then commanding 'A' Flight, recalls something of Johnny from around this time:

> I was flying on a patrol from Manston with another pilot as No.2 when we pursued 2 Fw190s across the Channel and I shot one of them down near Boulogne ... before the action, we had an unplanned meeting with another section led by Johnny. For some strange reason my usual Typhoon PR★A was being flown by my No.2 and I was flying PR★R, so when I asked Johnny afterwards whether he could confirm my victory he, being unaware of the swap of machines, said that he could not do so but had seen an aircraft shot down by my No.2.

This confusion was obviously quickly resolved but it is indicative of Johnny's meticulous and matter-of-fact approach. 'He was always immaculate but quite a self-contained individual, a private type who didn't wear his heart on his sleeve. Yet a good companion, and if ever you wanted a sensible view on any-thing or a practical solution to a problem, then Johnny was the first one to ask.'

Throughout March 1943, despite bad weather, a distinct pattern of activity emerged. Constant standing patrols remained de rigueur, sometimes enli-vened by the appearance of enemy fighters making 'tip-and-run' raids up and down the south coast. These raids, difficult to counter, created a lot of trouble for the British defences, invariably resulting in flat-out chases back across the Channel at nought feet, often in indifferent weather.

During the phase of a full moon, a full programme of solo night intruder sorties was maintained with Typhoons ranging far and wide across north-ern France and Belgium. Occasional 'Roadstead' missions also made a nice change, with the Tiffies teamed up with a squadron or two of Spits to trail their coats over the enemy coastline seeking E-boats or other shipping to strafe. These missions attracted plenty of flak but they saw very few E-boats and rarely spotted any enemy fighters.

One highlight of the month, which provoked some hilarity amongst those not personally involved, was the arrival of the artist Cuthbert Orde. In the course of a week he completed portrait sketches of pilots including the CO, both flight commanders, Frank Ziegler, Moose Evans, Cheval Lallemand, Peter Raw and Johnny, who found sitting for his portrait an interesting though tedious exercise. He also felt the finished likeness did him scant justice, making him look too sombre.

By April 1943 the Luftwaffe had curtailed their cross-Channel forays and even enemy rail targets had seemingly dried up, the Germans finally realising just how dangerous it had become to run their trains during periods of moonlight. More offensive operations were called for and Rhubarbs were back on the menu. So, late in the afternoon of 4 April, Johnny flew one of nine Typhoons escorting Whirlwind fighter-bombers in an attack on Abbeville marshalling yards. Taking off from Manston at 1816hrs, they rendezvoused with two squadrons of Spitfires from Hornchurch and set course for the French coast at Cayeux. The bombing went ahead unopposed and during the return flight, when most of them were looking forward to tea followed by a pleasant evening in some welcoming hostelry, the Typhoons were vectored by Swingate Control to a 'special target' off Boulogne. This turned out to be several E-boats plus a flak ship – how absolutely bloody charming.

Beamont, leading them up-sun to attack the ships from astern, managed to achieve surprise for no return fire was experienced until after their first attack. It may have been slow in coming but once the flak opened up it was hot and heavy. Instructing the pilots to make only one attack, Beamont led four Typhoons down on to two E-boats which were bringing up the rear of the small convoy. Simultaneously, Johnny and Moose Evans took on the flak ship.

Johnny squinted at the target dead ahead as the horizon tilted crazily first one way then the other. His cannon shells whipped the sea to foam as they converged towards the squat, grey shape in the water; high-explosive strikes winking up its sides and onto the superstructure. Holding the sights square on target, Johnny did his best to ignore the return fire which seemed to snake and spiral around him. But the enemy gunners had been fooled into splitting their fire, for not too much was coming directly his way. The smoke shrouding the enemy vessel started getting thicker; then a small explosion, probably ammunition, as the ship caught fire. Out of the corner of his eye he saw one of the E-boats stopped in the water and burning, its crew leaping overboard to escape the fire.

Leaving the convoy scattered, and with several vessels ablaze, the Typhoons climbed away, reforming in the climb, and headed for home assessing their damage. Blanco had caught a real packet and seemed to have lost half his rudder, and F/O Raw was reporting engine trouble; but they both made it back to Manston safely. Then, as they all joined the circuit prior to landing, a Typhoon broke formation and headed straight in to land. The pilot was obviously in something of a hurry, which prompted a radio call from Mony van Lierde, 'Who is that cunt landing downwind?' 'Crooner Leader if it's of any interest, Van,' Beamont replied, wrestling with the controls of his rapidly ailing Typhoon. There followed a brief pause before abject and profuse apologies poured forth from the hapless Belgian amid hoots of mirth from others.

The April moonlight offensive kicked off on the night of the 15th when the CO, Johnny and F/O Payne each went off to make more mischief with enemy rail communications. For once, Beamont was out of luck, but the others both found worthwhile targets. Johnny, headed for Charleroi, struck lucky, claiming two engines probably destroyed near La Louviere. He went on to attack a convoy of six trucks on the road outside Enghien, attracting some light flak for his pains. He landed back at Manston at 2334hrs.

Two nights later he was back over Belgium in his favourite PR★N Nuts on yet another Rhubarb, taking off from Manston early on the 18th. It was a quiet night with little or no traffic about, or so it first seemed. Train-busting was a waiting game, so Johnny scoured the tracks from Dixmude, Roulers, Thielt, Ghent to Oudenarde, before finding a long train of covered goods wagons beetling along the line just outside Middlewijk.

His first attack brought the engine to a grinding halt in the usual clouds of steam, before Johnny switched fire on to the trucks. Unopposed by ground fire, he made a succession of attacks which left the wagons in the middle of the train a sea of flames visible for miles around. Well pleased with his night's work, he returned to base to find that he had just destroyed the squadron's 100th locomotive. This, of course, was just and righteous cause for later celebrations having evoked a signal of congratulations from the C-in-C. Later it transpired that a tactful conspiracy to award this honour to the CO, who also got two locomotives and landed a quarter of an hour before Johnny, had been foiled by a clerical error on the part of the IO when totting up the squadron's bag for the night. But Beamont wasn't too fussed – his personal tally of trains now stood at twenty-five, all proudly emblazoned on the side panel of his aircraft PR★G.

On the evening of 7 May there was a gargantuan thrash, starting with a private squadron do at the Old Charles and later moving back to the mess at Doone House, which was arranged to take leave of the CO who had completed his second tour of operations. Clearly an epic binge, even by 609 standards, Beamont was to be found, at a fairly late stage in proceedings, sitting on the floor in a sea of beer crooning quietly to himself and wearing flowers in his hair. The eloquence of the Operations Record Book in describing the aftermath cannot be bettered:

May 8. Hangovers of different degrees and kinds. F/O Smith is accordingly adjudged a hero when he leaves the ground 2 minutes after being scrambled at 0703, in weather anything but sympathetic, for a bandit invading Canterbury. Further flying is discouraged by a gale which reaches 60 m.p.h. accompanied by rain … Scrambled by F/Lt Wells with a verey pistol, S/L Beamont makes a good getaway in his M.G. Sports despite a super 'line' occasioned by the presence on the number plate of the aforementioned panel bearing 5 crosses, 25 locomotives and a seeming battleship to represent half an R-boat. F/Lt Wells then spends the rest of the day causing much sawing to be done in the erection of bunks at Dispersal … 'B' Flight actually sleep there rather than go to Westgate for a mere 5 hours or so. Roused by the voice of Cpl. Hinchcliffe at 0500 hrs, F/Lt Wells looks up and is surprised to see noone there - till he remembers he is in the upper berth.

Beamont went back to Hawkers for another spell of test flying during which enforced 'rest' from operations, he spent much of his time diving Typhoons to terminal velocity to try and establish exactly why their tails sometimes fell off. Some rest! Word got around that he had dived one at over 500mph which went a long way toward improving confidence in the aircraft. His award of a well-deserved DSO was announced on 15 May.

The new CO, S/L Alec Ingle AFC, had an unenviable task in taking over from someone as charismatic as Beamont, particularly at a time when the squadron was doing so well. But bringing his own brand of leadership he was well liked and respected. He also had his own views on future tactics. So anti-shipping attacks using cannon against E-boats, minesweepers and flak ships became the order of the day, No 609 Squadron Typhoons often flying in support of No 137 Squadron Whirlwinds.

Due largely to the stormy weather, there had been little activity since Ingle took over and he was keen to see this change. Accordingly, after a conflab with the flight commanders and the IO, offensive operations resumed on 11 May when Johnny, together with Mony van Lierde, Moose Evans and Johnny Baldwin, took off at 1637hrs under Swingate Control and found a 500–700-ton coaster about 400yd from Calais harbour entrance. Johnny, first into the attack, drew fire from three guns on the ship. They were soon augmented by intense light and heavy flak from the shore. All pilots reported strikes on the vessel which they left smoking as confirmed by their camera gun films. But clearly, if such attacks were to be successful in future, they would need something a lot heavier than their existing cannon armament. It was like throwing marshmallows at a coconut shy.

Not easily dissuaded, Ingle continued to press the case for launching more daylight anti-shipping strikes and finally got permission from Group to go ahead. Consequently, shortly after dawn on 14 May, he took Johnny, Johnny Baldwin and Pinky Stark on an anti-shipping patrol off the French coast from Dunkirk to Cap Gris Nez. As Stark recalls:

> Alec Ingle and Beamont were as different as chalk and cheese. He didn't like trains and as there weren't too many aeroplanes around he went for shipping – and that was 'orrid! We would take off from Manston in the morning before daylight, flying on navigation lights, straight across the water at nought feet and get to the enemy coast just as dawn was breaking. Inevitably, these little coastal convoys all had a bloody flak ship.

Another Typhoon pilot, Desmond Scott, CO of No 486 (NZ) Squadron based just down the coast at Tangmere, recorded:

> Attacking E-boats in the Bay de la Seine was among our primary objectives. Thin-skinned they might have been, but they made up for this deficiency by carrying a large number of 20 mm and 37 mm guns. Their most dangerous weapon was the quadruple 20 mm cannon which for some reason or other we called a 'Chicago piano'. The volume of coloured tracer sent up by the E-boat flotillas was a frightening spectacle and our chances of collecting a packet were very much in the enemy's favour.

Two hundred yards outside Boulogne Harbour the four Typhoons spotted a minesweeper – or was it a flak ship? It was of little consequence: they knew that either could be a lethal target. Catching even the slightest hit from return fire at the heights at which they were forced to fly in and attack would usually prove fatal. The ship sat close inshore and light flak snaked up towards them from what looked like barges moored alongside the harbour mole. This was interspersed with some fairly heavy AA opening up from harbour gun emplacements. All surprise was gone and the enemy gunners had them well bracketed. But to everyone's immense relief, for the sky above Boulogne was suddenly a very noisy and thoroughly inhospitable place, Ingle decided to leave the ship well alone and they returned to base.

That night No 609 Squadron had cause for a double celebration. Its first bombs dropped in anger and their first night kill – a Heinkel He111 shot down into the sea off Ostend by Mony van Lierde. Two hours after the first load, Johnny dropped the squadron's second bombs of the war: two 250lb GPs dumped across the runway at Abbeville/Drucat in disgust, having found nothing worth blowing up at St Valery-en-Caux.

Another Rhubarb the next night was much more successful when he dropped his bombs on barges between Ghent and Aeltre. Whatever the cargo, when the smoke cleared three of them had completely disappeared and the rest were a total shambles. He then went on to attack a powered barge with his cannon before withdrawing back over the coast at Bray Dunes.

On 16 May, all squadron records were broken with a total of eighteen night sorties being flown. The previous night the Luftwaffe had launched more than forty against Harwich from Schiphol and the squadron was keen to repay this unwelcome attention. Johnny was one of those off just before midnight on an intruder sortie to Amiens/Glisy airfield. But he got no trade there, everything was quiet, so he diverted to Abbeville/Drucat, where he found flare path and perimeter lights on. There must be an aircraft expected or already in the circuit. Throttling back and dropping to 600ft over the runway approach, Johnny spotted the navigation lights of an aircraft going in to land below him and gently dropped in behind, stalking his prey. Following it, he waited until it had touched down before dropping one of his bombs on the runway immediately ahead of it. Then, continuing the dive down to 300ft, put his second bomb straight through the roof of a hangar. This resulted in a most satisfying bang followed by a huge secondary explosion with vivid red and orange flames lighting up the surrounding countryside, sending a pall of smoke over 2,000ft. Somewhat belatedly, the airfield lighting was doused as Johnny did a final circuit to admire his handy work before heading for home. At the English coast, he was engaged by searchlights and guns, which were obviously more alert than their German counterparts. Never a dull moment!

On 19 May, the squadron paraded for a visit by the AOC, Air Vice Marshal Saunders, who presented a well-deserved DFC to Cheval Lallemand and went on to speak highly of the squadron's achievements in 'more than any other putting the Typhoon on the map'. After taking tea with the AOC, the squadron went back on readiness and flew two more patrols before nightfall.

Then, in the middle of the night, an unexpected visitor dropped in at Manston. This was not unusual for Allied aircraft were often dropping in and some of them quite literally. It was a common enough sight to find another strange wreck adorning the airfield when you arrived at dispersal early in the morning. Being the foremost airfield on the southern tip of England, Allied aircraft of all shapes and varieties frequently limped in to land there, either with battle damage or having lost their bearings during operations over the Continent. This one was no exception for the pilot was totally disorientated. What made it unusual was that it was an Fw190.

It was a busy night with most of 'B' Flight up on various intruder missions. The CO, along with Johnny and a few others, were waiting for Johnny Baldwin to return from a trip to Amiens-Glisy, when around 0330hrs they noticed an aircraft being homed by the searchlights. Puzzled, they all watched it land and roll down the runway towards dispersal, when Mony van Lierde recognised it as a 190. There was a sudden mad dash for the Hillman parked outside. When they screamed to a halt alongside, the Fw190 was stationary but with the engine still running. Alec Ingle vacated the car at speed and, pointing a finger at the pilot in what he hoped was a threatening manner, shouted 'Hands up!' at the bewildered pilot. Bundling the hapless German into the back of the car where he sat wedged between van Lierde and Renier, Ingle turned to Johnny who was in the front passenger seat: 'What the hell do we do with him now?'

Johnny lit a cigarette and offered one to the German pilot. 'All pilots landing from an operational patrol must report at the Intelligence Office,' he offered, citing regulations. So off they went to deliver their prize to the duty intelligence officer, F/O Treweeks, who refused to be impressed and pointed them to the back of a long queue of pilots awaiting debriefing.

This was only the second intact Fw190 to land in Britain and the following day Johnny insisted on having his photograph taken with the disconsolate pilot, Uffz Ehrhardt of 2./SKG210. Apparently, he had mistaken the Thames Estuary for the Channel and thought he was landing safe and sound back at St Omer. He went off to the slammer while his aircraft went off to A&AEE at Boscombe Down for evaluation and later became a welcome addition to No 1426 (Enemy Aircraft) Flight, the RAF's growing collection of airworthy enemy machines.

Two days later, shortly after 2130hrs, Johnny led one of two sections ordered to patrol Clacton in marginal conditions, low-level haze and twilight combining to reduce visibility. Arriving over the designated area they patrolled up and down the Essex coast in the deepening gloom awaiting further instructions. Off Harwich, F/O Renier came under light AA fire from what appeared to be a destroyer which was soon swallowed in the swirling mists below.

After what seemed like hours, Hornchurch Control put an end to their misery and vectored them back south over the Thames Estuary towards Manston. Visibility, still poor with patchy haze, made flying conditions irksome. The Typhoons forged through the clag while pilot's eyes bulged with the strain of trying to see ahead through misted armoured-Perspex windscreens. Instinctively they eased formation to increase the distance between each aircraft and were flying two very loose pairs, each wingman barely visible as shadows. Midway across the estuary Johnny noticed the haze directly ahead of them start to darken, the swirling mists forming almost solid shapes. Christ almighty! 'Balloons!' a blurted warning as he went into a steady climb and waited for an almighty crunch. Some twit at Hornchurch Control had vectored them slap bang over a convoy flying balloons.

Johnny called up on the radio and took a quick headcount. Through sheer good fortune tragedy had been avoided and all four Typhoons returned safely to Manston. Later, Johnny's caustic comments on the telephone to someone in authority at Hornchurch, which he delivered quite calmly and deliberately but with acid menace, were said to have made strong men blanche and go weak at the knees.

An influx of new pilots fresh from OTU kept Johnny busy supervising the training of those allocated to his flight. As the squadron ORB records: 'Several new pilots embark on their first solos and F/L Wells, watching the landings, gradually becomes a spent man (he is nearly taken away in the ambulance when Sgt Bavington writes off the undercarriage of the Hurricane by means of a ground loop).'

On 31 May, during an attack on shipping off Blankenberghe, Johnny's aircraft was hit by heavy flak but, fortunately, not seriously damaged. Standing patrols continued unabated until a serious shortage of Sabre engines curtailed operations reducing defensive operations to cockpit readiness with the occasional scramble. The main activity was now anti-shipping strikes, often operating in conjunction with No 184 Squadron Hurricane IVs armed with rockets and No 3 Squadron whose Typhoons, carrying bombs, were labelled 'Bomphoons'.

For the squadron, 1 June was a red-letter day, and for Johnny in particular. Along with F/O Davies, they had taken off at 1220hrs to form a section as a precaution against enemy activity detected over the French coast. They flew in a wide arc at 1,800ft, circling Manston and awaited further instructions. At 1305hrs Johnny spotted three aircraft heading away from Margate towards Broadstairs at nought feet. Leading Davies in a steep diving turn towards them to investigate, they saw bombs impacting in the town and a gasometer explode in gouts of flame and smoke. Johnny, radioing 'Bandits, Tally Ho!' dived to attack as a loose gaggle of twelve more Fw190s appeared below. Closing he fired a snap burst at one of the enemy fighters before being forced to break and take avoiding action from light AA fire that peppered the sky around them. His PR★N took some hits, which he later found had shot an engine bearer away, and he realised that there was no sign of Dave Davies – he was on his own.

The enemy formation was going flat out for home, exhausts smoking, and right down on the deck skimming the waves. Choosing to ignore the tail-enders, Johnny set off after the leading vic of three about a mile ahead, gradually closing on them. He fired a short burst at extreme range trying to make his target weave, but the lead Fw190, obviously experienced enough to ignore this, just kept on going. Out of the corner of his eye, Johnny was acutely aware that the rest of the enemy formation was flying on either side of him. With the range down to 200yd, Johnny fired three short bursts closing to 150yd for a final three-second burst which tipped the Fw190 on to its starboard wing. At this height and speed it was an impossible situation to retrieve and the enemy fighter tumbled into the drink, sending up a fountain of water. Flying through the plume of spray, Johnny, in danger of over-shooting the leading pair, throttled back while selecting another target. A couple of bursts from 200yd sent the second Fw190 into a prolonged skid to starboard, allowing him to close right up to 150yd for a three-second burst which sent it crashing into the sea in a gout of spray and debris.

Ignoring the streams of livid red and green tracer now passing over his wings from behind, Johnny set his sights on the remaining Fw190 which sat square in his windscreen 200yd ahead, jinking gently from side to side. Stabbing the firing button, after a one-second burst Johnny was disgusted to find himself out of ammunition so pulled up into a steep-climbing turn, seeing the enemy formation sweep past below him.

On return to Manston, Johnny was relieved to find Davies already back with three claims of his own to equal the squadron record of a hat-trick on a single sortie. Between them they had accounted for five Fw190s. Another, crashed at Lydden quite close to the airfield, was credited to a Bofors gun crew at Margate. There was some serious celebrating that night at the Old Charles and congratulatory signals the following day from the C-in-C, the Secretary of State for War, and formal thanks to both pilots from the citizens of Margate. High praise indeed.

The days blurred into a routine of cockpit readiness, standing patrols and uneventful scrambles, interspersed with increasingly dicey anti-shipping strikes. An occasional social event did much to relieve the constant stress as an alternative to simply getting plastered nightly in the bar. One such, on 9 June, was at Grosvenor House in London to celebrate Biggin Hill's 1,000th victory of which No 609 Squadron were reckoned to have notched up half. Johnny attended, along with Alec Ingle and Cheval Lallemand. The party was reported to have been 'a wow' as both Johnny's appearance and delicate con-dition the next morning readily affirmed. Wisely, he grounded himself for the rest of the day.

On 21 June his award of the DFC was announced, the citation being pub-lished in the Supplement to the *London Gazette* 6 July 1943:

Acting Flight Lieutenant John Christopher WELLS (45883) No. 609 Squadron. This officer has completed many hours flying, involving sor-ties both by day and by night. He has achieved much success in attacks on enemy lines of communication, while in air combat he has destroyed at least 3 enemy aircraft, 2 of which he shot down in one engagement. Flight Lieutenant Wells has displayed commendable courage and tenacity.

It was thirteen months since he had first joined the squadron at Duxford, during which time he had logged over 237 hours on Typhoons and flown close to 200 sorties. He had been promoted flight lieutenant with effect 27 May 1943 and was credited with three enemy aircraft destroyed and one damaged. He also had a very respectable bag of seven locomotives, assorted enemy shipping and barges to his name, along with sundry miscellaneous mischief and mayhem inflicted on the enemies of the realm. He was due a well-deserved rest on completion of his first tour of operations and by dint of some judicious string pulling had contrived a spell as a Development Test Pilot with Napier's at Luton. Cheval Lallemant was to join him. Following a particularly spectacular display of low flying one day, the young Belgian had incurred the dire wrath of the station commander, who was in the process of having him posted to an OTU. Thanks to a timely intervention by Johnny, who had a few conciliatory words in certain ears, it was arranged for Lallemant to join him at Napiers, where the Belgian's flying skills could be put to better use.

As the squadron diary for 24 June 1943 records: 'Departure today of F/Lt Wells DFC and F/O Lallemant DFC (Belgian), the former in a sabre-toothed Battle, the latter at 0600 (noisily) in his Opel motorcar. As two of 609's most experienced, distinguished and senior pilots, their departure will cause quite a gap.'

Pleased to step aside from the constant strain of operational flying for a while, a rest period may have followed, but Johnny's logbook over the next few months still reveals a gruelling daily schedule of endurance trials and engine-cutting tests on Typhoons. He was embroiled in development flying for the new Sabre IV series of engine and this involved often two or three flights a day testing fuel flows, oil dilution 'boil-off' and supercharger clutch tests in a variety of simulated operational conditions. It required disciplined flying and was fascinating work for someone with his mechanical bent and operational experience. He soon settled in and was enjoying every minute.

On 9 October, he logged his 500th hour on Typhoons during a flight to test the effect of negative gravity. And the following month he recorded an indicated air speed of 403mph in level flight at 3,000ft in Typhoon DN561, a feat eliciting a double exclamation mark alongside his logbook entry.

Just before Christmas, having been at Napier's for six months and nearing the end of his term, he was starting to feel just a bit too comfortable for his own good, when an urgent message came through from Group. The CO of No 609 Squadron had been shot down and killed. Johnny was to return to Manston immediately and take command of the squadron.

12

'DISPLAY' LEADER

It was great to be returning to 609 as their CO and Johnny was understandably delighted. He only wished that circumstances had been different. The loss of Pat Thornton-Brown had been a tragic waste, as the squadron intelligence officer, F/L Frank Ziegler, recounted:

> 609 was detailed as close escort to American Marauder bombers. It only had six aircraft, and with the bombers strung out in three boxes over ten miles, there was nothing for it but to appoint two Typhoons to each box. Again it was the old sad story: they were attacked from astern by a swarm of American Thunderbolts, and recognition signals were given in vain. Arty Ross was hit by his countrymen in both wings, and two pilots never returned: 'Chuck' Miller, a Canadian, and the CO, Pat Thornton-Brown. It was typical of Pat that his last words on the RT expressed concern, not for himself, but for Miller. His DFC was announced a few days later, and his wife was due next day to join him for Christmas.

So, on Christmas Eve 1943, Johnny Wells returned to No 609 Squadron, his appointment as CO being confirmed five days later. It was barely nineteen months since he had joined them at Duxford and he couldn't have wished for better. This also perpetuated a growing tradition as Pinky Stark, later to become their seventeenth and last wartime CO, explains:

> 609 was a very good school. The squadron produced quite a number of their own COs who came up through the ranks, as happened to me. They didn't often promote from within, but a lot of the chaps had been on 609, learned their trade, gone somewhere else, and then came back (as CO).

There had been some changes in the squadron (call sign then 'Display') with a few new faces around, but enough of the 'old firm' were left to make him feel right at home. Soon after he had joined Napier's the squadron had left Manston for Matlaske in Norfolk to be rested for a month. Then, prior to their return to No 11 Group in August, Alec Ingle had left on promotion to wing commander to be succeeded by Pat Thornton-Brown. Moving back, they were initially based at Lympne, a satellite airfield, where conditions were cramped and unsatisfactory, reaching their old stamping ground at Manston ten days before Johnny's return.

At Manston they formed the first long-range Typhoon wing with No 198 Squadron, commanded by Johnny Baldwin DFC, another ex-609 veteran. As Frank Ziegler, squadron intelligence officer and chronicler, puts it, 'For two months a friendly rivalry developed between the two Johnnies, both of them reared in the same fold, and their two squadrons as a team superb.'

Even the aircraft looked different as many were now fitted with a drop tank under each wing to extend their range. 'Ranger' sorties now penetrated the enemy's hinterland far beyond the Typhoon's usual operational sphere to seek out Luftwaffe inland airfields, where targets were in abundance. One of Johnny's flight commanders, F/L L.E. Smith, had even reached Germany, becoming the first Typhoon pilot to do so. A few weeks earlier, on 2 December, the Manston Typhoons had caught an entire gruppe of Dornier Do217 bombers taking off from Eindhoven and left eleven of them blazing hulks littering the surrounding countryside. Operating in close conjunction as a long-range strike force, the Typhoon squadrons were currently accounting for more enemy aircraft destroyed than the whole of the rest of Fighter Command put together.

In addition, the aircraft could now pack new armament: eight rockets, four under each wing fired in pairs or in a full salvo of eight. These potent missiles were simply short lengths of steel tube packed with propellant and fitted with vanes at the tail to improve stability, each carrying a warhead of 60lb of high explosive or 25lb of solid shot. It was said that they were deadly when used against all manner of ground targets and would transform the Typhoon into the RAF equivalent of heavy artillery. Armed with eight rockets and its four 20mm Hispano cannon, each Typhoon could deliver a broadside equivalent to that of a RN cruiser.

Rockets had been introduced back in October but it was the following month before the squadron could undertake operational testing. Adapting to the new weapons took time and practice, as Pinky Stark recalls:

I suppose that I preferred the low level fighter role – I think most of us did. But we were stuck with bombs and rockets and had to get used to it.

The original idea was that you came in at nought feet and when you saw the target approaching you pulled up slightly and then did a shallow dive. Nobody hit anything – and we were trying!

'We were very well placed at Manston as there were two wrecks out on the Goodwin Sands and we used those as targets. I could stand on the blast wall outside dispersal and see the chaps diving on these things.' One day, as deputy flight commander, he was watching two NCO pilots, an Australian and a Canadian, whom he had sent off to practise rocket attacks on one of the wrecks:

Instead of shallow dives I saw them in screaming dives and they hit the thing every time. That became the standard system for the whole of 2nd TAF eventually. This low-level nonsense was a waste of time. The intention coming in at nought feet was surprise. Sitting up there somebody knows you're going to be diving any minute now, but in a 60 degree dive you were going fairly fast down at the bottom.

As pilots gained experience of the new weapons, they found that ground attack using rockets needed a technique but nothing too fancy. A swerving attack proved best, straightening up as you came on target and keeping the aircraft steady prior to release. But when aiming, allowance had to be made for a greater drop in trajectory than conventional high-velocity weapons like cannon or machine guns. As there was no appreciable recoil from rockets, keeping on target was fairly straightforward.

Flight Lieutenant Eric Roberts confided to his diary concerns which were omnipresent in most Typhoon pilots' minds: 'We will probably come in for a lot of casualties from flak … and personally, I don't think a lot of damage will be done by the rockets because of the many factors governing their accuracy when there's ten-tenths flak around.' Later events would prove him right but only in regard to future casualties.

Weather permitting, the squadron flew operations daily, penetrating deep into France in search of targets or flying joint missions with the Typhoons of No 198 Squadron, also based at Manston. On 3 January, Johnny led six aircraft on a Ranger to the Paris area and, on the following day, two fighter sweeps of enemy airfields in Holland; broken cloud making the first uneventful, but the second proving very different.

Nine aircraft joined No 198 and crossed the Channel at low level heading for Gilze Rijen, where they planned to separate; 609 going on to Volkel. Avoiding Roosendaal put them a little off course and they were approaching Gilze from the south when F/L Davies reported an aircraft low ahead and to port. Two more were then spotted – Do217s – and there were others in the circuit preparing to land. They had caught a Luftwaffe bomber unit with its pants down.

Davies, crossing the airfield under 1,000ft to avoid intense flak, fired at the first Dornier, which burst into flames and crashed. His wingman, F/O Watts, flying straight up the runway at 100ft, met another coming towards him, which he attacked, knocking several large chunks off it. A disappointed Johnny, who was about to attack this from astern, watched it crash in woods west of the airfield. Manu Geerts and Pinky Stark put paid to another 10 miles to the south after a short chase, whilst F/O Detal shot down a fourth, which crashed east of Gilze after three of the crew bailed out. Three more bombers were destroyed by P/O McLaughlin ground-strafing, and a Do217 that ground looped attempting to land crosswind in a hurry was later awarded to G/C de Goat by general consent. F/O Daix suffered engine failure halfway back across the Channel and ditched with his port auxiliary tank still in place, the aircraft sinking within five seconds. The squadron circled the spot, transmitting for a fix, but nothing more was seen.

It was an auspicious start to the new year and the month after Johnny took over was the squadron's most successful since the Battle of Britain, with eighteen enemy aircraft destroyed – thirteen in the air and five on the ground. But it was not without difficulties. On the 28th, the Manston Typhoon squadrons took off at first light for Coltishall to escort Beaufighters on a coastal Roadstead operation but, due to poor weather, the mission was postponed until mid-afternoon. Halfway to the Dutch coast, staggering along close to stalling speed a mere 100ft above the choppy sea, they flew into thick mist. Avoiding collisions while trying to stay in contact with the Beaus was taxing, just flying in such conditions being hazardous enough. They pressed on, tired eyes peering through the swirling clouds enveloping them, ears attuned to the faintest sound of trouble from their engine – it was hellish.

After what seemed a lifetime, they reached the Dutch coast where two Beaufighters collided, another going down to ditch in the sea. Several convoys were then seen off Borkum, but the Beaufighters made for home without attacking and the untidy formation struggled back to Coltishall where they landed after three hours in the air. Thoroughly dispirited Typhoon pilots, making their feelings clear, were only placated when both COs, Wells and Baldwin, submitted a strongly worded report on the futility of such operations.

By way of contrast, two days later, the Manston squadrons scored the biggest Typhoon fighter victory of the war, claiming twelve Fw190s between them, and their combined total for the month reached forty-three enemy aircraft destroyed or, put another way, three-quarters of the entire No 11 Group total. This prompted a flurry of congratulatory signals from the top brass and much celebratory raising of elbows.

It was to be another joint effort, Ramrod 498, flying in support of Marauders bombing Melun, north of Paris. No 609 Squadron was to sweep the area Montdidier–Melun–Bretigny, No 198 operating further west. At Roye airfield, Johnny spotted a Ju88 being refuelled and went into the attack followed by F/O Shelton. Sweeping low over the airfield boundary to avoid flak, Johnny watched his cannon shells snaking across the tarmac towards the aircraft dead ahead, winking and flashing as they exploded on target. Ground crew, toppling from the wings, scattered and fled, the Ju88 lurching drunkenly as a small explosion caused the undercarriage to collapse in clouds of smoke and dust. Two more bombers parked a little further on got the same treatment.

Reforming at low level, they reached the fog-shrouded Marne then headed north away from Paris. Veering west they crossed Creil airfield, attracting some flak, and were north of the Seine just south of Gisors when they met a gaggle of Fw190s. In a hectic series of combats at heights ranging from ground level to 1,000ft, three 190s were claimed, the squadron returning without loss. Honours go to 198, however, who scored nine without loss. Signals of congratulation arrived from Air Chief Marshal Leigh-Mallory, Air Marshal Hill and Air Vice Marshal Saunders. Not too bad a result from a mission that, they later discovered, had been cancelled soon after take-off.

February proved something of an anti-climax due in part to poor weather. Johnny was confined to bed with a severe attack of tonsillitis prompting a visit from the new MO, George Bell, who had only just arrived on the squadron. It was their first meeting and it made a lasting impression on the young medic:

When I saluted and introduced myself, he croaked painfully, 'Not another bloody Scottish MO'. I was then ordered in colourful language to do something so-and-so quick to get him out of his such-and-such bed and get my so-and-so posterior along to Doon House to meet the such-and-such pilots. I didn't know that squadron leaders were as profane as that!

On the 8th, the squadron moved to Fairwood Common outside Swansea in South Wales for a month of gunnery practice. It was routine to send squadrons on these courses so that every unit got its fair share of firing at ground targets and air-to-air firing at drogues. As Pinky Stark, one of the squadron's top scorers modestly put it, 'It helped to maintain reasonable standards and gave the new boys something to shoot at'.

They were housed at Kilvrough House, 2 miles from the airfield, where conditions were somewhat spartan. One of the squadron's promising young stalwarts, F/O Shelton, incurred Johnny's legendary 'rain of terror' by taking a hot bath one evening which meant no hot water left for others to even shave. Berating the culprit, Johnny ordered the batman to fill the bath with ice water at 0730hrs the next morning and call them both. He then took great pleasure in watching Shelton immerse himself and slowly turn blue. A sure case of 'the punishment fitting the crime'.

This period was an important time for Johnny and his pilots in getting to know one another better and letting off steam before returning to the fray. The inevitable horseplay which resulted was not entirely frivolous high jinks but rather an essential means of retaining some sense of normality in a world seemingly gone mad and helped them face the deadly demands of daily combat flying.

Several of their haunts around Swansea, like the Langland Bay Hotel, paid gracious host to Johnny and his merry men that month and, doubtless, some still bear the scars with something akin to pride. One evening, sick of trying to get near the fire in the officers' mess due to the customary throng of ATS and naval types, someone secreted a couple of Coffman starter cartridges in the grate which duly exploded, dispelling both fire and throng in that order and sending glowing embers into the farther reaches of the room. A subsequent investigation into the incident by an indignant mess secretary got nowhere.

With over 216 hours flying completed at Fairwood in just ten days, and pilots finally starting to hit the drogue, a succession of aircraft needed to be flown back to Manston for inspection and repair. They returned there on the 20th to receive the news that they were to become Bombphoons and part of No 123 Airfield in No 84 Group, 2nd Tactical Air Force (2 TAF).

'Airfield' was a somewhat misleading designation adopted for the highly mobile units in 2 TAF later superseded by the more appropriate term 'Wing'. It was all part of the advance planning and reorganisation taking place in readiness for the expected forthcoming invasion of Europe. But it meant that 609, leaving No 11 Group ADGB, ceased to be a fighter squadron and, as many pilots viewed it, was relegated to the bomber role. Making matters worse, most of the ground crews were replaced by new personnel, even the IO, F/L Ziegler, being posted away after three years with the squadron. Johnny had his work cut out keeping up morale.

Some pilots, however, were simply irrepressible. On return from another Ramrod on 25 February, a Typhoon broke formation and dived through cloud off Ramsgate to hurtle over the coast at nought feet, taunting the AA guns and prompting swift rebuke from Johnny: 'Red 3, you're a clot.' F/L Ross, flying Red 3 and still in formation, replied somewhat frostily, 'Would you repeat that please?' After a brief pause, Johnny's voice came again, 'Red 4, you're the clot.' The real culprit, Manu Geerts, remained tactfully silent.

Four days later, Nos 3, 198 and 609 Squadrons took off on a series of fighter sweeps supporting another Ramrod mission. They attacked a variety of targets, including barges west of Namur, before engaging two Ju188s flying at 1,000ft west of Cambrai. Not surprisingly, both bombers were shot down with their engines on fire, shared amongst Johnny and six other pilots. F/O Shelton failed to return, victim of flak during an attack on barges south of Douai.

On 16 March, No 123 Airfield moved to Tangmere for intensive dive-bombing practice under G/C Denys Gillam, formerly Johnny's wingco (flying) at Duxford. After a week they moved on to Acklington in Northumberland to hone their newly acquired dive-bombing skills. It was while there that their future role was finally decided. With mixed emotions they learned that they had escaped being designated a Bombphoon squadron – deep joy! Future operations would be as R/P fighters – universal consternation! They now faced returning to the fray with largely untried and (to them) unproved weapons.

On 1 April they moved back down south to Thorney Island, living under canvas to prepare for the conditions they would face operating from temporary airstrips on the other side of the Channel. On arrival, Johnny took great relish in announcing that, in spite of the appalling rain and fog, they could also look forward to three weeks of intensive practice flying with rockets, each pilot to complete twenty hours. Nor was that all, he continued with a ghost of a smile, he had also decided that there would be some night flying. All of which was, of course, received with what the squadron diary records as 'more enthusiasm than ever before'. Johnny knew full well that one sure way to avoid discontent among pilots was to keep them flying.

Flying in sections of two or four they practised 30- and 60-degree dives on ground targets day after day until after three weeks they were starting to feel quite proficient. On the 21st, General Eisenhower, the Supreme Commander of SHAEF, visited Thorney Island and spent some time with the squadron. He sat in on one of Johnny's briefings for a rocket show scheduled later that afternoon, as MO George Bell recounts: 'J.C.'s language was ... colourful, and I am sure that listening to J.C. the General would have been impressed with the amount of fornication that went on among the enemy.' The operation was later postponed and subsequently cancelled.

The following day they moved camp to Llanbedr, where they spent the next week practising rocket-firing attacks on the ranges every day, still living under canvas. Individual scores were assessed and reported and each day continued to show consistent improvement. Some unforeseen snags were revealed, not every worry over the weapons being dispelled, but pilots were forced to conclude that rockets could be very accurate indeed. By the end of the month back at Thorney Island they were eager to try their new weapons on operations and felt ready for anything that 2TAF planned for them.

Within days they were making regular rocket attacks on targets in France: road bridges, railway sheds, marshalling yards, canal locks, shipping and barges. When operations were cancelled they unloaded their rockets on targets set up in Studland Bay or practised low-level strafing runs on the railway line between Godalming and Haslemere. The pace was definitely quickening and everyone confidently expected an imminent launch of the long-awaited invasion.

On 10 May 1944, Johnny led the squadron on Ramrod 861, to attack railway lines and a bridge between Yvetot and Buchy in company with No 198 Squadron. Crossing the French coast near Dieppe at 8,000ft they went into a 30-degree dive towards the target, which was clearly something the enemy wanted left alone. They were met by intense flak which broke up the formation, damaging several aircraft. Leading the formation, W/C Brooker took a hit in the petrol tank which mercifully did not explode or catch fire. Johnny also came close to disaster when his brand new PR★Z was lifted vertically about 40ft when a shell exploded directly beneath it, miraculously without damage. Flying Officer 'Spud' Holmes got back with a neat hole drilled straight through the middle of his port wing roundel. A portent of things to come?

The following day, as part of a wing attack late afternoon, twelve aircraft took off for the German radar installation at Etretat, situated near Fecamp on the Cap d'Antifer, reconnoitred by W/C Brooker and Johnny the previous day. It was their first foray against one of these tricky targets, attacks that continued right up to D-Day in an effort to blind the enemy defences.

'Beauty Leader going in now.' Johnny led them down. They were last in to the attack, and the German guns had their range almost as soon as they started diving. Bracketed by fire and buffeted by explosions, Johnny had never experienced such accurate heavy flak. It was awesome. Perversely he found himself wondering if the flak bursts acted like cloud cover and offered them any sort of protection. Off to one side a direct hit blew a substantial chunk off F/L Wood's port wing. Woody's Typhoon steepened its dive and Johnny watched as it burst into flames, crashed to the ground and exploded. It was all over in a minute and there was no parachute.

Attack over, they reformed and set course for home. F/O 'Junior' Soesman, also hit, was forced to bail out about 15 miles off the French coast. They watched him drop into the water but, for whatever reason, he failed to inflate his dinghy – possibly he was wounded. Johnny and F/O Jimmy Stewart DFC orbited the position until lack of fuel forced them both to return, by which time an air-sea rescue Walrus and a section of Spitfires were on their way. But no trace of Soesman was found despite searches of the area throughout that evening and at first light the following morning. All in all, it was decided later, a 'ropey do'. Two days later, two more aircraft failed to return from an attack on a transport column escorted by tanks spotted heading west towards Boos. F/O Stewart baild out, hit by light flak near Fleury, and F/Sgt Fidgin went missing. Johnny, having problems with his radio and engine, did not find the target so brought his rockets back.

Weather permitting, sorties were flown every day to disrupt enemy communications: roads, railways and canals. German radar sites along the French coast also received close attention but, although 609 had no knowledge of the fact at the time, they were making two attacks outside the planned invasion area for every attack inside it. For them it was simply a succession of targets, usually defended by murderous light flak, with mounting damage to aircraft and casualties to pilots.

Johnny flew as often as his other duties allowed. He preferred to be in the air with his squadron than tied to a desk. On 23 May, he led two Belgians, F/L Cooreman and Manu Geerts, with the Argentinian, P/O Pagnam, on a Ramrod but found the primary target covered by cloud. Hugging the French coast, they found a likely looking alternative, a rectangular concrete tower surrounded by scaffolding near Caen/Douvres. Attacking with their rockets, they were delighted to note the occupants haring away from the target for dear life and they squirted them on their way with 20mm cannon fire.

Johnny, going in suicidally low, was almost blown to kingdom come when he flew directly over the explosion of a salvo of rockets fired by Cooreman. Not to be outdone, Manu Geerts came back with a radiator scoop full of concrete debris. But they all returned safe and in good time for lunch, after which Johnny went off to test a new type of 35lb incendiary rocket, four of which he fired into a creek just behind the flight hut with Spud Holmes following him down taking cine-gun shots. It was all in a day's work.

The following day they were back over France for an attack on a petrol dump cunningly disguised as houses just south of Amiens. Johnny, first into the attack, dived from 2,000ft and scored a direct hit on a large fuel tank which exploded sending debris, flame and smoke up 10,000ft. There was no flak to speak of, making a pleasant change, and weather conditions were perfect. Everyone agreed it was a 'wizard prang' but G/C Gillam, who had been flying with another squadron, topped this with the comment that in his opinion it had been 'honey pie'.

Whitsunday, very hot and hazy, Johnny collected more flak in his starboard tail plane during an attack on a German army HQ at Liebsiez during which Manu Geerts was also hit and lucky to get back. P/O Watelet failed to return, which depressed everyone, until he turned up later having landed at Friston short of fuel. Later that afternoon two more Typhoons were badly damaged in an attack on a German radar site near Boulogne. Things were warming up on the far side of the Channel. It was warm enough for most pilots to fly in shirt-sleeves – 2TAF fast becoming known as the Turkish Bath Force. That evening, released from operations, a bathing party adjourned to the nearby creek.

On the 30th Johnny led the squadron on a morning show to attack rail targets near Formerie and marshalling yards south of Abancourt. Leaving the target area they met intense and concentrated AA fire. F/O Thorogood was hit and his aircraft streamed coolant. Gaining height he attempted to reach the coast but was forced to bail out 15 miles north-west of Formerie, his Typhoon crashing into a wood. Andre Blanco was also hit and came back with his fuselage looking like the proverbial sieve. Inspecting the damage, the veteran Belgian, who had joined the squadron as a sergeant pilot way back in January 1942, merely remarked, 'If I had known it was that bad I would have had an "accident"!' Time after time Blanco would return with his aircraft shredded by flak but seemingly unaffected by the experience. The MO put this remarkable display of sangfroid down to the vast quantities of caffeine the Belgian consumed daily. He was rarely to be seen without a mug of tea in one hand and a cigarette in the other.

So May 1944 came to a close. During a very hectic month, the squadron had flown over 250 operational sorties (Johnny himself logging twenty-two) attacking enemy radar installations, rail, road and canal networks. The new R/P weapons had been thoroughly put to the test and not found wanting. But it had cost them five pilots – two of whom they learnt later survived in captivity.

In the week preceding D-Day, the softening up of the enemy coastal defences was pursued with vigour. As the official history of the RAF relates:

> assaults were delivered for the most part by the Typhoon and Spitfire squad-rons of Nos. 83 and 84 Groups. The targets were very heavily defended by light flak and to attack them 'demanded great skill and daring'. The losses in aircraft and pilots was very heavy. Of the many assaults made, Leigh-Mallory in his despatch selected three as worthy of special mention. There was that of 2nd June carried out by eighteen rocket-firing Typhoons of Nos. 198 and 609 Squadrons on the Dieppe/Caudecote station …

This particular attack involved 609's 'A' Flight, led by F/L Davies, who was lucky to get back with severe flak damage; Johnny led a similar attack on another radar installation at Cap Gris Nez later in the day. But during these attacks on the 2nd, No 198 Squadron lost their CO, S/L 'Nibby' Niblett, who was replaced by Davies a few days later.

At 1900hrs on 5 June 1944, Johnny took off with seven aircraft to attack Field Marshal Rommel's HQ which Intelligence had located in a chateau at Livetau on the Cherbourg peninsula. The Typhoons obliterated the target leaving it wreathed in smoke, but assessing the actual results of such attacks was always going to be difficult. However, according to subsequent Swiss radio reports, they only just missed the 'Desert Fox' who had left the chateau minutes before they arrived. Returning back across the Channel in the gathering gloom Johnny and his pilots witnessed an unforgettable sight, unique in history. Below them the invasion armada headed for Normandy – it was on at last! Maintaining strict radio silence, as ordered, the pilots exchanged excited thumbs-up and waves.

Later that evening, all pilots were assembled for a briefing and told of the launch of the long-awaited second front: Operation Overlord was under way. The general air of excitement and expectancy generated by the news that Allied paratroops were landing in France was tangible. Everyone was suddenly aware that they were party to momentous events and history was in the making. It was quite a sobering thought – particularly as, from now on, the entire squadron had to be at readiness every day before dawn.

D-Day itself seemed to pass very much like any other during the preceding weeks, with little interference from Luftwaffe fighters. The first squadron show on the great day itself didn't materialise until early afternoon when four aircraft went off to attack a German radar site outside Le Havre. Johnny led the next sortie which went off at 1710hrs to attack stationary enemy transport spotted on the road east of Lisieux. They all returned safely, claiming two tanks destroyed (the first of many to be claimed by the squadron) and two more damaged along with other mechanised vehicles. But on a similar show later that evening they lost an Australian pilot, W/O George Martin, who was hit by flak and bailed out south-west of Caen but successfully evaded capture; F/O Gibson returned with flak damage.

On D-Day +1 No 609 Squadron flew armed reconnaissance shooting up road and rail traffic. One of the eighteen squadrons of Typhoons from Nos 83 and 84 Groups involved, reinforced by Mustangs released by No 11 Group ADGB, they ranged across northern France beyond the beachhead area seeking targets. If no locomotives or vehicles were found then bridges were attacked, anything that would slow down movement of German forces. Weather conditions were atrocious, 10/10 cloud down to 1,500ft forcing them to fly dangerously low in search of targets. By the end of the day, the Typhoon and Mustang squadrons had lost seventeen aircraft to flak, many more returning to base with severe damage and/or wounded pilots.

On the credit side, their attacks had proved decisive. Near Falaise, five columns of the Panzer Lehr Division moving forward from Alencon were subjected to regular air attacks throughout the morning and by noon the attacks became incessant. By dusk they had lost a total of ninety vehicles containing stores and ammunition, forty lorries full of fuel and eighty-four half-tracks including some 88mm guns. The German commander, Generalleutnant Fritz Bayerlein, with the havoc and carnage on the road between Vire and Le Beny Bocage still fresh in his memory, described it as the '*Jabo Rennstrecke*' or 'fighter-bomber race track'.

Johnny in the thick of it, as usual, led nine Typhoons on an armed recce south of the beachhead. They had long-range tanks fitted to extend the time they could spend over the battle area and deposited their rockets in a stationary troop train found near Le Breuil. Another late afternoon operation on the 8th brought even better results, with three more enemy tanks destroyed, one damaged and cannon strikes on several others. Eric Roberts, now commanding 'A' Flight, having missed a tank with his rockets, was impressed by the effect of his cannon on such a heavily armoured target: 'Boy, did it go up! It just belched flame and black smoke – completely burnt out.'

Flying Officer Inches also returned from this attack with good cause to be impressed – with the sturdiness of his aircraft. Attacking a line of tanks on the road north of Aunay he flew along the road at what he reported was 'something like' 200ft and was breaking away when he hit something, probably a tree, which threw his aircraft into some telegraph wires. Collecting these around both wings, where they coiled round his remaining rockets, he struggled back to base trailing yards of French telephone wire and with several chunks of road paving lodged in his radiator scoop. He thought it a fair exchange for the wingtip he left behind.

Every day, weather permitting, they flew in support of the landings; pressing home attacks on enemy tanks, transport and communications or strong points identified by the army. Then, early in the afternoon of 14 June, the squadron took off from Thorney Island and on completion of its sortie landed on Emergency Landing Strip B2 Bazenville in France.

Emergency landing strips (ELS) had been established in the beachhead area, at Asnelles, Pouppeville and Saint-Croix-sur-Mer, within days of the landings. Using experience gained by the Desert Air Force during the North African campaign, specially trained Airfield Construction Groups of Royal Engineers, after detailed inspection of likely sites identified months earlier from aerial photographs, could clear and level a site and lay down a 3,600ft-long emergency runway in under twelve hours. These airstrips used perforated steel plate or, more generally, Sommerfeld track, a square-mesh steel wire mat laid upon impregnated canvas designed to cut down dust and prevent waterlogging. Each strip of high-tensile steel measured over 70ft long and 7ft wide and came in a roll weighing about 5cwt. They were literally pinned to the ground with screw pickets every 6ft around the entire perimeter, joints being clipped or welded together in situ. Designed to be moveable, they could be recovered and transported elsewhere if required. But, in practice, once laid they were rarely ever taken up.

Dust was a serious problem in the beachhead area. It was thick and brown and infiltrated everywhere, clogging fuel lines and choking engines. The mechanics did what they could, and many aircraft were hurriedly fitted with air filters designed for use in North Africa. The canvas underlay was supposed to reduce the dust, but runways still needed spraying with water nightly to keep the problem under control.

Refuelling and rearming facilities came with the RAF servicing commandos, often operating under extremely hazardous conditions close to the front line within range of enemy shellfire. Local defence was provided by soldiers of the RAF Regiment, who cleared the immediate area of any landmines or snipers, and manned 40mm Bofors light AA guns surrounding airstrips. Certain strips, once established, had routine maintenance facilities added to create an Advanced Landing Ground with proper taxiways to secure dispersal points complete with blast pens. This whole complex organisation was kept supplied with fuel, munitions, vehicles and stores by dedicated RAF beach squadrons in the beachhead area so, by noon on 10 June 1944, the first squadrons to land in France began operating from ELS around Bayeux.

Wing Commander Brooker led the wing across with Johnny leading 609. Approaching the tiny airstrip, Johnny wondered what the surface was like when the wingco's Typhoon, landing immediately ahead of him, vanished in a thick cloud of dust. He needn't have worried for the landing run turned out to be far less than he expected – if anything, only slightly longer than landing on a pukka grass runway. Safely down, he was directed to the dispersal area by heavily armed and warlike ground staff and jumped down on to French soil. It was four years, almost to the day, since the squadron had last landed in France when four of its Spitfires had escorted Winston Churchill on his final mission to the French government prior to the collapse.

Targets were clearly plentiful and easy to find, though some were a mite too close to the airstrip for comfort but made for some very quick sorties. Johnny heard that over at Camilly, Typhoons had attacked enemy armour barely 1,000yd from their own runway. They spent the rest of that day in Normandy amid the dust, the sand, the constant noise of heavy guns, occasionally leaping into slit trenches whenever a shell screamed close overhead. Later they would become so used to it that they would be able to differentiate between enemy gunfire and their own. They returned to Thorney Island later that night having flown two operations from Bazenville against crossroads, enemy strong points and heavily defended rail targets at Bencaville–Campagne, where the intense flak that greeted them even shook a few of the more experienced pilots.

On 18 June No 123 Airfield moved to Funtingdon, where they continued to live under canvas, partly to keep them accustomed to the nomadic conditions they would soon be experiencing in France, but mainly because every airfield in southern England was now packed with aircraft either operating in support of the landings or waiting to cross to France. There were simply too many units for the permanent bases to accommodate. In the meantime, weather conditions remained poor which considerably reduced the overall effort.

Some pilots had taken to wearing khaki battledress in favour of air-force blue. It made them less distinguishable as pilots when operating from airstrips which were often within range of enemy snipers. They also argued that in the most unlikely event of being shot down and captured they could ditch their flying badges and pass themselves off as 'brown jobs'. Apparently Jerry was none too fond of the RAF, and Typhoon pilots, in particular, could expect short shrift if they ever fell into enemy hands. Despite these ugly rumours, not everyone adopted khaki, many preferring to remain faithful to air-force blue, Johnny being one of them, but some interesting combinations were paraded and the squadron began to take on a motley and villainous appearance, particularly as side arms had been worn for the past month.

Within a matter of days they were off again, this time concentrating at Hurn pending an imminent move to France. If nothing else, these moves were good practice for what was to come once they crossed the Channel for good, and everyone felt increasingly confident that life 'on the road' was not going to impair efficiency. But on their first joint operation from Hurn, No 198 Squadron lost Dave Davies, clobbered by flak during a close-support mission for American troops attacking Cherbourg. Previously a flight commander in 609, he had been 198's CO for exactly eighteen days.

Next day was enlivened by the long-overdue appearance of the Luftwaffe when some Messerschmitt 109Fs were encountered during an attack on enemy transport in the Lisieux area. Climbing to join what he took to be his section, Spud Holmes, suddenly realising they were 109s, let out a bleat on the radio that no one could understand. He jettisoned his rockets and tanks, forgetting to switch over to his main tank in the excitement, but managed to get into position to attack one of them before running out of ammo. During the brief but furious engagement which followed, the Typhoons claimed one Me109F destroyed and one probable, with four more damaged. Had they known it, this 109F, falling to F/L Eric Roberts, was the squadron's 232nd and last air-to-air victory of the war. One Canadian pilot, Buchanan, was lucky to escape serious injury when enemy cannon fire demolished his cockpit hood, splinters wounding him in the arm.

Then suddenly, on 24 June, Johnny was posted from them, handing over to S/L Manu Geerts DFC; yet another home-grown promotion and the squadron's first Belgian CO. Johnny was naturally reluctant to leave this, his first command, at such a critical time, but he had been leading them for the past six months and it was made clear that it was the right and necessary thing to do. There was a long way still to go, but officers with his experience would be needed to fill more senior operational roles as the war in Europe drew towards an inevitable climax. There also had to be scope to develop the next generation of flight and squadron leaders who could rise through the system, gaining their own experience of command.

So bidding a sad farewell to his pilots, not forgetting G/C William de Goat who Johnny had always saluted before every mission, for to do otherwise was 'tempting fate and sheer stupid bravado', Johnny was on his way. No 609 Squadron Operations Record Book for 24 June 1944 records: 'To-day comes news that the C/O is posted to Middle Wallop for Ops B work and so the squadron has lost a most experienced pilot and a good leader. Our good wishes go with him and the hopes that he will find us some good targets.'

13

STAFF WALLAH

Flak is where the enemy is.

No 84 Group ORB, August 1944

It was abundantly clear that after the invasion RAF aircraft operating from airfields in France would need their own independent control system. The Fighter Command system, designed for the defence of Great Britain, was organised into groups and sectors spread across the UK. As such, it was too centralised and would soon get overstretched and eventually redundant once the aircraft of 2TAF were based in Northern Europe. This apart, fighter-bombers flying in close support of ground troops needed a mobile control system to move forward as the frontline advanced.

Valuable lessons and good experience of this type of aircraft control, developed by the Desert Air Force earlier in the war, formed the basis of a separate operational control system initiated within 2TAF. A series of high-level meetings between senior officers of Nos 11 and 84 Groups recognised that a smooth change over from the existing sector control to the new system would need careful handling. So it was agreed that a small team should be set up within No 84 Group charged with the responsibility for implementing the necessary changes and managing the transition. Labelled No 84 Group Control Centre, it formed at Goodwood Park on 23 June 1944 to provide the necessary link between the operational wings forming No 84 Group and Group HQ. The team was commanded by G/C Gerry Edge DFC, when Johnny joined them two days later as one of two air liaison officers on the staff.

Johnny hadn't fully appreciated just how tired he was, but after a few fretful days adjusting to a non-operational regime he unwound and threw himself into his new duties with his usual drive and enthusiasm. He even got some flying in, ferrying himself around various out stations in the unit Auster. Understandably, he was a little apprehensive at his new appointment having no previous experience of staff work; also the prospect of rubbing shoulders with some of the staff types he had encountered over the years filled him with something akin to horror. But Johnny figured that he could rely on his intelligence and experience to see him through.

Much to his surprise he actually found himself enjoying some of the work – it appealed to his thorough and methodical nature. Never a pedant, Johnny simply approached each task with the aim of achieving the best possible result in the most practical and logical way. It was partly due to his engineering training, but he had always been precise in everything that he did, even as a lad. He took care in whatever he did. No detail escaped him, however small, and he derived great personal pride and satisfaction in a job well done.

The unit, based at Middle Wallop, continued to act in close conjunction with the Sector HQ but assumed immediate control of fighter-bomber operations within No 84 Group until Group Control could be established in France. Quite apart from the complex logistics involved, their duties included establishing a network of mobile radar beacons as navigational aids for aircraft operating deep in northern France. Selecting appropriate sites in France for these medium-range 'Eureka' beacons would be critical, for not only did they need to provide radar coverage beyond the immediate area of the beachhead, but they must also be sited to exploit any territory gained to maximise their effective range.

Communications between ground and air were fully co-ordinated, instructions being relayed to aircraft via Group Control Centres; 'Longbow' was the call-sign of 84 GCC and 'Kenway' that of 83 GCC. Mobile Forward Control Posts also accompanied every advanced element of the ground forces.

Using VHF radio-telephone, these advanced units were able to call for immediate air support from an aerial 'cab-rank' system of standing patrols. Normal procedure was for at least one section of aircraft to be airborne and kept on standby for fifteen minutes after which, if no calls were forthcoming, they went off to attack pre-planned targets, their place being taken by other aircraft.

This technique, first devised by the Desert Air Force, had been further developed by the 1st Tactical Air Force in Italy. It was a tried and tested system honed to perfection by 2TAF in the weeks following D-Day. 'Limejuice', No 83 Group's Advance Control Centre, is remembered to this day, with deep gratitude, by the author's father, a tank commander in the Guards Armoured Division, who had an abiding respect for the German Tigers opposing him. Army liaison officers attached to squadrons assisted at target briefings. They had all the latest 'gen' on what was happening on the ground which was crucial when aircraft were being called to provide close support against enemy targets often within 1,000yd of their own troops.

Amongst the mass of papers Johnny had been given as 'useful background to what goes on', was a lengthy report on a comparison of the effect of rockets and bombs when used against enemy tanks and transport. Naturally enough, this was of great interest as he had been delivering both for some time past. Compiled from an examination of results achieved in the three weeks immediately following the invasion, the assessment showed that rockets were far more effective than bombs when used against heavy armour but of considerably less value when used against thin-skinned vehicles. Overall, it seemed that bombs were achieving far better results – planning officers please note.

The report went on to summarise casualties to Typhoon aircraft during the same period. In terms of sorties per casualty, and damage inflicted per casualty, there was little significant difference between casualties to aircraft employing bombs or rockets. But most significantly, No 84 Group was suffering almost four times the casualties of No 83 Group and particularly in rocket attacks. The comparison was 40 opposed to 145 sorties per casualty. Johnny put this down to the fact that No 84 Group aircraft were obviously going in much closer to guarantee hits on target – their strike rate per sortie indicated that. But he also noted the suggestion that by penetrating deeper into enemy territory No 84 Group aircraft automatically accepted a greater risk of being shot down or damaged by flak. Somehow he doubted it. In his experience pilots didn't enjoy the luxury of making such clinical distinctions. On the whole they were a fairly fatalistic bunch. He read on.

Load for load, rockets were clearly shown to be inferior to bombs except when used against armour. And a combination of bombs and guns was achieving twice the results of attacks with rockets and guns. Now this was definitely useful knowledge and Johnny made sure that the information was incorporated in the weapons scheduling for future attacks. It was part and parcel of his work to see that the results of such analyses were distributed to the wings, where they would be used for selecting different war loads for specific targets.

Tables and graphs were produced showing the comparative results gained by bombs, rockets and/or guns used against enemy armour and mechanised transport. Johnny also took the opportunity to reinforce messages about minimum safe heights for bomb release (700ft for 250lb and up to 2,000ft for 1,000lb bomb with instantaneous fuse) and the lethal radius of damage from fragments or debris when firing rockets (250yd and 300yd respectively). Pretty coloured tables and graphs were produced for the sole purpose of increasing damage and destruction inflicted per sortie and reducing casualty rates. There were plenty of raw, relatively inexperienced, replacement pilots arriving in the squadrons just now, and he knew only too well how easy it was to press home an attack and leave the pull-out too late.

Chillingly, the report concluded that No 84 Group's use of rockets was only superior if the objective was to inflict damage to the enemy as quickly as possible. But this was at the expense of aircraft and trained pilots. This was certainly something he would need to keep an eye on. Losing trained pilots was bad enough, but the loss of too many experienced section leaders and flight commanders at this stage could create serious problems downstream. Meantime, there was still a bloody war to fight, so Johnny figured that the whole sad, sordid business would have to carry on as usual.

On 12 July 1944, five weeks after the Normandy invasion, and with Allied ground forces pushing deeper into France, the decision was finally taken to switch operational control of 2 TAF aircraft to the Continent and sector control was superseded. Within a week, after a couple of attempts which had to be abandoned, Johnny was amongst those forming an advanced element boarding an Anson and crossing the Channel on the 20th to put down at B14 Amblie, where No 84 Group HQ was to be based.

Three days later, after completing preparations and making a brief visit to B7 Martragny near Bayeux, and No 123 Wing, commanded by New Zealander G/C D.J. Scott DSO OBE DFC, he borrowed the wingco's personalised Typhoon DJ*S and flew back to Westhampnett. The rest of No 484 GCC crossed to France the next day and started deploying their radar network, operations being controlled by their counterparts at No 483 GCC in the interim.

Within three weeks a fully functioning control centre would be established in France and all minor installation problems resolved. After all the preparation and planning it was something of an anti-climax, but with the work of No 484 GCC done the unit was officially disbanded and on 18 August 1944 Johnny transferred on to the staff of No 84 Group HQ at Amblie as substantive wing commander (plans). But his brief visit to Martragny had made him realise just how much he missed operational flying and the camaraderie of squadron life.

By mid-August 1944, the skies over northern France belonged to the Allied air forces and the threat of any serious interference by the Luftwaffe was becoming remote. German air force activity was reduced to such an extent that No 84 Group issued orders that aircraft could dispense with camouflage nets when grounded day or night.

After the carnage at Falaise, when retreating German forces had been caught in a pinch-point and subjected to almost continuous air attack, the deadly efficacy of the fighter-bomber was never again in dispute. Johnny had viewed the camera-gun films from attacking aircraft and poured over photographs depicting in graphic detail the aftermath on the ground. What a ghastly yet inspiring business it was. He certainly didn't envy the target assessment people their task. Poking around inside a burned-out Tiger tank to establish the destructive capability of a 60lb armour-piercing projectile and its effect on the occupants couldn't be enjoyable. But he realised that it was necessary, for the business of war had become a cruel science.

He spent the next three weeks familiarising himself with the work of Group HQ and putting his face around the various sections. There were seven operational wings in No 84 Group, comprising a total of twenty-six squadrons, so there was always plenty going on at headquarters. Their main priorities were to organise attacks on ground targets in response to army requests, to plan and issue operational orders to the wings, to record scores and casualties, to identify and reconnoitre fresh airstrips, and to keep moving forward. The rapid pace of advance saw Group HQ move to Franqueville-Brionne on 1 September only to up sticks for Cremont three days later, and thence to Pihem by the 9th. These were hectic times and Johnny got used to living out of a kitbag.

As a staff planning officer, he was immersed in the detailed planning of operations in support of the 1st Canadian Army for which No 84 Group provided air defence. He tackled the full range of ground support operations, from winkling out concentrations of enemy armour to attacks on observation posts or gun emplacements. He learnt a lot, understanding how concentrations of mobile flak were often a useful pointer to enemy intentions, and was involved in planning more complex operations, some of strategic importance. Each was approached with the same ruthless efficiency – innocuous codenames masking their deadly purpose. Johnny was engaged in the detailed planning of Operation Vitality and Operation Switchback, aimed at clearing up pockets of resistance on the south bank of the Schelde. Another undertaking, long in preparation, was Operation Longbow, the air-to-ground attacks in support of Operation Infatuate, which was an assault on the island of Walcheren by Canadian Second Corps. Successively postponed due to bad weather, it remained part of Johnny's brief for practically the entire time he was at Group HQ.

Shortly before his eventual return to operations, Johnny did the preliminary planning for Hurricane I. This massive operation, jointly planned by the RAF and USAAF, was to mount a maximum daylight assault against targets across the northern Ruhr. It would signal the destructive potential of the combined Allied air forces and demonstrate their overwhelming supremacy over a rapidly dwindling Luftwaffe.

Hectic as it all was, Johnny could not be content with merely planning, and on 28 September he wangled himself a couple of sorties with his chums in No 609 Squadron – then operating from Merville as part of No 123 Wing, having squared things with the CO, G/C Scott, during his visit to them the previous month. At Calais that afternoon they attacked gun emplacements, an observation post in a church and totally obliterated a strong point; all part of their contribution to Operation Undergo – an assault on German defence of the port. Johnny had been closely involved with the planning for this and was keen to see it through to the bitter end. Reporting back to Group HQ at Laethem St Martin next morning, he was gratified to learn that, following their attacks, the Calais garrison had finally capitulated; 84 officers and close to 4,000 men were captured.

During a second operation later the same day, an armed reconnaissance mission, they attacked gun positions and destroyed another strong point near Antwerp, before spotting a dozen or so barges on the River Waal, south of Zaltbommel. Johnny made one rocket attack before returning for three more runs at the target using cannon. His gunfire, raking the barges, whipped the surrounding water into foam, exploding shells winking back at him through all the smoke. In the absence of any secondary explosions or gouts of flame, he had to content himself with claiming three barges damaged, but for a few exciting minutes he was back in his element.

Beyond such excursions, Johnny spent two months in a blur of planning – successive operations following one after another as the Allied armies rolled across Northern Europe, their air support ranging far and wide. No sooner had he attended liaison meetings with army commanders and agreed priorities that it seemed targets were scheduled and attack orders issued to the wings before the whole process was being repeated. He was part of a well-balanced mechanism, an intricate machine designed to respond with devastating suddenness in support of an army hell bent on final victory.

Everybody knew their role and performed their duties with diligence, speed and purpose. His alert and agile mind was being exercised to the full and along with his logical approach to problems, coupled with his operational experience, he found the work satisfying and stimulating. It gave him a fascinating insight into the background to the familiar operational orders he had been used to receiving at squadron level. It also afforded him a glimpse of a much bigger picture from which came a growing belief in the absolute certainty of ultimate Allied victory.

It was during this time at Group HQ that Johnny took the opportunity to air his views on the tactical role of the Typhoon. These views, shared with others, were developed from his observations over the preceding months and supported with instances based upon current operational experience gained mainly at first hand. In typical fashion, his opinions were well thought through, his arguments solid and he could wax passionate on the subject often in fairly colourful language.

Johnny had long felt that the Typhoon was too often employed as the principal means of destroying German tactical weapon resistance: hull-down tanks, mortars, 88mm guns, observation posts, even snipers. The precision and power of the rocket Typhoon were fast becoming the first, and only, method of dealing with such targets and in his view, 2 TAF were making it too easy, too convenient, to use them that way. To his mind this was fundamentally wrong, and there was a growing danger that we could end up using the aircraft for the wrong purpose and blunting our own weapon.

The practice seemed to have originated during the fighting around Caen when close support by Typhoons undoubtedly proved of great assistance. But the Typhoon's primary function, he argued, must surely be to create disorganisation, destruction and demoralisation of the enemy in a campaign of rapid movement. Used to maximum effect against tanks, vehicles and enemy concentrations moving in the open, it could often prove decisive.

On 14 October, Johnny joined old friends in No 609 Squadron at their weekly supper in Merville; an enjoyable if noisy occasion. The business of the evening was to discuss a proposal that the squadron present to the town of Brussels an RAF uniform to adorn the renowned Manikin Pis in the city centre. After much sober discussion it was agreed that the statue should be dressed as a pilot officer with DFC and Belgian Croix de Guerre and the adjutant detailed to make the necessary approaches. What ultimately came of the idea went unrecorded.

After five months as a staff officer, Johnny was itching to get back on operations before the war reached its inevitable conclusion and the shooting stopped. He started making a real nuisance of himself around Group HQ, dropping less than subtle hints with senior officers, but when it came, the opportunity was totally unexpected.

On 26 October 1944, Johnny represented No 84 GCC at a conference on tactics held at Group HQ at Nachtegaelshoek in Antwerp. The meeting was chaired by G/C F.E. Rosier DSO OBE, in charge of operations, with the usual crowd including some familiar faces representing wings. Johnny grabbed a few words with S/L Deacon Elliott DFC from tactics as they jostled around the coffee table before joining 'Sailor' Malan from No 145 Wing and Marian Chelmecki from No 131 (Polish) Wing for a quick chat on how things were at squadron level. Then they all got down to business.

A crowded agenda ranged from the wrinkling of Spitfire wings due to excessive speed in the dive, to close support tactics and the success of 'Winkle' – the use of continuous white smoke for target marking when operating in very close support of ground troops. Johnny picked up a number of action points during discussion on the selection of targets and alternates, and providing guidelines on bomb fusing for specific targets. But, try as he may, he found his attention slipping towards the end of the meeting during a desultory exchange on pilots' clothing and whether khaki or blue battledress should be made optional. He caught the group captain's eye at one stage and tried to appear more interested.

With the meeting finally adjourned, Johnny was collecting his papers together when Group Captain Rosier beckoned him over. 'How long have you been with us now, Wells?' he snapped.

'Coming up to two months now, sir,' Johnny replied, mind racing. 'And are you enjoying the work?' Freddy Rosier fired another question, like a pistol shot.

'Yes, sir …' Johnny drew breath to continue but was cut short.

'Good, good,' the group captain went on as if thinking aloud. 'It's not often we get chaps with your organisational flair. I'm told that you're a real asset,' he paused, sitting forward with his hands folded together on the table in front of him, fixing Johnny with a steady but friendly gaze.

'Christ!' thought Johnny. 'He's going to offer me a permanent staff post.' His brain went to maximum boost striving to find the right words to turn it down and to convince dear old Freddy that he would make just about the worst staff officer possible and that he should be sent packing back to a squadron immediately. He opened his mouth to speak not knowing exactly what words were going to emerge.

Again, Rosier beat him to the punch, 'But itching to get back on operations if I'm any judge.' The group captain leaned back in his chair smiling broadly.

'Oh yes, sir,' Johnny stammered, wits now completely addled. 'Yes indeed, sir.'

'Good,' Rosier beamed at him. 'Johnny Baldwin is due to be rested so No 146 Wing at Deurne will be needing a new Wing Commander Ops in a couple of weeks. I believe you know their CO, Denys Gillam?'

'Yes, sir,' Johnny almost squeaked, desperately trying to keep mounting excitement in check. 'He was my Wing Commander Flying back at Duxford in '42 in the first Typhoon Wing, and we've met on and off since.'

'Well that's settled then.' Rosier got to his feet and came around the table extending a hand. 'Good luck, Johnny. You should manage to get a few more trips in before it's all over. Keep the buggers on the run, and thanks for all you've done.'

Johnny could have hugged him. Resisting the temptation to give the group captain a hearty slap on the shoulder, Johnny voiced his thanks and departed on a wave of euphoria, his ruddy face suffused with that characteristic grin which lasted for days. Just fancy, Johnny Wells, wing commander (flying) of a Typhoon wing commanded by Kill 'em Gillam no less. He could hardly believe his luck; it would be quite like old times, or maybe not, remembering all their early difficulties. Talk about see the war out with a bang!

14

TYPHOON WING LEADER

If you see planes which are silver, they are American.
If you see planes which are dark, they are British.
If you see no planes at all, that is the Luftwaffe.

German Army XX Corps Report No 222, April 1945

On 16 November 1944 Johnny started his third tour of operations, this time as wing commander (flying) of No 146 Wing, the largest Typhoon wing in No 84 Group, based at B70 Antwerp/Deurne. They flew in support of the 1st (Canadian) Army, in Montgomery's 21st Army Group, covering the front west of the Rhine; their counterparts in No 83 Group operated over the area to the east. Two wings operated out of Deurne: No 145 with four squadrons of Spitfires and No 146 with five squadrons of Typhoons. Already fairly familiar with things, Johnny still did the rounds of operations, planning and personnel before leaving Group HQ to check out the latest details of his new command.

Two of his squadrons, Nos 193 and 197, formed late 1942 had been equipped with Typhoons from day one. No 193 had just got a new CO, S/L Derek Erasmus DFC, promoted from No 266 to take over from S/L Guy Plamonden, while No 197 Squadron was led by a New Zealander, S/L A.H. Smith DFC. There were also two long-standing units, No 257 (Burma) Squadron under S/L D.P. Jenkins and No 263 Squadron led by S/L R.D. Rutter DFC, as well as No 266 (Rhodesia) Squadron under S/L J.H. Deall – and another link with his past. The latter had been one of the three original squadrons forming the Duxford Typhoon Wing back in 1942, though Johnny knew it was doubtful if there were any pilots from those days left in the squadron now.

Johnny's new role lacked the camaraderie of having his own squadron, but providing leadership to five squadrons and acting closely with his squadron leaders and flight commanders would suit the solitary side of his temperament and he relished the task.

The wing had earned the reputation of being one of the best in 2TAF with a string of notable successes to its credit. Only the previous month, led by Kill 'em Gillam, they had obliterated the German 15th Army HQ at Merwestein Park, in the centre of Dordrecht, in a brilliantly executed set-piece attack. According to reports received from Dutch resistance, almost 100 Germans had been killed, mostly staff officers including two generals. Johnny recalled that the Dutch had reported on arrangements being made for the extravagant funeral parades which were to follow, which No 146 Wing naturally planned to attend in force, but rain and low cloud on the day had prevented the attack.

Antwerp/Deurne was a well-established pre-war base that had been extended by the Luftwaffe. On his arrival, Johnny learned that the only real drawback was the frequency that V1 flying bombs came over. One had recently impacted barely 150yd from No 197 Squadron dispersal area, fortunately without causing damage or casualties. It was rumoured that Flying Control had been flashing red lights at it in an effort to 'send it round again'.

Two days later Johnny was flying on operations. He aimed to join each of his squadrons in turn over the coming weeks and on the 18th led a subsection of No 257 Squadron on interdiction in the Arnhem-Utrecht area which had to be aborted due to bad weather. However, later in the day, he flew a close-support R/P mission to neutralise enemy guns in a wood near Arnhem, this time flying Johnny Baldwin's old aircraft. Meanwhile, other squadrons in the wing attacked three bridges south-east of Roermond in an effort to isolate the enemy in the Heinsberg area. One bridge was destroyed by No 197 but the other targets obstinately remained intact despite two attacks during which No 263 lost another flight commander to flak.

The following day Johnny led No 266 Squadron in a wing attack on the Gestapo HQ in the Christelijke Burger School just north of Euterpestraat in the centre of Amsterdam. But this was also aborted due to poor weather in the target area, and they diverted to attack a rail bridge at Zwolle. Over this secondary target, F/O Broad, a Canadian pilot with No 257 Squadron, was hit by light flak. His aircraft burst into flames, turned sharp right, and went straight in with all his bombs. The wing had already lost another pilot earlier in the day during an attack on a train near Gouda, but he was to turn up again three weeks later having evaded capture with the help of Dutch resistance workers.

Poor weather and flak accounted for most of their casualties; the Luftwaffe, now a spent force, was rarely seen. In the first week after Johnny joined the wing, four pilots were killed and two went missing, and no squadron was spared. Replacement pilots and aircraft were quick enough to arrive, but some losses, particularly among the more experienced pilots who had endured and already survived so much, were hard to bear. Close-support ground-attack missions seemed all the more relentless the closer to victory they seemed to get. It was a grim business.

It was another week before the aborted attack on the Gestapo HQ could be tried again, by which time No 197 Squadron had left for Fairwood Common, officially for two weeks of armament practice – of all things! So a temporarily depleted No 146 Wing took off for the attack with Johnny again leading No 266 Squadron as they converged on Amsterdam. This time the weather held fair and prompt at lunchtime, when it was hoped that most of the Gestapo personnel would be eating together, thirty-six Typhoons followed G/C Gillam down on to the target. They came in low, streets and rooftops flashing beneath them, the horizon tilting crazily first one way then the other as they corrected course and jinked towards the target. The packed jumble of grey buildings, squares and roads below suddenly started to look strangely familiar and then, directly ahead, the unmistakable contours of the target appeared.

Gillam's marker rockets flared off their tracks and rippled away to impact on the buildings ahead but overshot slightly. Johnny, following directly behind with No 266 Squadron, corrected his aim and was pleased to count eight direct hits among the sixty four rockets they fired. Meantime, through the dust, smoke and industrial haze which blanketed the city, he could just make out the Tiffies of No 193, like so many midges, dodging the cranes and derricks to attack the flak ships in the harbour. While somewhere further west he knew No 263 were dive-bombing flak positions at Schiphol.

It had been a thoroughly well-planned attack with detailed briefings, employing target maps, photos and models, conducted over preceding days. And it paid off, for they suffered no casualties. The northern end of the target was completely destroyed and the southern end severely damaged; it was burning furiously when they left. Photo-recce later showed direct hits slap-bang in the middle of the building, while a smaller building on the eastern side, thought to contain Gestapo files, was untouched. Dutch resistance sources later reported that casualties amongst Gestapo personnel had been regrettably low.

Three days later, no doubt by way of an encore, this was followed by an attack on the Gestapo HQ in Rotterdam. Again flying with No 266 Squadron, Johnny led. He was first in to bat, going in to mark the target followed by his wingman, F/O Dodd. They put sixteen phosphorous rockets straight through the roof of the building and were closely followed by No 193 Squadron who came in low, dropping 1,000lb bombs while the other three squadrons kept the flak gunners' heads down. No 84 Group Intelligence Summary:

> No.146 Wing, who are expert in these affairs, once more carried out a difficult job with no casualties ... altogether an excellent outing. The Wing

again hit the highlights with a spectacular attack on the Gestapo HQ at Rotterdam. Four squadrons led by G/C Gillam and W/C Wells took part. The attack was brilliantly led.

Ever modest, Johnny was forced to agree but couldn't have known that, apart from destroying another Gestapo HQ, eleven prisoners had managed to escape in all the confusion. A squadron dance that evening rounded off the day nicely.

Day after day, Johnny accompanied one or other of his squadrons in attacks on ground targets all the while harrying the enemy back towards Germany. On 10 December, after a fairly heavy night celebrating someone's birthday at the Magic Palace in Antwerp, Johnny joined No 193 Squadron at lunchtime to bomb a dam near Rhenon, south-west of Arnhem. They attacked at low level in pairs, claiming three direct hits with 1,000lb bombs, also breaching a dyke a little further north. Anything to hamper enemy troop movements.

The following day, with W/O Walker of No 193 Squadron as his wingman, he observed Nos 257 and 263 Squadrons dive-bombing the V2 rocket supply dump at Leiden railway station, where they were treated to a gratifyingly large explosion. Damage to your own aircraft during such low-level attacks was an occupational hazard accepted with a degree of sangfroid by most ground attack pilots – along with the flak they had to face. Close-support work may lack the glamour, not to say the glory, of conventional fighter combat but it took a particular type of pilot to be good at it. Diving on well-defended targets up to three times a day was no less harrowing, and if the loss statistics were to be believed, often more dangerous than pitting your wits and flying skill against an enemy pilot in a dogfight.

Raymond Lallemant put it thus: 'Missions of direct air-support were unspectacular. They lacked both the prestige and attraction of fighter missions. They brought little reward to the pilots, and the losses incurred were grave. The true fighter pilot hated all the ground-attack apparatus that festooned his aircraft like a Christmas tree.' There are no ground-attack 'aces' to be found amongst close-support pilots; but they flew, fought and died just as hard as their often better celebrated day-fighter comrades.

Johnny's next sortie was a combined show leading Nos 257 and 263 Squadrons in a low-level dive-bombing of a German barracks at Soesterberg. They off-loaded a mixture of incendiaries, cluster bombs and 1,000-pounders in the target area, hitting three of the barracks and experiencing some unexpectedly heavy AA fire from Gorinchem on the return flight.

Christmas Eve arrived with a totally unexpected and most unwelcome surprise in the shape of the Luftwaffe operating in force for the first time in months. It started as a routine long-range armed-recce mission south of the

Rhine during which four Typhoons of No 193 Squadron suddenly came up against more than fifty Me109s and Fw190s east of Enschede. Not surprisingly, the German pilots adopted a thoroughly belligerent mood so the Typhoons went to full boost to defend themselves. During the opening attacks P/O Freakley was shot down and another Typhoon was badly damaged prompting a distress call.

No 197 Squadron, airborne in the area, flew to their assistance, but nearing Gronau, F/L Curwen's section were 'bounced' by a mixed gaggle of enemy fighters, losing P/O McFee and W/O Read. Nos 263 and 266 Squadrons, also operating nearby, failed to engage. Neither did Johnny, whose logbook entries for the day merely record that 266 claimed one train destroyed, another going to 193 who also claimed one enemy aircraft shot down and another probably destroyed. Against this, No 146 Wing lost five Typhoons with two more damaged – bad arithmetic!

Christmas Day brought no respite. Johnny led two squadrons on another armed recce late in the morning, a sweep north and west of the Ruhr. This flushed out some tempting targets but also provoked further violent reaction from the Luftwaffe, with more than eighty Me109s and Fw190s being engaged 10 miles west of Munster.

Having just destroyed a train, 'B' Flight of No 266 Squadron were attacked by enemy fighters and lost F/O Scott-Eadie and F/Sgt Green before their escort could intervene. Flying top cover, No 193 Squadron arrived on the scene and waded into the enemy fighters, claiming one destroyed and another damaged in the fleeting but bitterly contested engagement which followed, F/L Smith limping back to land at Deurne with severe damage.

Johnny again seems to have missed out on the action, which is possibly fortunate for he was one of those operating at low level and therefore particularly vulnerable to attack. Flying with No 257 Squadron that morning, he led a raid on Heerenberg airfield, attacking some Bf109s on the runway and, for good measure, deposited their 1,000lb anti-personnel bombs on a nearby building. Next, they strafed some aircraft spotted dispersed in a wood east of Nijmegen, counting the target area well covered, but later suspected that these may have been dummies.

While Johnny will have undoubtedly regretted the loss of another two pilots, his mood must have lifted later that evening with W/C Johnny Baldwin joining them for Christmas dinner. 'Baldy' now sported a well-earned bar to his DSO, and it must have been quite a reunion for these two old sparring partners who traded yarns well into the night.

With a clearing of the weather on 29 December, Johnny recorded his first sortie flying a Typhoon 'personalised' with his initials J.W. Until then he had been using squadron aircraft or Johnny Baldwin's old machine. It was customary for RAF wing commanders to fly aircraft carrying rank badges and their initials instead of the usual squadron codes, and it is clear from his logbook that Johnny had two such Typhoons (JW1 and JW2) allocated to him, which he flew for the remainder of the war.

In a combined show, Denys Gillam and Johnny led four squadrons, attacked a complex of buildings forming the German 88th Corps HQ at Bilthoven, south-east of Utrecht. As usual, a meticulously planned affair, each of the four buildings making the target was allocated to a particular squadron.

The first wave of Typhoons broke away and fanned out over the target area to go in low to deliver a package of bombs and rockets. Surprise was total with the second wave following up by dive-bombing while No 193 Squadron flew flak suppression. After the third wave every building was either reduced to rubble and totally destroyed or hit and badly damaged. The Typhoons reformed and set course for Deurne. Again they suffered no casualties.

Two days later, New Years Eve, another hectic day, started with a two-squadron show south-east of Utrecht at 0945hrs. Johnny took eight aircraft of No 197 Squadron, along with 'B' Flight of No 193 Squadron, to dive-bomb railway bridges crossing the Maas at Culemborg and Tricht. Leading the attack, Johnny took his section down through intense light flak; even when not particularly accurate, it was always terrifying. Last section into the attack, led by S/L Smith CO of No 197 Squadron, went in low but caught an awful packet. Smith was in obvious difficulties as they left the target area but managed to put his aircraft down on the other side of the river, about 2 miles south-west of Culemborg. Pilots saw him running from the aircraft. 'Yet another senior pilot lost,' Johnny mused. But the way things were, 'Smithy' now had a better chance of surviving the war than most of them probably did. At least they had scored two direct hits on target with several near misses.

The key event of the day was still to come: a low-level mission by sixteen Typhoons from Nos 197 and 257 Squadrons against the German 88th Corps Tactical HQ, located in a villa at Gameren, near Zaltbommel. Johnny again led the show, taking eight aircraft of No 197 Squadron off early in the afternoon. They had no trouble in locating the target and the Typhoons winged over and dived to the attack in pairs, following each other line astern. Johnny circled above watching them close on target like swallows streaking low across the patchwork landscape. Twin puffs of smoke punctuated the air as each aircraft in turn reached the release point and fired its rockets, the smoke trails streaming away towards the target daubing giant exclamation marks in the sky. The vivid smoke slowly blurred and dispersed in the turbulent air to form ghostly reflections of the fresh trails made by following attacks. Aircraft veered up and away from the explosions of their rockets, as one after another they sliced through the thickening clouds of dust and smoke which then obscured the target.

Three direct hits totally demolished the main building. Later a 1st Canadian Army intelligence officer, who visited the scene and saw the aftermath of this attack, commented that the villa had been 'stubbed out like a cigarette end'. The German staff was wiped out; only the GOC, temporarily absent, escaped.

That night, New Year's Eve, gave cause for rowdier than usual squadron celebrations, with a wing dance in Antwerp. Everyone sensed that 1945 would herald the long-awaited end to the war. But the following morning it was business as usual with early shows planned and briefing for all squadrons scheduled before first light.

Bleary-eyed pilots crowded into the briefing room, more than a few nursing tremendous hangovers and looking forward to a good whiff of oxygen to clear their heads. But Johnny had barely identified the target selected for a wing attack when the power supply failed and the lighting went off. Not best pleased at the inevitable delay that would follow, he dismissed all but one squadron and reverted to individual squadron briefings using temporary lighting that was hurriedly set up. To add to his growing irritation, there would be a further delay as one of the runways was covered in ice and unfit for take-off. Most of the ground personnel had already been herded out to clear the fresh snow which had fallen overnight. At least the weather seemed reasonable: clear with a slight haze. He joined some of the pilots outside the briefing room as they all huddled together around an oil-drum fire awaiting further orders.

It was bitingly cold and there was little idle chatter but no doubt this was due to 'the morning after the night before'. They communicated in gestures and glances, sharing cigarettes and rubbing gloved hands together as they stamped their feet to keep the circulation going. Johnny moved amongst them, his caustic often ribald comments filling the silence, but inwardly he was fretting – they should have been off long before now. He checked his watch, it was approaching half past nine.

The noise of engines caught his attention – seemingly, someone in 2TAF had managed to get up and about this morning. A gaggle of aircraft appeared over the railway embankment bordering the airfield. Bloody untidy formation and too damned low, Johnny thought to himself as he glanced toward them. By God, he'd have them on the carpet before lunchtime if they were his. Probably some split-arsed colonial types or Americans celebrating the New Year by beating up the airfield. These particular aircraft made a real change for, as realisation and recognition slowly dawned, the lead aircraft opened up with its cannon and Johnny was bowled over in the undignified scramble for cover. They were 109s!

For the next fifteen minutes, Antwerp-Deurne was subjected to a series of attacks by up to thirty enemy fighters in successive waves. The lads from

II./JG77 and III./JG77 had flown close to 200 miles from Osnabruck via Rotterdam to deliver their New Year's greetings. Fortunately, having got the jump on the defences, their attacks seemed quite disorganised, delivered from between 150 and 300ft and not pressed home. That at least was the general opinion of grounded British pilots forced to watch; and they should know – they considered themselves something of ground-attack experts.

Most of the grass run-off areas at Deurne were waterlogged due to recent rain so the Typhoons were parked on the eastern side of the airfield along-side the railway embankment and not too well dispersed because there were simply too many, about eighty all told. But, to Johnny's great relief, the German pilots failed to exploit their advantage and made a complete hash of their attacks, the Typhoons getting off lightly with little damage.

In the main, the German pilots came in straight and level, making perfect targets for the ground defences. Flight Lieutenant Ronnie 'Bentos' Sheward, acting CO of No 263 Squadron, was scathing. Standing on top of the embank-ment with some of his pilots during the attack he was heard shouting, 'Weave you stupid bastards!' Denys Gillam was also heard to remark, 'If any of my boys put on a show like that I'd tear them off a strip!' But, despite volumes of pointed advice and a great deal of invective from the watching pilots, the RAF Regiment gunners manning the airfield defences proved equally inept, loosing off close to 1,300 rounds and only laying claim to a solitary 109 – and that was only 'damaged'.

Eventually, the sound of enemy aircraft receded and the guns fell silent. Smoke billowed from several fires around the airfield and shouts rose above the noise of trucks and jeeps which roared past, horns blaring. Somewhere an alarm bell shrilled. With the excitement over, they started to take stock of the damage. Johnny dusted himself down and went hunting for his cap.

In all only seven Typhoons had been hit, one No 266 Squadron aircraft being a complete write-off. This was actually quite good news to the long-suffering squadron engineering officer as, apparently, it was just about the worst 'clapped-out' hack on the unit and he reckoned that he owed the Luftwaffe a personal vote of thanks for helping him get rid of it. No 257 Squadron reported two aircraft badly damaged, while the rest of the wing had five more aircraft needing repair, plus a few others with minor damage. An RAF Regiment corporal was the only casualty, hit in the mouth by flying shrapnel.

Even as the attack was taking place, priority calls and urgent teleprinter messages had been flashed from HQ 2TAF to indicate that this was no iso-lated event but part of a carefully planned and co-ordinated Luftwaffe strike against Allied airfields on the front. Eindhoven, Brussels-Evere and Melsbroek had been particularly badly hit, and other British and American airfields had suffered extensive damage and casualties.

Some time later, Johnny learned via RAF Intelligence that this ambitious operation, codenamed *Bodenplatte*, had been conceived to support the German offensive in the Ardennes, but was delayed by bad weather. Planned by Luftwaffe Generalmajor Dietrich Peltz, commanding Jagdkorps II, it was a bold effort aimed to inflict potentially crippling losses on the Allied air forces in north-west Europe and restore some measure of German air superiority. Over 800 German aircraft had been involved and close to 300 of them were lost, with 200 of their pilots killed, wounded or captured. In total, they managed to destroy some 200 Allied aircraft, which was serious enough losses but made good within days. For the Luftwaffe, already crippled by losses, it proved a disastrous, desperate and despairing last effort.

A little later that morning, S/L Arthur Todd, newly appointed CO of No 257 Squadron, arrived from England. 'Sorry you weren't here earlier for all the fun and games, you missed quite a party,' Johnny greeted him. 'I'm afraid that you're already down a couple of crates damaged before you even get started!' As it turned out, Todd had not missed a thing. He had been en route to Deurne when news of the attacks broke, and had diverted to St Denis Westrem where he arrived just in time to witness the Polish Spitfire Wing, fortunately airborne at the time of the attack, wreak havoc among the attacking German fighters. They had claimed over twenty destroyed for the loss of two of their own pilots. All things considered, he felt, the Luftwaffe had laid on quite a reception for him.

HQ No 84 Group had already been on the wire to ascertain the extent of the damage and to stress the importance of getting aircraft up in the air and back over the front as quickly as possible. It was crucial that operations go ahead as usual and that the Germans be given no grounds for suspecting they had inflicted any significant damage. So by late morning No 197 Squadron took off from Deurne to attack enemy positions in the village of Meeuwen, closely followed by 'A' Flight of No 193 that went off to bomb a bridge at Vianen. Johnny was happy to report that No 146 Wing was back in business with a vengeance.

Mid-afternoon, S/L 'Rastus' Erasmus led eight Bomphoons of No 193 against an important road junction which they cut 'quite nicely', while S/L Deall led No 266 in an attack on a factory in Keizersveer which they left ablaze. Then eight Typhoons of No 263, responding to urgent army requests, put sixteen rockets through the spire of Hedel church, which housed a German observation post.

Rounding off what had been quite a hectic day, a V2 impacted on Deurne that evening causing a huge crater but little other damage. These ballistic missiles arrived without warning and there was no defence against them. Travelling at supersonic speed, the sound of their approach arrived after their impact. The devastation they must cause to heavily populated targets like Antwerp didn't bear thinking about.

Days passed in what was fast becoming a continual grind of targets as the Allied armies pushed ever closer to Germany and final victory. Bridges, factories, railways, defensive strong points, store dumps and rocket launch sites were all obliterated with ruthless efficiency. Even losses from flak and the appalling weather conditions remained an unvarying constant – as if there was a deadly monotony to it all.

No 257 Squadron lost another pilot on 5 January 1945, when P/O Gerry Jones died crash-landing near base after a bombing attack on Veen village. Before the end of the month they lost four more, F/L Lao, P/O Whitmore and W/O Button all missing on the 20th when an attack on a bridge at Leiden had to be aborted due to dreadful weather conditions of ¹⁰⁄₁₀ cloud and snow squalls. And four days later, F/O Johnny Lunn's Typhoon exploded as they were reforming after an attack on bridges south of Utrecht, probably victim of heavy AA fire.

On 8 February 1945 the wing moved forward to B89, a newly laid airstrip at Mill, south of Nijmegen. This put them 70 miles closer to the front and a mere 12 miles from the German border, improving their operating range. The landing strip at Mill was good and long, but slightly too narrow for them to take off in pairs as was usual. And after the superb facilities they had enjoyed at Antwerp-Deurne, the conditions at Mill came as a bit of a shock.

B89 Mill could, at best, be described as a hutted encampment, so it was back to a spartan existence and living rough again. For the first thirty-six hours, the mess was an unlit sagging tent hurriedly erected in a sandpit. The pilot's billets were cramped Nissen huts set amongst the pine trees bordering the landing strip, and when all five squadrons were together it was very crowded indeed. There was no proper plumbing so everyone had to wash and shave in the open air, which, in the depths of a very cold winter, caused more than a little 'binding' among the more fastidious pilots.

One of Johnny's chums from Manston days, Pinky Stark, then CO of No 164 Typhoon Squadron in Johnny Baldwin's No 123 Wing, recalls, 'One got used to it. Bloody great mess which accommodated all four squadrons, then a brand new metal strip with a tented camp in the forest about 4,000 yards from the front line. The occasional shell came over.'

The site was littered with tree stumps where the ground had been cleared, narrow footpaths winding through the woods to cross clinker roads which had been hurriedly laid over the sandy soil. Nissen huts were just visible dotted amongst the trees with field latrines somewhere off to one side, to judge from the pungent disinfectant smell which occasionally wafted their way. The whole place had the distinct air of a frontier town like Dodge City or Tombstone, only without the tumbleweeds. Somewhere off in the distance, the sound of artillery could be clearly heard and the occasional shell exploded in the woods nearby.

Eventually the officers' mess, a long low wooden hut built by local labour adjacent to the runway, was ready and they vacated their marquee. Trestle tables and wooden benches were arranged down both sides of the room. Chipped and broken crockery and dirty cutlery littered a long counter at the far end. It was damp and airless; the cold penetrated everywhere, rising from the red-tiled floor. Small pools of water puddled on the tiles, reflecting the harsh light cast by light bulbs gently swinging from the ceiling in the chill draft from the door. There was no heating. Truly a miserable place.

Johnny kept them hard at it. There was no other choice. If the German army had been stubborn in its resistance to date, they were becoming increasingly fanatical in defence of their homeland. Demands from ground forces for close support against enemy tanks, artillery or pockets of resistance were almost non-stop, and he was insistent that response times be kept to an absolute minimum. It was not unusual in No 146 Wing at that time for aircraft to be scrambled to attack army demand targets, return, re-arm and re-fuel while the pilots debriefed, and be back in the air again en route to their next targets within thirty minutes.

Operating at such a pace at peak efficiency enabled them to attack thirteen different targets in a single day. On the day of their arrival at Mill No 146 Wing flew 156 sorties. No sooner had they landed on that first day, the aircraft were refuelled and at noon Johnny led No 257 Squadron on a special mission: the first use in No 84 Group of Mobile Radar Control. This innovation enabled them to bomb through cloud, when visual identification of the target was impossible and, better still, when the attacking aircraft were equally invisible to flak gunners. It worked by sending the aircraft directions by radio from a Mobile Radar Control Post located in a forward position, often near the target.

Approaching the target area straight and level at a predetermined course and speed, the Typhoons would be tracked by the MRCP which then sent a radio signal when the aircraft reached a certain point. They then went into close formation for a blanket bombing run and started a steady countdown to the release point. It was ideal for use against fairly large targets and accuracy was reckoned to be within 150yd with an effective range of 25 miles. Johnny had tested the new system as early as 4 January but this was the first time that it was to be used on operations.

The first attack using MRCP was with a mixed load of 500lb and cluster bombs dropped by No 257 Squadron on enemy troop concentrations at Miel. They followed this with a second MRCP sortie to Materborn later that afternoon while No 266 flew their first MRCP attack west of Cleve. The fifth mission of the day for a weary No 257 was at 1615hrs, when Johnny took them back to Materborn, this time for strafing runs and visual attacks with more cluster bombs – somehow infinitely more satisfying than simply pulling the toggle and watching your bombs vanish into a layer of cloud, although it had to be admitted that dodging light flak was never much fun.

February 1945 saw the Canadian army launch a major offensive east from Nijmegen through the Reichswald forest in preparation for an assault across the Rhine. This thrust would result in a particularly intensive period of operations for the whole of No 84 Group. Every squadron in the wing was now flying two or three times a day as a matter of routine, but 14 February was to prove exceptional. That morning Johnny led another big show, taking Nos 193 and 257 Squadrons against the German 180th Division HQ at Wetten. Placing their bombs bang across target they totally demolished the HQ and other buildings in the village but lost W/O Points of No 257 to flak. Over the radio he was heard to say that he was bailing out but didn't make it. Mercifully this was the only loss on a day in which every one of Gillam's increasingly weary pilots felt they had earned their flying pay.

From the Intelligence Summary of No 84 Group:

Today we have written more Group history. In a war remarkable for its air actions we have concentrated into an area of not more than 300 square miles, 804 fighter-bomber attacks. It is perhaps invidious to single out any wing for special commendation but when records are broken they should be mentioned. No.146 Wing today beat its own record for the number of sorties flown in any one day.

Then, on the 22nd, Operation Clarion was launched aimed at destroying the enemy transport system still remaining in central Germany. Not just road and rail traffic, but railway marshalling yards, signal boxes, level crossings, bridges, garages, repair depots, canals and locks. Everything was to be pulverised and brought to a halt with close to 10,000 Allied aircraft flying from bases in England, France, Holland, Belgium and Italy, deployed against targets covering the rest of Germany. Two hundred targets were specified within an area of 250,000 square miles, so the long-range fuel tanks went back on again.

That day Johnny flew an attack against the German HQ at Weeze which was left in ruins. They had received a warning to keep a wary eye out for the new Hawker Tempest, two squadrons of this potent fighter operating for the first time over in No 135 Wing, but saw no sign of them. Johnny just hoped that the Luftwaffe would play ball and send up something for them to shoot at. Even the latest German jet fighters were pretty thin on the ground these days.

Just before the end of the month Denys Gillam, having completed yet another tour, went on a well-deserved rest from flying, posted to No 84 Group HQ (Operations). He was loathe to go, but they gave him a truly monumental farewell thrash on 27 February when he announced his successor – some clot by the name of Johnny Wells DFC, promoted Group Captain OC No 146 Wing 2TAF. Not bad for a Trenchard Brat. A beaming Johnny acknowledged the noisy congratulations and inwardly prayed that he could afford the resulting drinks bill.

The following day it was again business as usual. During an attack on a factory south-west of Xanten, 'A' Flight of No 266 Squadron lost another pilot to flak; P/O Shepherd seen to bail out, so hopefully with a good chance of seeing out the war as a prisoner. On 18 March, they mounted a long-awaited 'Tit Show' – a wing attack on the German 9th Army HQ at Gorssel, south of Deventer, where they hoped to find generals Blaskowitz and Student in residence and possibly even Field Marshal von Runstedt. Flying with No 197 Squadron, W/C Deall led the formation accompanied by Johnny, who was orchestrating the whole affair as 'Master of Ceremonies'.

Thirty-six Typhoons took off late afternoon and flew direct to the target in the rapidly failing light. They had five specific targets. Reaching the target area in the gathering gloom, Johnny wasted no time and rapped out his orders before going down to deliver his calling card, with three Typhoons of No 197 Squadron following close behind him. Coming in low and fast, he put eight rockets through the first-floor windows and watched in fascination as bombs from the aircraft behind him bounced off the cobbled courtyard in front of the building, skipped towards the entrance and exploded on impact, the entire front elevation collapsing in clouds of smoke and dust.

Meanwhile, Deall took another section of three Typhoons down through moderate flak to attack the second target which they left severely damaged. Reforming after the attack, W/O Samuels' aircraft of No 193 Squadron was seen trailing vapour, evidently having taken a hit in the radiator, and was lost in ground haze between Zutphen and Arnhem during the return flight. He was posted as 'missing'. This attack was covered by the British popular press with a story by war reporter Lawrence Wilkinson, appearing in the *Daily Express*. Johnny said that he wouldn't be satisfied until they all featured in the more salacious columns of the *News of the World*.

Three days later there was another 'gigantic wing show', with forty-eight aircraft off early to attack the German 25th Army HQ in the Hotel Bosch van Bredius at Bussum. A similar effort against a fuel supply dump 5 miles north-east of Deventer took place later that afternoon where they 'managed to express a lot of ill will'. On both operations, three squadrons went in with bombs, while No 263 Squadron, rapidly becoming acknowledged as flak-suppression experts, was armed with rockets. Describing the morning attack, the No 84 Group Intelligence Summary noted that: 'The hotel was demolished in the first attack. The villa opposite also. There were eight killed and some wounded. The General had left for Bilthoven the day before after the attack on Rudelsheim but other officers and documents were still there.'

So, once again, their bird had flown. Obviously severely rattled by the increasing frequency of fighter-bomber attacks on their headquarters, disturbed senior German commanders were choosing to keep on the move.

The assault crossing of the Rhine began at 2100hrs on the 23rd, when the British 1st Commando Brigade advanced on Wesel. At first light the following morning Johnny's Typhoons were over the battle area with orders to neutralise enemy flak positions prior to the arrival of the British 6th Airborne Division. But plans came close to disaster when they were prevented from neutralising local flak by the early arrival of towed gliders and paratroops.

There were close to sixty Typhoons operating over the landing zones when the gliders arrived and Johnny made sure that there were never less than thirty-seven overhead throughout the entire day to provide close support for the ground forces. But smoke from the bombing of Wesel made targets difficult to locate and they were not too successful, only two flak positions being knocked out. Johnny flew one rocket attack with No 193 Squadron on a flak site hidden in a wood but was only able to claim a fire started.

It was clear to everyone that the end of the war in Europe was drawing to a close. So it was decided to start winding up and unravelling some of the machinery and organisation of war before the last shot was actually fired. Britain was tired of war and needed to prepare for whatever followed, even an uneasy peace. So some months before, plans had been set in motion throughout the RAF to disband units when opportunities arose, within an approved timetable of change aimed at creating an effective and sustainable peacetime air force.

Naturally, Johnny was closely involved with the organisation and implementation of changes affecting his wing. Within a very short time of arriving at Mill, he had already been overseeing arrangements for No 257 Squadron to fly their last sorties. They did so on 3 March prior to disbanding two days later; five of their aircraft and pilots were transferred to No 263 Squadron to complete operational tours.

By late March 1945 the 45-gallon long-range drop tanks had become an almost permanent fixture on their aircraft as the bomb line was pushed ever deeper into Germany. Operating in pairs, the Typhoons flew far-ranging armed-recce sorties, seeking worthwhile targets often in marginal weather conditions. But on 1 April, after losing another two pilots to the weather, and with cloud base down to 1,000ft, Johnny called a halt to further suicidal low-recce sorties. It was a sound decision. No 84 Group lost nineteen pilots that day, by far the largest proportion of the twenty-four lost by 2 TAF in only 300 sorties.

Meantime, they had to continue flushing the enemy out of northern Holland. On 12 April, the Canadian Army advancing on Emden were particularly well supported by No 84 Group. At the village of Friesoythe, set ablaze in rocket attacks, their close-support work brought loud and lavish praise from the commander of local ground troops. That day Johnny led three squadrons of Typhoons loaded with incendiary bombs against targets in Arnhem, but were forced to bomb in zero visibility.

Then on the 16th, a red-letter day for the wing, three squadrons were deployed to B105 Drope, leaving a thoroughly disconsolate No 193 Squadron languishing behind at Mill. Their disappointment was understandable for Drope, over the frontier north-east of Lingen, was in Germany. The end of the war was surely imminent.

The Canadian II Corps advancing towards Zutphen finally reached the Zuider Zee on 18 April 1945 while Typhoons bombed German gun emplacements on the island of Texel, where the garrison of Russian 'volunteers' had mutinied. Throughout the foggy, misty days that followed No 84 Group concentrated on enemy airfields around Oldenburg, shipping off the Hook of Holland and the mouth of the Elbe. There was no let up, but with targets in No 84 Group area getting increasingly scarce, Nos 123 and 146 Wings transferred to No 83 Group 'Kenway' Control for attacks on enemy shipping in the Baltic.

The 25th saw another maximum effort by Johnny's squadrons. Taking off from Drope at 1105hrs with No 197 Squadron leading, they attacked a hutted camp at Brake placing 80 per cent of their bombs on target. Circling high above to watch each squadron in turn deliver its bombs, Johnny later admitted that he 'was pleased with the performance' while the squadrons deemed themselves 'bloody well chuffed'.

Though it was clearly 'last orders', the Luftwaffe still managed a few surprises. Mid-morning the following day, four pilots of No 263 Squadron were attacking a train in Niebull station when one, P/O de Morgan, was hit by the ever-present flak. With his aircraft smoking badly he pulled up to gain height and radioed to say he was going to attempt a forced landing. His wingman, W/O Barrie, following him down to 200ft, circled to watch as he put down safely. At that moment, two Me262 jet fighters, dropping out of 9/10 cloud, attempted to 'bounce' Barrie but were spotted by the other section of Typhoons who immediately engaged. One of the jets was claimed shot down and the other escaped, but it was a fine show by the pilots concerned who were clearly 'on the ball'.

By the end of the month No 146 Wing had vacated Mill and settled at B111 Ahlhorn in Germany – their final wartime base. No 266 Squadron, who had left for Fairwood Common shortly before, joined them there five weeks later. Then, on 4 May 1945 Admiral Friedeburg surrendered to Field Marshal Montgomery all German land, sea and air forces in north-west Europe. Four days later, at 0116hrs on 8 May, ratification of the German unconditional surrender was signed at Karlshorst, in what was left of Berlin. This naturally resulted in one hell of a party, but Johnny found it a strangely muted affair, though there was some fairly hard drinking done by a few old-stagers who seemed to need rapid total oblivion.

Quite suddenly it was all over. A signal from the GOC 1st Canadian Army to the AOC No 84 Group RAF was copied to units. It read:

> On behalf of all ranks I desire to express our admiration and appreciation of the magnificent support afforded to 1st Canadian Army by 84 Group RAF throughout the operations in NW Europe now concluded in outstanding victory. This Army/Air combination has had to face and solve some tough operational problems but with the fine team work of our respective HQs and the skill, gallantry and determination which all ranks 84 Gp RAF have consistently demonstrated in action we have always accomplished what we set out to do.

Celebrations on the officially designated VE Day a few days later were more like old times. Possibly things had time to sink in properly. Pilots served the airmen lunch, after which things degenerated fairly rapidly and culminated in a riotous and extremely dangerous pitched battle which involved much firing of Very pistols. Strange to relate, there were no reported casualties. Then, on 15 June, the Belgian authorities saw fit to award Johnny the Croix de Guerre with Palm, which was deemed an excellent excuse for another epic thrash by all who remained standing.

Life seemed to be a constant round of visits and impromptu parties, old friends and comrades seeking each other out for 'one last jar' before they were demobbed and dispersed across the globe. Johnny's logbook records plenty of movement: Twente, Wilhelmshaven, Hamburg, Hanover, Celle and Hildesheim, all subject to local recce flights during this period. It was a wild, hectic time, a bit like final exams, prize giving and end of term all rolled into one. An old friend of Johnny's, Pinky Stark, remembers one such night spent with No 146 Wing which was by then based at R16 Hildesheim: 'It is an occasion I shall never forget.'

Johnny had invited Pinky to attend, along with two other officers, and they drove over from Gilze-Rijen in a V8 Ford Utility. Somehow they managed to get lost and stranded in the middle of a sewage farm when their rear wheels were trapped in a concrete culvert. Two hours later, thanks to a very impressive rescue convoy incorporating a Coles crane which eventually hauled them out, they arrived at Hildesheim to find the party well under way:

> We were a bit late getting to the party by which time most of them were fairly drunk. Johnny Wells was leaning back against the bar and sitting on the bar was a Canadian Flying Officer, obviously very drunk, holding a pint of beer over Johnny's head. Johnny looked up and said, 'If one drop of that hits my head, I shall hack you in the fork.' More than a drop landed on his head. He just stepped forward, turned around and said, 'Come on, down off the counter.' This chap jumped off the bar and up went Johnny's foot. I don't know how bad the damage was, but by God that chap screamed.

Along with many other units in 2TAF, plans to disband No 146 Wing were brought forward; tactical ground support wasn't needed any more and while Johnny approached the task with his usual thoroughness and eye for detail, unravelling the threads forming his last wartime command must have been difficult. He shared in the relief and joy of those who, jobs well done, returned home to loved ones. Others, exhausted by the constant strain of operational flying, simply went blank as if something inside them had suddenly switched off. He knew that many of these young men, who knew little else but flying and fighting, would face uncertain futures in civilian life. And for those who remained, now counting the days, having to endure the increasing anxiety and stress of still having to fly dangerous missions was made all the more difficult by memories of all those who would never see home again.

Group statistics were circulated – the sombre mathematics of mayhem. Johnny knew it was necessary; someone had to count the cost, draw a line, foot the bill. He scanned the columns of figures: since D-Day No 84 Group had flown more than 90,000 sorties – over a quarter of them ground support. They had shot down 200 enemy aircraft, claiming another 113 damaged, destroyed a further 81 and 203 damaged on the ground. Close to 4,000 mechanised vehicles had been destroyed and another 4,609 damaged, as well as 93 trains destroyed and 502 damaged.

He read on. They had dropped nearly 43,000 assorted bombs, totalling 19,400lb, and fired over 79,000 rockets and over 5 million rounds of 20mm ammunition, a million of them in the last month. Impressive totals certainly, but wasn't there something awful about them as well? Something too ugly to contemplate; the unspoken, imponderable, immeasurable factor – the cost in terms of human suffering. He pushed the thought aside; he must be overtired.

In the eleven months since D–Day No 84 Group lost 56 aircraft in combat, 415 to flak, 61 to unknown causes, and 96 in accidents not due to enemy action; totalling 628 aircraft. That had cost them 407 pilots killed or missing. Johnny reflected on just how many his own wing had lost in the six months since he had joined them; it was 38 or close to 10 per cent of the overall total. What a terrible waste.

On 16 May, Johnny drove to Amsterdam with the wing padre and others taking supplies of food and cigarettes for distribution. It was a voluntary goodwill gesture by members of the Allied forces that would be repeated countless times in many places throughout Europe during those days when civilian supplies were scarce and an emerging black market thrived. Johnny and the padre, S/L Perkins, will have enjoyed the trip for they had much in common. They had both joined the RAF as apprentice fitters over, what now seemed, several lifetimes ago.

It was a time for flags and cheering, celebration parties and parades. On 27 May, 'after much practice over preceding days', a formation flypast was undertaken by No 84 Group at Celle, followed by another at Nijmegen on 2 June for Queen Wilhemina of the Netherlands. Then on the 26th, a farewell display at Brussels for Air Marshal Sir Arthur Coningham, AOC 2TAF and, on 6 July, a flypast by 280 aircraft over Brussels.

The Typhoons stood in immaculate rows still facing east; cockpits cocooned in neat tarpaulins, cannon covered over with tape. Early morning dew dripped off them on to the glistening black tarmac and gently steamed from wings unencumbered by bombs, rockets or long-range tanks. They stood silent but expectant, still powerful and menacing in their drab grey/green camouflage, but their work was done. It was over at last.

No 266 Squadron were next to leave, lifting off from R16 Hildesheim for the last time on 31 July 1945. Within a month, in a sudden flurry of activity, No 263 departed on 28 August to be followed in three days by Nos 193 and 197 – the last of his squadrons to go. No 146 Wing was officially wound up and ceased to exist. Johnny's thoughts could once more turn to home.

15

PEACETIME COMMAND

After winding up No 146 Wing Johnny returned to the UK for a welcome spell of leave. It was good to get out of uniform and act civilian for a while, although the austerity of post-war Britain came as a bit of a shock and the novelty began to pall. Misery and hardship had been suffered by many back at home while he and others had been slogging across Northern Europe enjoying a relatively comfortable existence – if avoiding death on a daily basis could be considered that.

Johnny had to make up his mind what to do next and, while he remained open-minded and 'live' to opportunities, the prospect of leaving the service held little attraction for him. There seemed to be little or nothing for him in civvy street and the RAF was all he had known since leaving school. It was his life. Fortunately, he was still a free agent with no ties to consider. Marriage, or other close personal relationships, had passed him by. He favoured, and was well used to, his solitary lifestyle, which he felt best suited a military career. Even as a boy, though warm and loving to those dear to him and always personable and sociable in company, he was of a solitary nature and generally happiest on his own, comfortable in his own company. So with no one to please but himself, he decided to remain in harness and accepted the permanent commission he had been offered in the peacetime RAF. It was an easy decision to make.

He returned to duties in late October 1945 and spent the next two months being schooled for senior command in the fast-growing sphere of logistics, in what was then Transport Command. The ability to deploy military resources swiftly, to trouble spots maybe thousands of miles away, was fast becoming a critical factor in maintaining the delicate balance of peace worldwide and Johnny's natural flair for organisation and thorough planning had not gone unnoticed.

He attended a month-long course at the School of Air Transport, passing Class A, and spent another month on a senior course at Digby, which he also passed with flying colours. Admittedly, it fell somewhat short of leading an operational fighter wing, but those jobs were already becoming scarce in the peacetime air force, and realistically he knew that an administrative post or staff position would get him up the chain of command equally quickly.

In January 1946, he commenced a two-year stint as executive wing commander and station senior administration officer of No 17 Staging Post, Castel Benito. This was in Tripolitania on the Mediterranean coast of Libya in North Africa. As he had always promised himself, he was going back again to the Middle East. He travelled by RAF Dakota from Hurn with an overnight stop at Istres and arrived at Castel Benito within a few days of a visit by Air Marshal Sir Charles Medhurst, who brought with him the new station commander, G/C H.J. Kirkpatrick CBE DFC.

Castel Benito was an important staging post for refuelling and servicing particularly aircraft troop transports travelling between the UK and British bases in India, Australia and the Far East. During the war it had been an important Italian air force base, later used by the Luftwaffe, and piles of abandoned aircraft littered the outlying areas of scrub. He walked amongst the hulks, those creaking, rusting monuments to ideals of conquest. Macchi 202s, Messerschmitt 109s and Junkers Ju88s, all still recognisable but stripped bare of anything of interest, value or use. He contented himself with a few photographs.

In a typical month aircraft movements could total 350 troop transports and 300 other aircraft, with an average of 300 troops a night needing accommodation. It was the military equivalent of a busy city airport. The nearby and aptly named Transit Hotel, and every mess on the base, was sometimes filled to capacity requiring troops in-transit to sleep aboard their aircraft.

Checking movements within a few days of his arrival, Johnny found to his astonishment that on one day recently there had been over a thousand troops, crews and other passengers needing overnight accommodation, while another thousand had already passed through during the course of the day – a staggering total of nineteen eastbound and twenty-three westbound flights. Administrating that lot on a daily basis, along with all the other duties associated with routine station administration, took some organising. With that amount of traffic it was inevitable that the occasional accident occurred. Within a month of his arrival, a Liberator from Bassingbourn undershot the runway with the result that the undercarriage collapsed on landing and it was written off in the ensuing prang. Fortunately nobody was seriously injured.

As often as not the so-called routine station administration was far from routine. On 20 February 1946, a warrant officer, one of a training crew from No 220 Squadron en route to India, went missing overnight. The rest of the crew carried on to their destination without him, but despite an investigation and search of the area the disappearance remained a mystery. Two months later they found his body at the bottom of a septic tank adjacent to the hotel.

It was good to be back in khaki drill again, though it was now far better tailored, and Johnny spent the first few weeks getting to know the ropes and grabbing the occasional opportunity to visit some of his old haunts in the Delta and beyond. During February 1946 he was even given the exalted job of completing the station Operations Record Book – no doubt in order to become familiar with every aspect of the station's activities. Although probably well-intentioned, it was an irksome and somehow demeaning clerical chore, and he vowed it was something he would never do again. And he didn't – during the whole of his time there.

The following month, Johnny was busy with inspection visits to facilities inland at Fort Tarhuna and the emergency landing ground on the coast at Misurata, between Benghazi and Tripoli. There he found the runways and ground-control system in good order. This was just as well for, in addition to their normal load of traffic, BOAC Avro Yorks were going to be routed through Castel Benito instead of their usual route via Luqa, where essential runway work was being completed. So everything had to be on absolute top line.

Apart from the daily round of transports which passed through, groaning with fresh-faced conscripts, there was also the occasional dignitary or VIP requiring hospitality and accommodation. In the course of a single month, Castel Benito played host to Field Marshal Smuts, en-route to England, the Aga Khan, 'just passing through', and marshal of the RAF, Lord Trenchard, who arrived from Malta and departed for Cairo the following morning. How many of these, if any, Johnny ever came to meet is not recorded, but Castel Benito was clearly a posting where a surprising degree of etiquette and social graces could prove useful. You never knew who you might meet. One day, the legendary Douglas Bader, then a representative for Shell Oil, arrived in his Percival Proctor V to 'fill up with gravy' and stayed overnight. He had arranged to meet up with someone at Castel Benito before flying them both on to Tunis. Johnny was tickled pink to meet one of the RAF's most famous pilots, but was even more surprised when Bader's passenger arrived next morning. It turned out to be none other than Lieutenant General Jimmy Doolittle, who had led the famous carrier-borne bomber raid on Tokyo and was a Shell USA vice-president.

In May 1946, in view of possible disturbances by the Arabs, the station defences were ordered to 'stand to'. It was a timely exercise for, the following month, the political situation threatened to turn distinctly ugly after statements on the future of Tripolitania by Mr Bevan to the House of Commons.

The station was brought to full readiness but there were no disturbances of any note and before long everything returned to normal.

In July Johnny was formally granted his permanent commission in the RAF confirmed in the rank of squadron leader, which seemed to bear little or no relationship to the work he was doing nor his acting rank of wing commander. On reflection, he had first led a squadron back in 1943, but it was another step forward. Within the year, BOAC took over responsibility for handling civilian flights in and out of Castel Benito, taking a load off his shoulders; then, in October 1947, he learned that he was appointed commander of the Order of Orange Nassau by Queen Juliana of the Netherlands, in recognition of his wartime service to that country. In due course, he was invited to attend the Royal Netherlands Embassy in Portland Square, London, where, on 27 July 1948, he received the award from Prince Bernhard. It was a most prestigious award, an impressive medal worn from a ribbon around the neck – he was beginning to look quite the beribboned warrior. His promotion to wing commander, with seniority back-dated almost a year, was announced the next day. It was a fitting conclusion to his two-year stint at Castel Benito, and on 19 December he took a Dakota to Luqa where, four days later, he picked up a York, returning to the UK just in time to be home for Christmas.

16

RAF GUTERSLOH

A desultory two years at the Air Ministry followed, working for the Deputy Directorate of Intelligence. Until in February 1949, after an interval of almost three and a half years, Johnny finally got the chance to return to an active flying role. He was posted wing commander (flying) at RAF Gutersloh, BAFO Germany – the British Air Forces of Occupation.

After a ten-day course at No 1 Pilot Refresher Flying Unit at Finningley, where the OC, S/L Stapleton, checked him out day and night flying on Harvard IIBs and a Packard-Merlin engined Spitfire LF16, Johnny was champing at the bit and simply bursting to take on his new role. His brief was very clear, his main task being to see that RAF Gutersloh maintained a full flying training programme while ensuring that re-equipment of its squadrons with Vampire FB5 fighter-bombers went ahead smoothly. It was right up his street.

Much had changed since he had last held such a job, with many technical developments and advances in place, but he was pleased to find that in many respects essentials remained the same. Pilots may be more qualified and better trained, and their aircraft, equipment, systems and procedures more complex, but they still needed good leadership both on the ground and in the air to instil confidence in them, their aircraft and their ability to locate and destroy hostile targets. Johnny picked up the reins with gusto.

His new posting was no easy number. Gutersloh was a crucial link in the NATO defence chain opposing the Warsaw Pact forces in Eastern Europe. Five squadrons based there came under his control: No 3 with Vampire F1s, No 16 already with Vampire FB5s, Nos 26 and 33 both operating Tempest F2s and No 80 with Spitfire F24s. Some 350 RAF officers, NCOs and airmen, plus 70 WRAFs, made up the establishment under the overall command of the station CO, G/C W.B. Murray OBE DFC.

Johnny arrived in a period of atrocious weather across Northern Europe which seriously threatened to curtail flying. Nevertheless, with typical drive and ruthless efficiency Johnny saw to it that Gutersloh maintained a full flying programme by clocking up an impressive 937 flights for the month despite the appalling weather. First challenge over.

On top of this he started his own programme of conversion on to jets with his first recorded flight in Vampire FB5 VV456 on 20 February 1949, within two days of his arrival. Unfortunately his impressions of piloting a modern jet fighter were not recorded, but with well over 2,500 flying hours the transition cannot have been too difficult.

He also took the opportunity of flying multi-engine aircraft for the first time in eight years. It was February 1941 since he had last flown a twin-engined type; if a mere twenty minutes in an Airspeed Oxford counted, and even that as second pilot. This next experience was also as second pilot but in a Gloster Meteor T7 WA662 with S/L Lambert, making practice interceptions at 20,000ft somewhere over Germany. So, after a fairly brief conversion on to twin-engined types, Johnny was regularly seen flying the Meteor, as well as a variety of other types, including Ansons, Oxfords and Devons.

On 7 March, splendidly polished and buffed, he formed up with the welcoming committee for a visit by the prime minister, accompanied by the Under Secretary of State for Foreign Affairs, the air officer commanding BAFO and the AOC No 2 Group, along with other dignitaries who partook of morning coffee in the officers' mess. Johnny, never totally at ease at such formal gatherings, recognised their value and importance only too well. Oiling political wheels was never his true forte and his mind was undoubtedly on more pressing things – a busy programme of flying demonstrations to organise and a full-blown interception exercise to arrange.

The interception exercise, involving four squadrons from RAF Gutersloh operating in conjunction with Mosquitos from RAF Wahn, took place later that month and resulted in a spectacular wash out. Only No 16 Squadron managed to make contact, the other three squadrons failing to receive any vectors from ground control. Spitting feathers and with much colourful language, Johnny instituted an immediate post-mortem with dire threats on the consequences. But fortunately for all concerned no serious system failings were revealed, though certain people were actively encouraged to 'pull their fingers out'. After which, Johnny's colour slowly returned to normal.

Come the spring and the first of his units, No 26 Squadron began relinquishing their Tempests for Vampire FB5s, occupying them in a hectic conversion programme throughout April. Then after a pause in May, during which Exercise Unity Two resulted in over 300 flights from Gutersloh with No 16 Squadron Vampires and No 33 Squadron Tempests giving a stunning demonstration of low-level tank busting on the ranges at Caen, No 3 started rearming with the Vampire FB5. Re-equipment completed, they took their shiny new aircraft off to armament camp at Sylt, while Nos 33 and 80 made final preparations for their transfer to the Far East on 2 July 1949.

Johnny, down to three squadrons, all Vampire FB5 equipped, drew breath before throwing them into another furious round of flying demonstrations and command exercises which lasted the entire summer. He flew as often as his other duties allowed, logging seven flights during July and six in October. He also took command of the station for a period pending the arrival of a new CO, W/C J. Stewart DFC, who arrived in November. Meantime, a well-deserved bar to Johnny's DFC was announced on 20 October, resulting in a moderately riotous celebration.

Bad weather clamped down towards the end of the year and brought an inevitable increase in flying accidents, mostly slight. But No 26 Squadron lost one pilot who died of injuries after a forced landing when he was out of fuel. It was the only serious accident to occur during Johnny's time at Gutersloh.

By the following August, Johnny was ready for a change of scenery but determined to depart on a peak of activity. So, in addition to the usual full flying training programme, the nucleus of a new No 67 Squadron was created and preparations put in hand for no less than four major exercises: Lamplight I, King Pin, Cupola and Hot Dog. During these exercises, two Gutersloh squadrons flew over 160 close support and low-level intruder flights, Johnny obviously deciding that their low-level navigation needed more practice.

Pleased with things at Gutersloh, and content in the knowledge that he had done a good job in the eighteen months since he arrived, Johnny handed over to W/C A.R.W. Wickham, who arrived from Tangmere on 5 August 1950. After an epic send-off leaving him curiously subdued for at least two days he left for RAF Wunstorf.

He was to do an equally good job as wing commander (flying) at Wunstorf during the coming year, where the station commander was G/C F.S. Stapleton DSO DFC. The station was home to another three Vampire FB5 squadrons: Nos 4 and 11, together with his old friends No 26, who had escaped from Gutersloh the previous January in order to get away from him – or so they insisted.

The routine was much the same as at Gutersloh and Johnny soon had the flying programme running the way he liked. It is also clear from his flying log that he was able to get in a lot more flying than before. He was on top of his job and enjoying the company of flying men which he had always considered a privilege to be cherished and made no secret of it.

Squadrons and personalities came and went with the ebb and flow of service life, and Wunstorf was certainly no different to any other station in that respect. In July 1951, No 4 Squadron left for Lake Constance on an exchange visit, No 26 Squadron returned from detachment to the UK and a Royal Norwegian Air Force exchange detachment flew in; all in the space of a single month. On the 26th, the whole station formed up to take their leave of the C-in-C, Air Marshal Sir T. Williams, and within two weeks it was Johnny who was making the rounds to bid his own farewell.

He made his last flight from Gutersloh to Wunstorf on 15 August 1951. His days as wingco flying were over. Indeed, it seemed his flying days may be over permanently for his next appointment was to HQ Allied Air Forces Central Europe at Fontainebleu. He was back flying a desk again – but for how long this time?

17

STATION COMMANDER

Two years later he relinquished the staff work at Fontainebleu for what he no doubt considered was a proper RAF job. His promotion to group captain was effective 1 July 1953, the same day that he took over as station commander at RAF Church Fenton in Yorkshire. Home base to three squadrons of Meteors, this was an important station in the defence of the UK, although when he arrived it was completely devoid of fighters. Nos 19 and 72 were both detached south to North Weald in readiness for the queen's coronation flypast and Johnny's old unit, No 609, was in Malta for a month of exercises. Meantime, building contractors were completing long-overdue runway lengthening.

Johnny did the rounds of introductions familiarising himself with his new command. His predecessor, W/C Irving 'Black' Smith OBE DFC, a New Zealander, had led the historic Mosquito attack on Amiens prison in February 1944. He had put together a good team at Church Fenton, which included Bobby Oxspring DFC AFC, as wing commander (flying) among other familiar faces from the past. Visiting the sergeants' mess, Johnny spotted another. The unmistakable and imposing figure of Darkie Hanson, whom he had first known back in far-off Duxford days as senior technical NCO of No 609 Squadron. 'So I've got you again have I, Darkie?' Johnny greeted him airily. 'I'm the new station commander.'

'That's OK,' Hanson grunted through his magnificent, luxuriant RAF moustache, 'I can always bugger off home.' Native of Yorkshire, with family home in nearby Leeds and years of service under his belt, Darkie was wont to speak his mind. It occurred to Johnny that he wasn't entirely joking. Many years later Hanson, with a wry smile, confided to the author that, 'Johnny Wells didn't cause us any inconvenience as Station CO.'

Church Fenton suffered the usual crop of flying accidents; though, for some reason, No 19 Squadron always seemed to bear the brunt. In Johnny's first three months as Station CO, they lost two pilots killed while practising low flying, with another aircraft extremely lucky to get back after a bird strike during ground attack exercises. Along with the squadron commanders, Johnny saw to it that the squadron kept to its full programme of low flying and that morale stayed high, so that early in the new year he deemed them in excellent shape when they flew off to RAF Jever on an affiliation exercise. To his delight the squadron later won the RAF's coveted Dacre Prize for weapons training efficiency, presented by the C-in-C Fighter Command, Air Marshal Sir Dermot Boyle.

Much of the daily routine on the station involved sector exercises, weapons training, flying training and practice interceptions in order to maintain a constant high state of readiness to counter potential threats by hostile aircraft. Semi-informal visits by the AOC No 12 Group were also a regular feature.

Johnny got in as much flying as he could, which was not much, but in October 1953 a new ground-control approach system was installed prompting a hectic programme of practice approaches and landings for all three squadrons over the rest of the month. With this all neatly done and dusted, every aircraft on the station then had to be taken out of service in strict rotation to be fitted with the latest Martin Baker ejection seats. And all without affecting alert response times – naturally. Then, somewhat abruptly, Johnny moved on, relinquishing command to G/C Colin Gray DSO DFC, who arrived from Stradishall and took over as station commander on 22 March 1954.

This move, coming much sooner than anyone could have expected, was surprising. So much so that it gave rise to speculation and rumour-mongering. Obviously, it was argued, some skeleton had been rattled deep in Johnny's cupboard and his past was threatening to catch up with him, necessitating swift removal. But the truth behind his sudden departure is more prosaic. Johnny's administrative skills had come to the fore yet again. Apparently, some bright spark in RAF Personnel had him earmarked to succeed as senior administration officer (SAO) of No 63 Group, where the existing incumbent, G/C D.M. Gordon CBE, was shortly due to retire.

Whether he got wind of this or not is unclear, but No 63 Group, with HQ at Hawarden, was responsible for Air Training Corps (ATC) units in the West Midlands and Wales. Administering to the demands of ATC squadrons in Birmingham, Manchester and Wales, and keeping the training wings and gliding schools across Cheshire, Lancashire and Staffordshire up to scratch, probably held little appeal for Johnny. If Group SAO it was to be, then better an operational group than a training command in his view. He needed to stay closer to the action.

Suddenly, and out of the blue, nature intervened to resolve things in a totally unexpected fashion. For some months past Johnny had been recognising the first signs of what would subsequently culminate in his nervous collapse. Clearly, he was long overdue a rest from the constant strain of command and was sensible enough to seek the help and advice of the medicos. It was a typically brave step to admit to any such failing; the service ethos was very much dominated by success and achievement. But the consequences of not seeking help could have been dire, even catastrophic. So after two months in the equivalent of air-force limbo, while his future was being decided, another door opened and on 3 May 1954 he was appointed to the Air Ministry in London as a deputy director of operations. That was more like it!

The next few months were possibly the most enjoyable, yet demanding, he had ever experienced. The work was challenging and exacting, and he approached each task with his usual thoroughness and eye for detail. He drove himself relentlessly, taking every opportunity which presented itself to avoid becoming office-bound. It was as if he constantly had to prove to himself that he was fully recovered and back on top form.

In November 1954, attending a refresher course at Central Flying School, he went through much the same sort of lessons he had at Sealand twenty years earlier, but this time the old Avro Tutors had been superseded by Jet Provosts. Then, in the following March, he joined a VIP inspection tour of RAF units in the Middle East, flying the round trip from London to Nicosia, Fayid, Amman, El Adem and Idris in an RAF Hastings. It was an all too brief return to some of his old haunts and a most welcome excursion. Later that year he was regularly piloting Avro Anson PH814 from Hendon to Jersey, via Charmy Down and Dieppe, as his duty, mood or the vagaries of weather dictated.

Johnny, spending two years with the Operations Directorate in London, rose to become director general of organisation at the Air Ministry – albeit in an acting capacity. With such credentials, and his health now no longer a problem, he was obvious choice for a senior position of some political importance if the occasion arose. When it did materialise, his new role took him back to the Middle East.

18

BAGHDAD

REQUEST SITREP NOW AND AT TWO HOURLY INTERVALS
IN THE FUTURE GIVING ALPHA GENERAL SITUATION AS
YOU UNDERSTAND IT AND BRAVO LOCAL SITUATION AT
HABBANIYA AND ON THE PLATEAU AIRFIELD.
SECRET from SASO HQ MEAF to RAF Habbaniya, 1300hrs,
14 July 1958

Over five years since he had held a flying job, Johnny was heartily pleased for the chance to escape the corridors of command and get back amongst aircraft and pilots again. So, after a month at No 4 FTS on a refresher course, this time on Vampire T11 trainers, and two weeks' Christmas leave back home in Norfolk, he arrived in Baghdad in early January 1957 to start a two-year stint with the British Liaison Party Iraq, acting as air advisor to the Royal Iraqi Air Force.

According to his brief, Johnny's main role was to see through the results of some protracted and delicate negotiations between the British and Iraqi governments over previous months and implement an agreement to extend the runway at Habbaniya from 6,000 to 9,000ft. He was also responsible for arranging delivery of fifteen Hawker Hunters, which Iraq had purchased to re-equip a squadron of their air force, and supervise conversion training. Back in the Middle East at long last, Johnny fully intended to enjoy himself, as far as other duties would allow. His new job was an absolute plum, the facilities and accommodation first class, and the climate sheer heaven.

Britain had held mandate in Iraq until 1932, when the kingdom ostensibly became independent, but in order to protect its strategically important oil interests, Britain still maintained a presence and exerted strong influence on Iraq through its union with neighbouring Jordan. Since independence there had been a period of relative peace and prosperity right up until the July immediately prior to Johnny's arrival, when the debacle over British and French involvement in the Israeli military invasion of Egyptian Suez had unsettled the entire region. A backlash of fundamentalism ignited throughout the Arab world, but things had eventually quietened down again and everything returned to normal. Or so it seemed.

Johnny got to know the region well in the course of his duties, flying himself around in a variety of aircraft available to him: Devons, Doves, Herons and Provosts. From Habbaniya to Raschid, Shaibah, Kirkuk, Mosul, Amman and Diana, visiting the forward bases or the plateau airfield; he even made the occasional trip to Nicosia to attend conferences.

His main job, the extension of the runway at Habbaniya, was important to the UK Government, who agreed to fund up to £100,000 of the total cost. Amongst other things, the RAF planned to employ the upgraded base to train Jordanian pilots. A tender for the project from Wimpey had been accepted and work commenced almost as soon as Johnny arrived. But within a few months, difficulties began to surface and in May all work on the runway was suspended as no formal contract was forthcoming from the Iraqi authorities. Johnny cajoled, connived, begged, pleaded and inwardly fumed but all to no avail. If he had any hair to spare he would have pulled it out by the roots, but within a matter of weeks his mounting problems with work on the runway extension were thrust into insignificance.

Iraq was an inherently unstable country, its people an eclectic mix of mainly Shia and Sunni Muslims, the Sunni being the ruling minority and running Baghdad. With Kurds dominating the northern provinces and a few Nestorian Christians, the Iraqis had, over centuries, resisted all efforts by outside powers to dominate them. Despite their mutual loathing, all three main groups had deeply entrenched nationalist, anti-colonial, sentiments.

The ruling Hashemite monarchy, installed by the British after the First World War, had never been popular and, as a result, the new regime of Abdul Karim Kassem had no difficulty in overthrowing the government. Widespread unrest in the capital followed, with freedom of movement restricted and curfews imposed, while armed militia prowled the streets. There were frequent and increasingly violent anti-British demonstrations.

Johnny was too busy to take much notice, besides which, life on the base was to a great extent divorced from outside events and continued much as usual. On 9 July 1955 he made a routine flight from Mosul to Baghdad in Dove, taking his total flying hours to over 3,727 hours. He could not have known it at the time, but this would be his last flight in a flying career spanning twenty-four years.

The military coup erupting five days later proved a bloody affair. King Faisal II and his brother were both assassinated in the royal palace and their wives shot. The pro-British prime minister, Nuri al Said, was hunted down and killed, his mutilated body dragged through the streets of Baghdad behind a motorcycle, another victim of the volatile and brutal politics of the country. Other pro-British sympathisers suffered similar ugly fates as angry mobs took to the streets, attacking foreigners on sight. Armed militia groups flourished as Iraq floundered. Transport and fighter units in the Middle East Air Force were brought to readiness and warned of possible Allied activity to the south and east of Cyprus. A flurry of 'Urgent' and 'Top Secret' signals were exchanged as the situation deteriorated.

The base at Habbaniya was home to 1,200 RAF personnel, including 89 wives and 159 children, the old airfield at Hinaidi having been taken over by the Iraqi air force some years before. As soon as it had become obvious that the latest troubles were serious, the station commander, G/C Edwards, immediately ordered the base on to an emergency footing, instituting well-planned procedures which had been in place for some time.

It was crucial that the base stayed in British hands and remained fully operational; either as a foothold for supplies and reinforcements if a decision was taken to send in UN troops to re-establish stability or as a haven for British and other foreign nationals seeking a means of escape. Either way, as one of the senior officers in charge, Johnny had to see to it. By the following day, vital equipment and security-sensitive material at Habbaniya had been destroyed or rendered useless. Throughout the night documents were burned and machinery smashed. RAF personnel hurriedly vacated the airfield buildings literally a few hours before they were occupied by Iraqi army forces. The military were extremely jittery and announced, with no obvious show of willingness and a seeming total lack of conviction, that they were now responsible for the safety of the base and its occupants. The base was secured but none of the RAF personnel or foreign nationals caught there felt particularly safe. Adding to their overwhelming sense of isolation, the routine staging of RAF aircraft through Habbaniya ceased. Over-flights were suspended and air traffic diverted. So any escape route for RAF personnel and their families was closed; the 'back door' was slammed.

On the 16th, the Defence Committee met in London to discuss the situation and Operation Valiant was high on the agenda. This contingency plan had already placed the 16th Parachute Brigade, plus the Guards Brigade, at high readiness. They were ready to fly in to Amman, via Israel, in the event that King Hussein requested assistance. A squadron of Hawker Hunters was to provide necessary local air support. A parachute battalion was also readied to be dropped into Kuwait. As discussions went on, news was received that all communications with Iraq had been cut. At Habbaniya, they were now on their own and completely in the dark. Johnny sensed that things were turning decidedly ugly.

With the collapse of the Iraqi monarchy, the Baghdad Pact effectively disintegrated and pro-Western states in the Middle East found themselves exposed and vulnerable. So to bolster some semblance of stability, American marines landed in Beirut in response to an urgent request from President Chaumon of Lebanon, while all American nationals were evacuated from Baghdad. Meantime, British troops flew into neighbouring Jordan. Tension in the region was building and during the next few, increasingly nervous, days the British Foreign Office speculated on Soviet intentions and possible Russian military intervention. The possibility of a pre-emptive attack on Iraq by Jordanian forces, supported by the British, was even mooted.

The British embassy in Baghdad still had contact with the Foreign Office in London and on 20 July reported that the situation was still unpredictable, and that the safety of foreign nationals depended on the Iraqi army which was endeavouring to exercise firm control. But more encouraging, the report went on to say that British subjects and foreigners had been circulating freely in Baghdad for the past two days. This was indeed welcome news but the situation remained extremely fraught.

Most of the foreign community in Iraq at the time of the revolt had managed to get out quickly. Yet many of the British had elected to remain, most of them oil worker employees of the Iraqi Petroleum Company which had pumping stations along the 550-mile pipeline to Haifa on the Mediterranean coast. Almost 6,000 British subjects remained in Iraq after the coup and they lived a precarious existence. They needed to be circumspect in everything they did, the people they met, and everyone with whom they associated. They were under constant close scrutiny by the internal security forces and, if they ventured out at all, they tended to congregate at the Alwiya Club, a well-known expatriate watering hole. Many of them were frequently rounded up for questioning, and most would be expelled over time. It was a dangerous time to be British.

A statement issued by the new regime announced that Iraq was an independent republic and that any union with Jordan was forthwith dissolved. It went on to say that Iraq expressed a desire for friendly relations with all countries, including the West, and confirmed that foreign nationals who wished to leave were free to do so. However, as Johnny would subsequently discover, such evacuation would proved infinitely more difficult to arrange in practice. When the new regime did eventually get around to letting people leave the country, only small numbers were allowed out. They left every Monday and Wednesday by scheduled airlines, the first Viscount carrying British families leaving Iraq on 28 July.

Within a week, the British ambassador, who had been the only means of communication between Habbaniya and the Foreign Office in London, would report that the atmosphere at the base was normal and very friendly, salutes and official courtesies by the Iraqi military being observed and maintained. The base was well stocked with supplies and there was freedom of movement within the perimeter, but anyone wishing to venture outside the boundary needed special permission and was normally only allowed out with an armed escort.

For those, like Johnny, who were still confined on the base, it must have been very restrictive. But from a security point of view still necessary. The constant strain of having to live in an enclave, cut off from all outside support and communication, and completely surrounded by a potentially hostile regime, must have been extremely stressful. Being in a position of authority only made it more so. It was tantamount to being under siege.

Doing his best to maintain some semblance of normality, Johnny tried to maintain his outside contacts and continued to press ahead with the planned modernisation of the Iraqi air force. But he found himself experiencing increasing difficulty at every turn. He put this down to a natural reluctance of senior Iraqi officers to be viewed as perpetuating a redundant cause or usurping the new regime. But the truth is that he was an unwitting pawn in what was turning out to be a much bigger political game than anyone had anticipated.

When the coup took place the Royal Iraqi Air Force had three squadrons based at Habbaniya; one equipped with fifteen Hawker Hunter F6s, another with fourteen Venom FB50s and a third with eight Vampire FB52s. A training flight of six Vampire T11s was also based there. In addition, they had forty elderly Hawker Furies which were used for ground attack operating out of Shaibah, plus some communications and Auster observation planes based at In'askar.

According to estimates he had been given, Johnny knew that they needed nineteen trained pilots per annum to maintain front-line strength, and these were to come from an annual intake of thirty-eight recruits. Until quite recently, most Iraqi pilots had received advanced flying training in the UK, but that experience had proved unsatisfactory to both sides as they invariably fell short of the stringent and exacting RAF entry standards.

With the new regime in power, the Iraqis were more anxious than ever to update their air force with high-performance day fighters, ground-attack aircraft and fighter reconnaissance machines. But past experience suggested that the British would be slow to assist them in developing such a capability, so they turned elsewhere. As was to be expected, there was no shortage of willing suppliers keen to obtain influence in this oil-rich region. Consequently, it

transpired that fifteen F-86 Sabres were going to be delivered with the USAF
taking over the training of Iraqi pilots. This was to be done at Habbaniya,
particularly as the runway was currently being extended. When he learned of
this, Johnny didn't know whether to laugh or cry.

The political ramifications of this move rumbled all the way to the top. They
were even discussed by the British Prime Minister, Harold Macmillan, and
the US President, Eisenhower. During these discussions, Eisenhower referred
to a report submitted by US General Twining on a visit to Habbaniya by an
American survey mission. Apparently, this adverse report was highly critical
of RAF Habbaniya, which was 'jam packed with equipment and that there
would be no room for the aircraft'. Needless to say, this particular bombshell
dropped from a very high level soon impacted on Johnny's desk.

According to his principal private secretary, the prime minister was said to
regard the situation at Habbaniya 'a most serious affair' and on his return from
Washington wasted no time in bending the ear of Sir Norman Brook about
it. As hot potatoes go, this was pretty damned hot and it was still sizzling nicely
when HQ Middle East Air Force passed it on to Johnny to frame a response.
After a brief pause for reflection, and a quick glance out of the window, he
reported back tersely, but truthfully, that 'no real grounds are known for the
US comment'. He must have impressed them with his economic prose style,
for nothing more was ever heard of the matter.

To Johnny's immense relief, work on the runway extension resumed in
January 1958 and the BLPI team was back in business – only to grind to a halt
again twelve weeks later when tests revealed that the asphalt already laid was
below design strength. Johnny, resigning himself to grinding his teeth, was fast
becoming sick of the whole affair. What a bloody shambles this was turning
out to be.

Then, at a Chiefs of Staff Committee meeting in London on 23 September,
it was revealed that a squadron of United Arab Republic aircraft was expected
to arrive at Habbaniya imminently. This was a gross breach of protocol which
would clearly put the RAF complement still based there in an impossible situation. The Foreign Office recommended their immediate withdrawal while
leaving the BLPI, Johnny and his team, in situ. As the minutes of this meeting
show, the early withdrawal of all RAF personnel, apart from a small care and
maintenance party, was considered to be essential. But as only one of the 145
men in the BLPI had done any work at all in the last two months, it was felt
that a decision about them could wait.

Johnny stood on the tarmac at Habbaniya watching Viscounts take off for
Cyprus carrying those scheduled to go. It was hell knowing that his name
wasn't even on a passenger manifest and that his turn may not come in time.
But he concentrated on getting as many out as possible.

He finally got out on 28 October, with G/C Edwards who had been replaced, and just before another bout of violent anti-British riots and serious civil disturbances. Five months later, the final withdrawal of 100 RAF personnel and their families took place from Baghdad West. Even at that late stage, conversations were still taking place about a possible joint military intervention in Iraq by America, Britain and Turkey. Over forty years later, a military intervention by the USA and Britain would ultimately take place which would force a change of regime but seemingly resolve little or nothing. And so we continue to ignore the lessons of history.

His experiences over the preceding months, plus the constant strain and heavy responsibilities which couldn't be shared, had taken an awful toll. Way beyond the end of his tether, Johnny was physically exhausted and emotionally drained. He was heartily relieved to get out of Iraq, and this time was glad to be leaving the Middle East.

★★★

His next posting was to RAF HQ Germany and in June 1959, while visiting Jesolo in Italy, Johnny suffered a heart attack. Air-lifted back to RAF Hospital Wegberg, in Germany, his condition was closely monitored over the next two months. Eventually, with his heart disease seemingly under control thanks to regular doses of Warfarin, he was able to return to light duties; but he remained under close supervision by the hospital until the following March. Despite this, two months later he suffered another attack and was invalided back to England. From August 1960 he was an out-patient at Cromer Hospital in Norfolk. He took time to consider his future.

On 12 August 1960 he was summoned to attend a medical board at the RAF Central Medical Establishment where his condition was assessed as 'permanently unfit'. Feeling as he did, he was not particularly surprised and over the preceding months had been contemplating the inevitable prospect of having to call it a day. Official notification arrived during six weeks' sick leave and he was invalided from the RAF on 23 September 1960. The following December he was placed on the retired list. It seemed to have happened with alarming speed.

Wed to the service for over 33 years, Johnny had enjoyed a very successful career. Joining the RAF as a boy aircraft apprentice, he had risen to group captain and acting director general of organisation at the Air Ministry. He had travelled the world and received honours and distinctions beyond the dreams of a young lad from Sheringham. He had learned and experienced the thrill of flying over 3,500 hours, shared in the joys and endured the sorrows of airmen at war, flying some 400 sorties, and still relished the enduring warmth and companionship of service life. He knew that leaving the air force would be a most painful wrench. But the world was changing faster than ever and in his heart of hearts he knew that he was 'tour expired' and long overdue a rest. His time was done.

EPILOGUE

After a lifetime spent in the service, settling back into civilian life was not easy. But Johnny threw himself into things and soon established a comfortable routine. He set up home with his sister Margaret in a big house nestling on the cliffs overlooking Sheringham beach. Like Johnny, Margaret had never married, so he designed the house to provide self-contained accommodation for both of them, leaving most of it available to holiday visitors arranged through local agents. Mother lived nearby in her own house. So, following long-established family tradition, Johnny let the house every summer and, towing his caravan, would head off to look up chums from his RAF days. His sister, left in charge, handled the bookings.

Five years passed in what must have seemed a tranquil idyll after the traumas he had experienced. Johnny was content and life was good. But, on occasions, he will have missed the challenge of command and, almost certainly, lamented the seemingly general lowering of standards, lax modern attitudes and lack of discipline in civilian life. He was no martinet, but had lived his life abiding by simple rules of decent conduct and saw no reason why others should not do the same.

One day he was involved in a minor dispute with neighbours spraying their car who managed to daub Johnny's fence with paint. It was an accident, not malicious, but nonetheless a careless act, slapdash and entirely remote from Johnny's own meticulous approach to things. He was incensed and angry words were exchanged. Things became heated and an altercation followed. It prompted another massive heart attack. Johnny was rushed to Cromer Hospital where he suffered a second attack from which he never recovered. He died there on 12 February 1965.

Characteristically thorough to the end, Johnny's will ensured that his beloved mother and sister were secure for life. His mother, Mabel, lived on until 1975 when she died aged 93 – still mourning her youngest child. Johnny's elder brother Robert died that same year; their elder sister, Margaret, lived on until 1998, when she died aged 92.

His well-tended grave lays in the middle of Sheringham cemetery, situated on the western outskirts of town aside the road to Wells. A handsome black marble headstone commemorates his achievements; a smaller plaque remembers his sister Margaret. Close in death, as they were throughout life, they overlook the golf links fringing the railway line to Weybourne and the grassy hillocks where they once scampered as children with the dull roar of waves pounding the beach below and the keening of gulls wheeling overhead.

> *Here fell the daring Icarus in his prime,*
> *He who was bold enough to scale the skies;*
> *And here bereft of plumes his body lies,*
> *Leaving the valiant envious of that climb.*

Desportes

APPENDIX I

AIRCRAFT FLOWN

Details of all aircraft flown either as a passenger or pilot between the dates shown

No 35 (B) Squadron – Bircham Newton

Apr. 1931–Jul. 1932	Fairey IIIF Mk.IIIB	S1532
	Fairey IIIF Mk.IV(GP)	J9785, J9798, J9820, J9822
Oct. 1932–Sep. 1934	Fairey Gordon	K1762, K1776, K1777 (converted IIIFs), K2626, K2685, K2689, K2690

Air Armament School – Eastchurch

Aug. 1932–Sep. 1932	Westland Wapiti IIA	K2252, K2254, K2255, K2256, K2258, K2259, K2260, K2264, K2265, K2266, K2268, K2269

No 5 Flying Training School – Sealand

Oct. 1934–Aug. 1935	Avro Tutor	K3242, K3246, K3248, K3252, K3253, K3263, K3264, K3265, K3266, K3267, K3269, K3271, K3307
	Bristol Bulldog TM	K3185, K3186, K3929, K3930, K3931, K3932, K3933, K3934, K3947
	Bristol Bulldog IIA	K2957, K2959, K2962

No 45 (B) Squadron – Helwan

Sep. 1935–Jan. 1936	Fairey IIIF Mk.IV	JR9162, JR9656, JR9677, J9817, K1708
	Hawker Hart	K4460, K4470, K4472, K4473, K4474, K4477, K4896

No 6 (B) Squadron – Ismailia & Samakh

Jan. 1936–Nov. 1936	Hawker Hart	K3956, K4457, K4458, K4460, K4470, K4472, K4473, K4474, K4475, K4477, K4481, K4487

No 4 Armament Training Camp – West Freugh

Apr. 1937–Sep. 1938	Avro Tutor	K3259
	Hawker Demon I	K5714
	Hawker Fury II	K8229
	Westland Wallace I	K3913, K5071
	Westland Wallace II	K6053, K6062, K6064, K6071, K8683, K8688, K8698,

No 1 Flying Training School – Netheravon

Sep. 1938–Mar. 1942	Fairey Battle I	K7559, K7575, K7600, K7609, K7610, K7614, K7626, K7627, K7632, K7637, K7651, K7680, K7687, K9388, L4958, N2049, N2098, N2100, N2101, N2235
	Fairey Battle (Trainer)	P6617, P6618, P6619, P6621, P6622, P6627, P6632, P6635, P6667, P6668, P6671, P6673, P6680, P6682, P6689, P6722, P6725, P6737, P6754, P6757, P6758, P6759, P6768

Hawker Audax I	K3059, K3064, K5143, K5148, K5160, K5243, K7325, K7328, K7342, K7382, K7482, K7489, K7550, K8324
Hawker Hart	K2435, K2452, K2458, K2461, K2465, K2467, K2966, K3010, K3861, K3880, K3890, K3957, K3960
Hawker Hart (Special)	K4366, K4367, K4368, K4375, K4380, K4409, K4413, K4423, K4436
Hawker Hart (Trainer)	K3762, K4941, K5816, K5819, K5823, K5861, K6463, K6478, K6507, K6508, K6519, K6520, K6534, K6537
Hawker Hind (Trainer)	K4651, K5374, K5440, K5447, K5450, K5468, K5506, K5522, K5524, K5540, K5542, K6615, K6619, K6644, K6651, K6653, K6679, K6680, K6685, K6713, K6730, K6737, K6756, K6759, K6766, K6783, K6784, K6806, K6827, K6834, K6856, L7175, L7183, L7188, L7205, L7212, L7219, L7231, L7233, L7235
Hawker Nimrod II	K3657, K3658
Miles Master I	T8485, T8507, T8512, T8522, T8727, T8732, T8739, T8759, T8760, T8762, T8763, T8764, T8767, T8771, T8776, T8777, T8778, T8825
North American Harvard I	N7011, N7044, N7045, N7046, N7048, N7049, N7059, N7061, N7062,

N7063, N7071, N7072,
N7073, N7119, N7124,
N7125, N7149, N7174,
N7187, N7188, N7189,
N7190, N7191, N7192,
N7193, N7194, N7195,
N7196, N7197, N7198,
N7199, P5787, P5788,
P5789, P5790, P5792, P5859,
P5860

No 52 Operational Training Unit – Aston Down

Mar. 1942–May 1942	Miles Master II	AZ364, AZ367
	Supermarine Spitfire I	AR227, P9306, P9433, R6913, R6959, R6975, R7157, R7159, R7200, X4059, X4175, X4414, X4773
	Supermarine Spitfire II	P7501, P8148, P8365, P8540

No 609 (West Riding) Squadron – Manston

May 1942–Jun. 1943	Hawker Typhoon IA/B	R7595, R7628, R7691, R7708, R7713, R7849

D. Napier & Son – Luton Airport

Jun. 1943–Dec. 1943	Fairey Battle	K9278, L5286 (Sabre engine test-beds)
	Hawker Typhoon IA/B	R7643, R7712, R7771, R7850, R8803
	Hawker Typhoon IB	DN549, DN561, EK208, EK209, EK498, EK500, JP673, JP746, JP940, JR141, JR336

From this point the logbook records aircraft codes rather than serial numbers.

NO 84 GROUP 2TAF

1st September 1944

Wing	Sqn No	Aircraft	Codes	Base
123	164	Typhoon IB	FJ	B7 Martragny
	183	Typhoon IB	HF	B7 Martragny
	198	Typhoon IB	TP	B7 Martragny
	609	Typhoon IB	PR	B7 Martragny
131	302	Spitfire IX	WX	B51 Vendeville
	308	Spitfire IX	ZF	B10 Plumetot
	317	Spitfire IX	JH	B10 Plumetot
133	129	Spitfire IX	DV	Brenzett
	306	Mustang III	UZ	Brenzett
	315	Mustang III	RY	Brenzett
135	33	Spitfire IX	5R	B17 Carpiquet
	222	Spitfire IX	ZD	B17 Carpiquet
	349	Spitfire IX	GE	B17 Carpiquet
	485	Spitfire IX	OU	B17 Carpiquet
145	74	Spitfire IX	4D	B8 Sommervieu
	329	Spitfire IX	5A	B8 Sommervieu
	340	Spitfire IX	GW	B8 Sommervieu
	341	Spitfire IX	NL	B8 Sommervieu
146	193	Typhoon IB	DP	B3 St Croix
	197	Typhoon IB	OV	B3 St Croix
	257	Typhoon IB	FM	B3 St Croix
	263	Typhoon IB	HE	B3 St Croix
	266	Typhoon IB	ZH	B3 St Croix
35 (Recce)	2	Mustang II	XV	B4 Beny-sur-Mer
	4	Spitfire XI		B4 Beny-sur-Mer
	268	Mustang II		B4 Beny-sur-Mer

BIBLIOGRAPHY

Action Stations by Michael Bowyer: Patrick Stephens 1979
Against the Sun by Edward Lanchbery: Cassell 1955
Air Command by Air Vice-Marshal Raymond Collishaw: William Kimber 1973
Cover of Darkness by Roderick Chisholm: Chatto & Windus 1953
Fighter Pilot's Summer by Norman Franks & Paul Richey: Grub Street 1993
Flying Start. A Fighter Pilot's War Years by Hugh Dundas: Stanley Paul 1988
Ginger Lacey – Fighter Pilot by Richard Townshend Bickers: Robert Hale 1962
One More Hour by Desmond Scott: Hutchinson 1989
Open Cockpit by John Nesbitt-Dufort: Speed & Sports Publications 1970
Pilot's Notes for Typhoon: Air Ministry 1943 reprinted by Air Data Publications
Pilot's Summer by Frank D. Tredrey: Duckworth 1941
Rendezvous With Fate by Raymond Lallemant: Macdonald 1964
Royal Air Force 1939–1945 (Vol. III) The Fight is Won by Hilary St George Saunders: HMSO 1954
Tha Battle of the Airfields by Norman Franks: William Kimber 1982
The Big Show by Pierre Clostermann: Chatto & Windus 1951
The Day of the Typhoon by John Golley: Patrick Stephens 1986
The Flying Sword – The Story of 601 Squadron by Tom Moulson: Macdonald 1964
The Greatest Air Battle. Dieppe, 19th August 1942 by Norman Franks: Grub Street 1992
The Royal Air Force in the World War (Vol. 4) by Norman Macmillan: Harrap 1950
The Squadrons of the Royal Air Force by James J. Halley: Air Britain 1980
The Story of 609 Squadron. Under the White Rose by Frank Ziegler: Macdonald 1971
To Live Among Heroes by George Armour Bell: Grub Street 2001
Toolbox on the Wing by Geoffrey Ellis: Airlife 1983
You Are Not Sparrows by S.J. Carr: Ian Allan 1975

INDEX

Other titles published by Spellmount and The History Press

The Battle of Britain
ROY CONYERS NESBIT

Riding high on the success of their Blitzkrieg campaign that had steamrollered France and the Low Countries into defeat, by June 1940 the Nazi forces were poised on the Channel coast ready to invade England. In the desperate air battles that followed, the 'Few' of the RAF succeeded in defeating a numerically superior Luftwaffe, preventing the invasion of England.

978-0-7524-5652-2

Last of the Ten Fighter Boys
JIMMY CORBIN

The Ten Fighter Boys, published in 1942, comprised the first-hand accounts of pilot officers and sergeant pilots from all walks of life. Among them was Sergeant Jimmy Corbin, a 23-year-old pilot standards based at Biggin Hill, Kent. Now, sixty years later, Flight Lieutenant Jimmy Corbin, Spitfire pilot and sole survivor of the 'Ten Fighter Boys' tells his extraordinary wartime story.

978-0-7524-5643-0

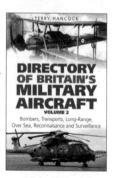

Directory of Britain's Military Aircraft Volume 2
TERRY HANCOCK

This directory details all the aircraft, airships and gliders which have served the UK's forces throughout the years of flight since the first powered flight, airship *Nulli Secundus*, in 1907. Each entry lists the type name and mark, role prefix, and comments on type, roles, crew, capacity, service period, units and countries, armament, engines, serials, and includes a performance and dimensions table.

978-0-7524-4532-8

Battle of Britain Memorial Flight
RICHARD WINSLADE

The Battle of Britain Memorial Flight – otherwise known as the BBMF or simply 'the Flight' – is based at RAF Coningsby in Lincolnshire. This lavishly illustrated tribute combines Richard's stunning colour photography with a personal and insightful narrative. His involvement with the Flight over many years enables him to give us a unique window on this priceless national treasure.

978-0-7524-5651-5

Visit our website and discover thousands of other History Press books.

www.thehistorypress.co.uk